Nanda's
Neelkanth

Nanda's Neelkanth

CHANDRA PRAKASH KALA

PARTRIDGE

A Penguin Random House Company

To order additional copies of this book, contact
Partridge India
000 800 10062 62
orders.india@partridgepublishing.com

www.partridgepublishing.com/india

To
my mother
Kamla Devi
&
my father
Sunder Mani

Contents

Tales

The Last Wish 13

My Favorite Medicine 19

The Prisoners of School 23

Riding the Best.. 28

Gaura's Home.. 32

Aunty.. 45

Nagrasani 49

A Killer in the Clouds 52

A Bull in the Leopard's Monarchy 55

The Tip of the Tail... 61

The Heavenly Leaf.. 66

The Forgotten Healers 70

Travelogues

Kafal Lore 74

A Job Hunter 77

My First Job 81

The Bear's Trail 98

A Non-vegetarian in the Holy Hills.................. 102

His Confession... 111

On His Wishes... 117

Seers of Pandukeshwar 123

Nanda's Neelkanth 136

My Maiden Visit to Penn State......................... 148

Battle between the Best 174

The Fragrance of Parijaat 178

Botanist of Surguja 185

The Childhood Friend.. 189

Ziro 194

A City of Biodiversity.. 202

The Silence of Candolim 208

The Land of Many Shades 215

Om Mani Padme Hum 238

The Roof of the World 269

The Floating Heaven 281

A Vagrant and the 'Queen of Mountains' 299

Hidden Gem of Europe.. 313

The Majesty of Mahasu 319

Acknowledgements

I wish to express my deep appreciations for all those who encouraged me through the long years of this work.

I thank Richa, my wife, and Shaurya, my son who supported me all along my long sittings for writing this book. I am grateful to Shaurya for his enormous patience, especially in the moments when I engaged in writing and he needed me desperately to chat and play.

I am indebted to my mother, Kamla Devi and father, Sunder Mani Kala who are my first teachers. Though, they are not physically present with me, their love and teachings will remain a source of inspiration for me forever.

At last but not the least, I thank my publisher Partridge for showing this book the light of the day.

Preface

Being blessed to wander in some of the most fascinating hills and valleys of nature, I have been endeavouring for long to put these stories together. I offer here the elements that appeal most to me during my wanderings in the jungles, meadows, villages and towns, especially in the abode of gods and goddesses – the Himalaya.

I pick up one of the tales as a title of the book '*Nanda's Neelkanth*'. *Neelkanth* is one of the several names of the Lord Shiva, the Hindu god. Many snow-clad peaks of the Himalaya are named after the gods and goddesses and *Neelkanth* is one of the most magnificent peaks. It attracts every human soul not only to its brilliant hues and majestic snowy peak but *Neelkanth*, as the Mahadev, also remains the source of spirituality for billions. Likewise, *His* consort, *Nanda* who is adorned with innumerable names including the Gaura, has been venerated in the form of beautiful mountains of the Himalaya. The quiet and unquiet woods, the elusive and elegant wildlife, the people and their culture and their struggle for living are the other elements in this bouquet of experiences.

This book is a tribute to Him - *Lord Neelkanth* - who inspires humans for philanthropy to an extent of consuming all the deadly poisons of this world so that others can enjoy the heavenly nectar. I hope the readers enjoy reading this collection of stories, as I have loved writing it.

1.0

The Last Wish

Everything was decorated nicely. Every person invited for the marriage party had dressed his/her best costumes. Ganesh was spraying perfumes on one of his friend's costumes. He wanted that everything should be in order and one and all in barat (marriage procession) must look attractive and handsome. After all it was his brother's marriage.

The barat had set off to Ashingee village, which about five km away from Sumadi, Ganesh's village in Garhwal region of Uttarakhand hills. Three musicians were leading the marriage procession through serpent hilly trails. The musical instruments of two musicians were hanging from their neck to belly. One was beating his hanging drum, which was smaller in size and locally called 'damoun', by two equal size sticks. The second musician was beating one side of drum by a stick and other side by fingers. The sound of bigger drum (dhol) was, obviously, louder than smaller one. The third musician in row had a pipe in mouth, which was connected with a puffed-up cloth pressed under his armpit along with four other colourful pipes placed one side of his shoulder and a flute in the hands. Some people called him a bagpiper.

Each one of them had attained mastery in playing with his musical instrument. Their coordination with every beat, rhythm, song and tune was commendable. The moment they began the journey to Ashingee, the tune was different. While walking in the dale, the tune was different than the tune they played on the mountain top and slopes. One of the elders in the marriage procession informed me that a tremendous traditional knowledge had been accumulated over the years by these local musicians. This knowledge was called as 'Dhol Shastra' in Garhwal.

After half an hour the barat had arrived in Khalu – a village in the valley, surrounded by green farmlands and famous for mangos. The young girls, women, men and children of Khalu had come out from their houses and assembled in small groups on the way to see baratis (people in marriage procession). Knowing that many beautiful eyes had close look on them and to attract their attention some barati started dancing and singing like birds to draw other's attention.

The barat walked on and arrived at Ashingee in dark; as usual tradition to reach at night in the bride's village. The patromax was lit and firecrackers were burnt to intimate the arrival of barat to the host – the bride's relatives. After sometime the musicians along with some hosts and priest from bride side had arrived to welcome the baratis.

Priest chanted some mantras and sprinkled water drops over baratis from a metallic goblet, religiously called kalash, placed on the head of a young girl. The bridegroom, his father and some elders were welcomed with garlands.

The barat then taken to a venue decorated with flowers, penchants and disco lights.

As soon as the cold drinks and tea were served to the baratis, girls sitting on the roof yet not clearly visible in the dark had started cursing the bridegroom and his relatives in sweet melodious tune.

"Hamra goun ma, pakni pakoda.
Adratyya ponoun tai, undoo khakoda.
Undoo khakoda, ta matu lapoda.
Matu lapoda, ta kandalin jhapoda."

'Snacks are fried in our village. Drag down these night-coming guests. Drag and paste mud on them. Paste mud and beat them with stinging nettle'.

Whosoever barati's name girls got to know, they cursed him in folksongs style by naming he and his relatives. Cursing baratis by host girls being a part of tradition nobody took it seriously rather everyone enjoyed them and laughed on each stanza. When there was no radio, TV and gramophone these girls made to enjoy the baratis by singing such readymade folksongs.

The delicious food at dinner with the melodious songs of host girls had entertained both guests and hosts. After this melodrama, the baratis in small groups were taken to different houses for night rest.

Next day morning after breakfast, I thought to walk up the hill top, close to the village in expectation of broad and larger view of the surrounding area. I asked Ganesh if he could go along with me. He agreed. It became killing two birds with one stone when a group of young girls voluntarily agreed to accompany us. I along with four beautiful young girls and Ganesh set off to climb the hill top. We passed through a relatively dense forest of chir pine. Many colourful birds were chirping in forest but their chirping had subjugated by the girls tweets. No one was listing to the jungles. Chatting with girls the time ran quickly and we reached on the hill top without much struggle.

There was a temple on the top. I bowed my head to the temple deity and asked the girls, 'whose temple is this, Durga or Laxmi.'

'It is neither Durga's nor Laxmi's temple. It is our village girl's temple.'

'Your village girl! You people make girl's temple. I don't understand. Do you worship village girls?'

'It is our village girl's temple. You believe or don't believe. It is upto you,' a sweet voice blown in the air.

'I trust you but ….,' I said.

'Ifs and buts have no place here. It is a fact and has a long story,' she interrupted before I finished.

'If you don't mind may I know that story?'

The young beautiful girl responding to my queries gazed at me but quickly dropped her eyelids. Her eyes were broad. Her reddish cheeks on whitish face with sharp nose had increased her beauty. She appeared to be shy enough to disclose the temple story. I sat on the temple's boundary wall and lift my eyes to see the panoramic views of the valleys and rolling mountains. I could see a part of my village, Sumadi, and hills around it. After a long silence, the girl whom I had asked about the temple by the time had made up her mind to speak out the temple's story.

She began to narrate the story and said, 'some decades ago, there was a girl, Madhu, in our village. She was very beautiful and fond of music and songs. She loved to sing and enjoyed listing music. Though she loved music there was hardly any occasion for such things except marriage party and Ramleela days. Ramleela was performed only in a few villages once in a year.'

'When she grew up to sixteen, her interest in songs was on climax. The Ramleela was performed in your village, Sumadi, during September and October in Navratras. She decided to go Sumadi with the fellow villagers for watching Ramleela. In Ramleela, she saw many good actors who performed their roles with interest and zeal. The Ramleela at Sumadi, as you know, was played with both acting and songs together, it made her to enjoy a lot. She enjoyed the play and songs of almost every actor. Though there were many women characters in the Ramleela, all the characters were played by men folks. Women were not allowed to perform in the Ramleela stage,' she said.

'Yes, I know. Still the roles of female characters are played by male members only,' I said agreeing with her description.

'After sometime, a young lad appeared in the stage in the Ram's character. His voice was so melodious and touchy that each spectator appreciated and applauded his acting and songs. He was really a great singer and actor. Madhu was not untouched from his marvelous acting and songs. She was so impressed and fell in love of his melodious songs and acting,' she took a deep breath and continued.

'She came back home but lost her heart in the Ramleela. The voice of Ram was still ringing in her ears. His face had overshadowed her mind and heart. Since that day, she walked up every night to Sumadi till the last day of Ramleela,' she said looking far away in the horizon.

'Do you know who was at that time in the Ram's character?' I quizzed.

'Sachan,' she said. 'But he was completely unaware of Madhu's condition and state of mind.'

'Ramleela came to an end but it became difficult for Madhu to live without having a glimpse of Sachan. She had a dream in her heart of being loved by Sachan. She started counting days for the beginning of next year's Ramleela,' she said.

'With this desperate long waiting, unfortunately one day she fell sick. Despite all possible attempts her health kept on deteriorating. Her parents lost all hopes. Lying on the bed, with broken voice Madhu pleaded for her last desire, 'papa please take me to the place from where I can see Sumadi.'

She continued the story with broken voice, 'there was not enough time left. Her papa lifted her in his arms and brought to here on this hill top. She looked at Sumadi with utmost satisfaction, tears rolled down from her beautiful eyes, and within couple of minutes she passed away.'

'Her parents were not so wealthy to make a big temple in her memories like Taj Mahal. Notwithstanding with their utmost capacity, they built this temple of Madhu,' she said and became silent.

I looked at the temple, which was shining just like the Taj Mahal.

2.0

My Favorite Medicine

Preparations were on to celebrate the first birthday of Sanju on a grand scale at Dharigaun village. I was eight then. I arrived at Sanju's house with my mother. Villagers had assembled at his house with variety of gifts. I saw a long row of married women applying auspicious turmeric paste one by one on Sanju's feet, hands, shoulders and head in a definite sequence. Close at hand a priest was chanting mantras. Two persons at one corner of the courtyard were beating drums hanging from their neck, as the mark of birthday celebrations. An aged woman was busy in distributing sweets to every person.

I entered the veranda. At a corner three grown men sitting on a string cot were cutting jokes and hence were laughing loudly at every now and then. Nearby to them, a person squatting on the floor was stirring something in an iron vessel placed on the fire through a large tablespoon. He took some soup in the spoon, dipped his finger in it, and touched his tongue by the same finger.

'Now it is perfectly cooked,' he said while tasting it.

'Would you like to have some soup?' he asked me.

'What is this?' I asked him back.

'It is wild chicken soup. It is really very tasty.'

'No, I don't.'

'Why?'

'I don't eat chicken and mutton. I don't like it.'

'Really, you have never eaten chicken and mutton,' he said with some surprise.

The conversations between us had attracted the attention of persons sitting on the cot, by now. They also insisted me to taste some soup. But I was not comfortable to taste it. I denied flatly and moved away from the veranda. I walked in the right side of the backyard where a white cow was tied with a stake at a corner by the rope. Her calf was tied at some distance. Cow being a holy animal, on every auspicious day including birthday some sweets and 'prasad' are given her to feed.

After sometime a person belonged to my village – Sumadi - came to me with a bowl of soup in his hand. He offered that soup to me. On my enquiry about the soup, he convinced me that it was an ordinary yet tasty vegetable soup. I took one spoonful soup and hesitantly put it in my mouth. It was really tasty. I asked him for some more soup, and I finished three bowls of soup then.

In the afternoon, I got to know that the soup I had consumed was not of vegetables rather it was of a wild chicken. I was surprised on its taste and had regret not taken it before. In the evening, once the celebrations had been completed, I bade adieu to our host and walked back with my mother to Sumadi. On the way, my mother thought to collect some grass from the nearby jungle to feed our milking cows at home. She asked me to wait for a couple of minutes so that she could gather some grass from the mountain slopes.

I sat down in the shade of a pine tree. There was a mug full of wild chicken among the gifts given to us by our host. I removed the cloth wrapped around the mug and opened its lid made of leaves to eat some chicken. I ate almost half of the chicken in the mug and closed it before my mother came back with two bundles of grasses.

While climbing further to Sumadi I felt some itching in my chest. By the time I reached at home in the dusk, the itching had become almost unbearable. I had red rashes all across my body, and I started crying. My mother washed my body with the warm water. She then massaged my body with the cow urine, and also asked me to drink a few drops of the same. I drank a small cup of cow urine and went to my bed. In the next morning, I had become completely fine. However, the itching I had felt made me to stop eating non-veg. again.

Later on, a day after winning a local cricket tournament a male goat was slaughtered by my colleagues to celebrate. My teammate had pressurized me to eat that mutton.

'There is nothing wrong in eating mutton. We all have been eating it since beginning and we have not had any problem. The day you ate it earlier, as you said, the meat would have been contaminated by some unwanted material. Your problem is psychological rather than physical,' said Ashu, one of my teammates. All others were agreed with him and hence nodded their heads. I had to make up my mind by force so I ate it.

After that, I tried to make myself busy in talking with them so that I could divert my attention from the fear of allergy. Alas!! Within two hours I had started feeling the same problem, as I had felt earlier. The itching started from my chest to belly and at last all over the body, including head. My entire body had become reddish and it had become unbearable to me to stay at one place. I remembered my mother's treatment of allergy. I drank a full glass of cow urine and also applied it on my body. I then went to bed to take the rest.

Luckily, the cow urine had worked again, and I began feeling better.

In due course of time with many such events and experiments, I learnt that my body was unable to digest mutton. Surprisingly, this was not the case with chicken and fish. I discussed it with some allopathic doctors but I did not get any satisfactory answer. I don't know whether there was some specific protein in mutton which was unsuitable for my body to adjust.

But, I was sure on the wonderful anti-allergic properties of cow urine, which used to bring me back from the deep troubles, as and when required.

3.0

The Prisoners of School

My grandfather and grandmother had passed away before my birth in late 1960s. I often heard my colleagues talking about their grand pa and ma, especially the wonderful stories narrated by them before going to bed. This made me to think about my grandparents. Photography at that time was not so common in my village and I can say in most parts of rural India. I had not even seen any photograph of my grandparents. I used to imagine their features, look, boldness and beauty on the descriptions of my parents, neighbours and other fellow villagers.

There was an old banyan tree in the middle of my village. Villagers used to relax beneath the long and dense branches of this magnificent pious tree. Children used to swing high and low by catching its long hanging aerial roots. Others used to play cards and 'chowsar'. There was a group of temples of Laxmi Narayan, lord Shiva and Hanuman. Overall, it was a perfect meeting and picnic place of men folks. Women hardly sat beneath the banyan tree as it was occupied by men and they were only seen for a short time worshipping gods and pouring water on the Shivaling.

I once asked my father, 'how old this banyan tree?'

'I can't say. But it was as such in my childhood. When I asked my father he spoke the similar words,' replied my father.

I felt the importance of the banyan tree that had seen many generations of my ancestors who had relaxed beneath its dense shade. Though it was alive, I was unable to understand its language. Otherwise, I would have requested him to tell about my ancestors.

My school route passed through just beneath the banyan tree. Quite often some school going children plucked its leaf and placed them inside their school books. Several times I attempted to know from my classmates the purpose of doing so. But no one disclosed this mystery to me.

While going to school, many of us remained quite tense and upset due to class activities and lot of homework allotted by different subject's teachers. Just after prayer at school, the tension increased with classes. The class teacher seemed to be a circus ring master who left no stone unturned in training his every object. The way of training was no matter to him. If someone of us could not satisfy his query then punishment was unavoidable. Some of the teachers slapped so hard that it shuddered the head to blackout.

Most of the teachers were in the race of discovering the unique methods of torture and punishment. The math's teacher – Gusain, was fond of five leaved chaste tree's flexible stick. He hit on the palm at least four to six times. The number of hits varied depending upon his mood. Every child in the class was so scared that rather than concentrating on the lecture we desperately waited for the bell to ring.

Some of us were strong enough to tolerate such painful moment but not all. Some sobbed quietly and others screamed in pain. Sometime the teacher hit so hard that it became impossible to stretch the palm for next hit. After each hit one had to either rub his palms together or rest them for a while across the armpit for receiving the next hit. Even being a first rank student of the class I had gone through this trauma once in a month and sometime in a week. After three to four hits the palm became so numbed that I felt myself almost without palms, and kept on stretching my hands as half dead or full dead till the last hit to receive.

All around the school campus there were many guava trees. Our English teacher liked guava and often broke its branches for this purpose. During guava's fruiting season if any student was caught plucking a fruit without prior permission from the agriculture teacher then punishment was sure. Rather eating guava fruit he was then beaten up by its stick.

The science teacher, Singh saab, was the source and sea of terror. No student could dare even to ask him a question. He first hit on palm and if someone did any delay in stretching his palm for next hit he was notorious to lose his temper and then could hit anywhere on the body even on the head, chest, belly, thigh and legs. Even after this, if his temper was not calmed down he hanged the culprit from the guava tree upside down. Sometime if this act did not satisfy his wish he then hit the body from the stick and if the stick broke down he did not hesitate to kick the hanging teens.

The biology teacher had denuded all the decorated bushes in the school premises. He did not send out any of us for bringing stick in anticipation that every passing moment may calm down his displeasure. Without any delay he broke down the branches of peacock feather plant planted in row for decorating the lone school building and set off his mission.

When I entered the eighth standard, I was ready to face a unique punishment discovered by our geography teacher, Khanduri. There was a black board, which was out of order. He was so lazy that rather going out of class for gathering stick or sending someone to pick up a stick for him, he discovered the use of broken black board as a punishment tool. He separated and picked up a piece of this board and started his job.

Before hitting hard he was kind enough to ask the defaulter, 'would you like cat or bat.'

Cat meant for him was to hit by vertical edge of the board's piece and bat stood for hitting by its flat surface. Naturally, everyone requested for bat as it was relatively less painful.

As the third law of Newton these actions had provoked some reactions among the students. Once in class ninth one of my classmates – Bhagat Singh, was beaten up continuously by biology teacher as he was unable to deliver the right answer. He ultimately could not tolerate such torture and while receiving the hit he caught the stick. This annoyed the teacher so much that he rather than speaking Hindi started cursing the whole class in English, which we then hardly understood. Most of us started giggling, which soon converted into laughs. This made the teacher uncomfortable and he felt better to leave the class room.

Hitting by stick for not delivering proper answer and for incomplete homework was one factor for punishment. But sometime, some teachers enjoyed kicking anyone of us without any reason. We used to sit on the mat or bare ground in the rows. While moving between the rows Tiwariji – a Hindi teacher used to kick someone of us making mimicry of our dialect – Garhwali.

One such day, about one and half km away a group of women were harvesting grasses from the mountain slope. They saw Tiwari kicking the innocent teens. They complained the same incident to the villagers at home, which aroused anger in the guardians. In the evening, some angry guardians gathered at Tiwari's residence and warned him not to repeat such act in future. The moment he accepted his misbehavior but soon he restarted his usual practice of hitting us without any reason.

No one of us ever dare to inform our parents and guardians about our school's trauma. We were always in the impression that informing to the parents could harm us both ways. The parents could take it otherwise and might have made us responsible for indiscipline and not attentive in classes. In other case, if parents became convinced and complained to our teacher, the teacher could have been more aggressive and could even failed us in the exams. The innocent childhood was ready to face the continued trauma and we were hanging just like the pendulum between the emotions of parents and teachers.

While going to school in the morning we did not forget to bow our head before the Hanuman, *Lord Neelkanth* and Laxmi Narayan sitting beneath the banyan tree in anticipation of receiving some blessings so that our teachers could be kind enough. A day after greeting the *Neelkanth* beneath the banyan tree, as usual, I saw some boys gathering fresh banyan leaf and putting them in their note books.

'What the hell is this? Could you please tell me why you put these fresh leaves inside the note book?' I asked desperately with some hope to get some answer of my long waited query.

'You don't know!!! If you keep fresh leaf of this banyan in your note book it must save you from teacher's fury. They can't beat you then so heartlessly,' one said with full of confidence.

4.0

Riding the Best

Sitting on a rock cliff above the pine forest, I saw an eagle soaring high up in the sky of pristine blueness. His free will and freedom that made him to fly high made me envy. I was upset over the rules to be followed, especially to be on the dot of time during the school days. Often, I was forced against my will to go school. I was pressurized to wake up early in the morning against my wishes of not leaving the bed early. I had no choice and say hence I released my frustrations in cursing such bonded system of education.

Binu, my classmate at Sumadi's Primary School, had similar opinion. Even, he was one step ahead of me. He mostly bunked classes. He had guts to bunk classes, but I could not do so.

One day, I and Binu were sitting together under a mango tree of the school garden during the interval. He seemed to be relaxed but I was tense.

'Yadav sir will again beat us in the English session,' I said. 'He is very particular of grammar and grammatical mistakes. I wish he should be transferred to some other school.'

'That's why I am not attending his class,' Binu disclosed his plan.

'Are you going home?' I asked.

'No, I shall remain hiding there,' he said raising his finger towards a nearby Lantana and small flowered poison sumac's bush.

'You don't scare to be caught by someone.'

'I hide into mango tree if I guess someone visit here.'

'Teacher may complain to your father. You will be thrashed,' I cautioned him.

'I don't care,' he said hastily.

'You are enough bold and lucky, too,' I said.

'Don't you wish to be lucky? Why don't you join me?' he asked. 'Trust me. I assure nothing will happen.'

'My father will kill me,' I said.

'Don't worry. Nothing happens. Even if someone complains say you had diarrhea and went to relieve in the jungle,' he aired a solution.

I liked his last suggestion, and therefore accepted his offer. Having a companion Binu became happy. We both climbed into a mango tree as soon as the bell ringed indicating end of the interval. Students playing and straying in the school ground and premises walked to their respective classes. School was two km away from village in the jungle. With the gathering of students in their classes the noisy environment had turned into complete silence.

The afternoon sun shimmered on the guava's garden spanned all around the school. Few women were gathering grasses on our right hill slope. On a newly constructed serpent hilly road leading to Srinagar, a nearest town, labours were loading stones in a truck.

'Have you ever enjoyed bus riding?' Binu asked me.

'No, never.'

'Would you like to ride?'

'Of course, yes,' I said.

'Let's go to enjoy truck riding. There is no difference between truck and bus. Both have equal size and shape. I am sure you will enjoy it. It is really very interesting,' Binu said convincingly.

'Come on Binu. It is not our truck. I don't have a single penny. Do you have?' I asked.

'I too don't have any penny. But don't worry. I know the truck conductor. He will accept our request,' he said.

'How do you know him?' I said.

'I have got into that truck, quite often. Only we have to assist labours in loading it,' he disclosed the secret of his success in riding the truck free of cost.

'But the stones are too heavy. I doubt to lift one,' I said.

'We only pick up some small ones,' he said cleverly.

We finally stepped down from the tree and walked uphill towards the truck. Binu greeted humbly with folded hands to both conductor and driver and so that I. Without wasting time he started loading stones in the truck.

'Come, you also keep some stones in the truck,' he insisted me to do so. I started following him with some hesitation as we did not yet have any deal with truck driver to ferry us. Once the truck was loaded Binu stepped up in the truck and climbed on the piles of stones, and indicated me to do the same.

Interestingly, neither driver nor any labour and conductor paid heed to us. The truck moved on over the mountains. The road went west, where there were no forests, just bare brown hill side and cultivated land. I stared out from the truck's backside the scattered roadside trees were running away from us. I noticed, first time, how trees looked like and moved away from the vehicle.

A horn blared, shattering the mountain silence, and the truck came round a bend in the road. A herd of cows was scattered to right and left. Some of them went uphill and some went downhill. Soon there were cattle all over the place. A cloud of dust raised and we had left them behind.

Dust was everywhere. The truck was full of it. For a moment I had difficulty to breath. I could feel dust in my mouth, nostrils and eyes. The laborers seemed more or less unaffected and acclimatized with the dusty road. They had continued their mountain song as the truck swung round the sharp bends of winding road.

After two and half km drive with the rattled sound, the shaky old truck stopped on the roadside at Kaanda bend. Laborers began unloading the truck and I stood at the edge of the road. Binu joined me. He was smiling, though he seemed to be just dug out from a quarry, full of dust. I broke out a twig of shrub and started beating my trouser and shirt. I cleaned my hairs, face and shoes.

Suddenly, I saw four of our classmates coming to us. I scared to face them. My heart started sinking in anticipation of something out of the blue. I cursed the moment I accepted Binu's offer. I shivered imagining my father's wrath. My classmates had reached very close to me. They smiled at me and without saying a word walked to unload truck. I now had a deep breath.

'Let's go home. The school time is shortly going to be over,' I said. 'We must reach home at time otherwise we may be caught.'

Binu agreed and we rushed back home, leaving truck on the roadside. My first experience of riding a four tired motor vehicle had come to an end. It was though suffocating and dusty I never forget my first riding of vehicle as one cannot forget his/her first Love.

5.0

Gaura's Home

In Garhwal, not only the Badrinath, Kedarnath, Gangotri, Yamunotri and Hemkund inspire the human soul for spirituality but every dale, mountain, river and even forest and rivulet are the source of heavenly feelings, mysticism, and holism. Here each village has its own village deity. Likewise, the Sumadi village, tugged deep into the mountains of Garhwal, has its village deity – *Gaura Devi*.

The villagers have been worshipping goddess *Gaura* since occupying the land on a mountain slope at Sumadi around a small lake in twelve century. The lake was so beautiful that the first settlers here named it as Gauri Kund after the name of their clan's deity. *Gaura* is another name of mother Parbati – the consort of *Lord Neelkanth*. The villagers of Sumadi have deep faith in their deity and land, like any other hill village of Garhwal.

'What does Sumadi stand for?' I asked my father when I was a child.

'Actually, it is not Sumadi. It is rather Surmadi, which means the 'house of Gods'. 'Sur' means god and 'madi' means place to live or home,' my father explained to me.

'Surmadi was more appealing and pious. Why do we call and write then Sumadi?' I asked.

'People prefer to choose shortcut and so that short forms, as much as possible. This tendency has changed Surmadi into Sumadi. In the race of shortcut, they hardly bother about meanings,' my father pointed out.

Quite often, my father used to offer prayers at the village temple of *Gaura*. On some occasions I accompanied him. One such fortunate day after offering prayers at the temple I asked my father, 'I heard every temple has some idols. But we don't have even one in our temple. Where is our *Gaura*'s idol?'

'It is in Devalgarh,' he said.

'But Devalgarh is quite away from our village. Why did we keep it there?' I hissed.

'Because She lives there only.'

'She is our deity. Why does she live far away from us?'

'My son, she lives with her husband like any other married woman. And Devalgarh is her husband's home.'

'Who is her husband?'

'*Neelkanth*.'

'If she lives there why do we offer her prayers here?'

'She lives here, as well. She is omnipresent. Whenever and wherever you call her she will be there. Being a daughter of this village, Sumadi is her first home. After her marriage to *Neelkanth*, Devalgarh has become her permanent home,' my father explained to me yet my small inquisitive brain was unable to grasp such mysticism.

'Do you visit her at Devalgarh?' I asked.

'Yes, I have been there several times. Every year on Vaishakhi the villagers from far and wide gather at her temple premises at Devalgarh for seeking her blessings.

'May I accompany you on the forthcoming Vaishakhi?' I requested.

'Yes, why not? I shall take you there,' he promised.

It was a day of November and Vaishakhi had to be celebrated in April hence there was enough time to visit Devalgarh. In an evening of November, villagers gathered in the temple premises. They had to fix a holy day for celebration of jaggi - a religious fair. After studying position of stars and planets in the astrological book the village Brahmin finally declared December eight for celebration of jaggi. Once the day was fixed, the jaggi was celebrated with great zeal and enthusiasm by the villagers. Being a religious fair it was attended by a large number of *Gaura*'s devotees from far and wide.

Likewise previous years, people of nearby villages and their near and dear ones were informed about the date of jaggi. On the day of jaggi, people started trickling down in the Sumadi village. Some vendors with their make-shift shops had also arrived for selling various shades of bangles, nose pins, earrings, necklaces, and toys. A couple of sweet sellers of Srinagar town had also put their stalls on the side of narrow footpaths below the temple square. All of a sudden, the calm and peaceful area had converted into a crowdy market centre.

A 'deepak' (lighting lamp) was brought from the residence of the main priest of *Gaura* where it kept on lighting day and night, uninterruptedly. A group of priests began to arrange things for yagya. They kept some sacred wood composed of mango, peepal, bel, deodar, and sandalwood in a kund (a square shallow ditch) and smashed them with ghee and coconuts before setting them into fire. They began chanting mantras. On particular intervals each one of them gathered a pinch of mixture made up of barley, ghee, til, saffron, sandalwood, cardamom, camphor, honey, and medicinal herbs and tossed it into the fire with chanting 'swaaha'. Sometime they tossed fruits and other food items into the fire exclaiming the same auspicious word - 'swaaha'.

On a corner of the temple's courtyard, the village musicians were playing dhol and damau - the local musical instruments. In the peak hours of jaggi and yagya, I saw a person in his fifties began to shiver. All men, women and children turned to bow their heads before him. I was told that the shivering person was the manifestation of the deity *Gaura* to her devotees. Within couple of minutes he ran through the crowd and jumped into the Gaurikund.

After diving in the Gaurikund, he returned to the temple courtyard where he was decorated with deity's cloths, ornaments and weapons. A yellow dhoti was wrapped on lower half of his body. A sacred red paste was applied on his forehead along with a few seeds of rice. A red scarf was wrapped around his head. He stretched his hands out asking for something. Immediately, a devotee brought a Gurkha knife locally called 'khukri' and handed over the same to him. He started performing celestial dance unfurling khukri in the air with the rhythms of dhol and damau. Devotees kept on offering him fruits and garlands and in return they got invisible blessings.

The celebrations came to an end by the evening. Prasad was distributed to the devotees. I received some fruits and flowers as a Prasad. Before turning back home, my father gathered some sacred ashes of yagya. He dipped his finger in the ashes and touched the same on my forehead.

'Why are people placing this ash on forehead?' I asked my father looking many people doing the same thing. 'Is it the end of yagya?'

'Applying ashes of yagya on forehead leads to ward off all misfortunes and diseases. The values and philosophy of yagya are not so simple. They are endless. Burning of ghee and herbs in holy fire with mantras purify the soul and surrounding environment. Yagya being a team work teaches us the way of living in the society with all humanity, compassion and cooperation. Yagya helps in curing the ailing human system at psychological, spiritual and physical levels. It fulfills all desires,' explained my father.

I saw a pundit who had heard our conservation came to us and smiled. Looking at my father he said, 'you are right on account of complexities associated with yagya. You know that fire is one of the five elements of life. Being hot and bright, the yagya's fire teaches us to be bright, active and full of brilliance. Its flame remains upward in all circumstances and pressures, which alerts us to be fearless. It accumulates nothing and whatever comes in its contact becomes fire itself. This teaches us not to accumulate things for our selfish gains rather use them for the welfare of others and make them generous.'

'Thanks punditji for enlightening. My son was asking me the use of applying ashes on forehead,' my father asked the pundit.

'Interesting! His question is very valid. Ash is the end product of fire. Likewise, the end of this physical form of ours has to be reduced to a handful of ashes. Generally, the people, being the worldly creatures, while busy in accumulation of possessions more often forget this eternal truth. Applying yagya's ashes on forehead makes them to remember the inescapability of death, the eternal truth.

Hence it teaches to utilize each and every moment of life in best possible way,' he explained philosophically. 'Next year we will organize the Dev Bhagwat right here. Since all about yagya is described in Bhagwat Puran, you will get then best explanation of yagya.'

We arrived back at home before sunset. Some of our relatives who came to see jaggi and lived in neighboring villages were waiting for us. They were desperate to go back home. My father offered them to stay back, which they denied, as they had some pressing work at home. One of the works that was common was to take care of cows.

Once they went off, my father asked me for a glass of drinking water. I picked up a glass and dipped it into a bucket of water. While pulling back the glass from water, I saw a tiny fish in the bucket. I was thrilled with joy. Her swift movements from one corner of bucket to other continued attracting my attention. I began playing with the fish and forgot to give water to my father. Realizing delay in my response, my father came forward to collect water from the bucket.

Peeping into the bucket he said hastily, 'this is *Gaura's* fish. Don't tease her.'

'*Gaura's* fish!'

'Yes, it is. It would have gone in the bucket while collecting water from the Gaurikund. We have to drop her there only,' he murmured.

'But my friends say fishes form a tasty food,' I hissed.

'This is not an ordinary fish. This is *Gaura's* fish. This is sacred and no one can eat her,' he said firmly. 'You know they keep Gaurakund's water clean from insects and harmful germs. Tomorrow morning it has to be dropped back in the kund.'

Weeks turned into months and the shivering winter began to dissolve with the banging of pleasant spring over the hills. Before the pleasure of spring turned into the heat of summer, my wish to visit *Gaura*'s temple at Devalgarh began to take shape. On a fortunate day of April, the residents of Sumadi gathered at temple premises of *Gaura*. It was Vaishakhi. The procession set off to Devalgarh with beating dhol and damau. While passing behind our house, I too joined the procession with my father.

The villagers kept on shouting slogans '*Gaura* mata kee jai'. Passing through some small villages such as Harkandi, Balodi and Jaletha, the march reached at Bughani.

'This is chief minister's house,' my father said raising finger to a double stored house on a hill slope to my right.

'Chief Minister! Who is that?' I asked.

'Hemwati Nandan. Hemwati Nandan Bahuguna. He was an ordinary village boy like any other boy of Garhwal. Today he is the most powerful person and head of the biggest province of our country, Uttar Pradesh. He born and brought up in this small village but his hard work and *Gaura*'s blessings made him bigger than these mountains,' he said in anticipation of inculcating values of hard work in my curious mind.

The caravan kept on rolling to Devalgarh on the serpent hill route. The size of caravan had inflated many folds before reaching the temple premises of Devalgarh, as the people straying on route had began to join the processes. A part of caravan entered the temple and began chanting hymns. Many people could not enter the temple and I was one of them. I stayed outside the temple's door with my father waiting crowd to be thinned. After a long wait, we got opportunity to have a glimpse of the *Gaura*. While bowing my head before Her I was extremely happy to see our clan's deity.

At four o'clock the deity was brought out by a group of priests. The crowd showered flowers and petals over the deity while she swung high and low in her swing. At last, the deity sat down on her throne in the temple. The crowd began to disperse. I turned holding my father's finger to the Raj Rajeswari temple. We offered our prayers to Raj Rajeswari, the goddess of Garhwal's king, and walked back to Sumadi.

Years kept on rolling. Life in hills between then and now had not been easy. I lost my father before completion of my matriculation. But his teachings remained live with me. He was my best teacher and perfect source of inspiration. Now his teachings were my sole property. The energy and spirit of this asset made me to continue my education and I completed graduation despite extreme hardships and adversities.

An evening while sitting in the shade of the old banyan tree at Sumadi, I came across the sad news from my village friends about Devalgarh temple. The *Gaura*'s idol went missing from temple, where it was secured for posterity. Most probably, someone had stolen *Gaura*'s idol.

'Is it true?' I asked Khunka who was sitting to my right in the circle around the banyan tree.

'It is hundred percent true. There is no doubt about it,' Khunka said.

'How someone dare to steal deity's statue?' I whispered.

'People believe that either someone from our village has helped the burglars or someone from our village has stolen the statue,' Mukesh added in conversation this time.

'What nonsense? We shall steal our own deity,' Gamma shouted.

'They have reasons to say so,' Mukesh replied.

'Reason! What do you mean?' I quizzed.

'Don't you know the traditional facts and beliefs?' Mukesh said.

'Please stop rambling and come to the point. What is that reason?' I asked being impatient to know the reason.

'Look, no one can lift, forget lifting, even can't shake an inch the *Gaura*'s statue. The muscle power and energy of a person does not make any difference to the deity. Even a large group of mighty people can't lift it without the assistance of Sumadi's residents,' he said.

'You mean, none other than our village residents lift the *Gaura*'s statue,' I said being flabbergasted.

'Yes, none other than our own village person, as it is *Gaura*'s wish. And against her wishes no one can succeed,' Mukesh said.

'I never heard it before,' I said.

'Since other villagers can't lift her idol, it is impossible to steal the same by other villagers and outsiders. That's why fingers are raising towards our own village,' Mukesh explained.

'It is amazing and unbelievable,' I said.

'It is absolutely true, and it has happened in past,' Mukesh said.

'I would wish to know that too. Will you please tell me?' I said.

'A long time ago, a severe dispute took place between the Sumadi's residents and rests of the villages in this region. All villages were against the special treatment given to the villagers of Sumadi in Devalgarh temple during the Vaishakhi festival. The villagers also raised questions on the authenticity of traditional belief, which claimed that without the support of Sumadi's residents one could not lift the *Gaura*'s statue. Looking into the gravity of disputes and subsequent war like situation, the villagers of Sumadi decided not to participate in the Vaishakhi festival held at that year in the Devalgarh temple,' Mukesh narrated.

'Well, what happened next?' I asked.

'On the fateful day of Vaishakhi all other villagers participated in the festival at Devalgarh temple. Initially, they waited for Sumadi's people and their procession to worship deity but when it got delayed they decided to perform prayers without Sumadi's residents. As per the traditional practice when they began to lift up *Gaura*'s idol for swinging they could not do so. They tried a lot and put their all strength in lifting up the statue but failed by all means. Now they had realized their mistake and pleaded forgiveness from the deity. They fell down on her feet. The very next day, all villagers of Sumadi went to Devalgarh and offered prayers to the *Gaura*, as per the traditional norms. Since then the traditional belief of lifting deity's idol with the help of Sumadi's residents has became more acceptable in the society,' said Mukesh.

'This is really a fantastic story,' I said. 'If it is so the people's apprehension in the society can't be ruled out.'

The rumors and tensions simmered for many days in and around Sumadi. Since there was no clue for getting back the *Gaura*'s idol, the residents of Sumadi finally decided to place a new idol in the Devalgarh temple.

An auspicious day was identified and marked with the help of village pundit for placing order to make a new idol. A village person was in touch with some idol maker at the pink city. His connection helped in placing order for making a good looking idol. The villagers of Sumadi working in various parts of the country and abroad were contacted to donate for this noble and religious cause. All these efforts had returned sweet fruits in terms of attractive amount of collection.

On an auspicious day the *Gaura*'s idol was brought from the pink city to the sacred city of Haridwar. When the people arrived at Har-Ki-Paidi with the *Gaura*'s idol, the evening aarti of Ganga had reached its crescendo. In the glowing lamps and ringing bells the bhajan rose above the din of the packed stands. With chanting mantras the idol was made to take a holy dip in the Ganges water. While bringing idol to Sumadi, a sacred bath was taken again in Devprayag by pundit and idol along with all people accompanying the idol.

Reaching at Sumadi with chanting mantras the idol was placed in the courtyard of *Gaura*'s temple. The villagers gathered around the idol and started shouting slogans 'Jai Mata Kee. Jai Ambe Jagdambe Mata....'. The religious music of dhol and damau had made the whole environment blessed with spirituality.

Devbhagwat (the story of gods) was organized in the temple premises before the *Gaura*'s idol that continued for the next nine days. Many Brahmins kept on reciting Vedic hymns and offering prayers in all nine days before the *Gaura*'s idol. The village environment remained embedded for days in the religious fervors and festivities. On the last day of Devbhagwat the yagya was performed with all zeal and passion.

The next day of yagya was the day of Vaishakhi. It was pre-calculated and decided that the idol would be carried to the Devalgarh on this pious day. In the morning of Vaishakhi as soon as the *Gaura*'s idol was placed in palanquin for carrying to Devalgarh, tears rolled down on the cheeks of villagers. With holy chorus and catchphrases the procession set out to march behind the *Gaura*'s palanquin to her destination at Devalgarh.

Number of villagers kept on shedding silent tears till the procession crossed the village boundary. Though, they were shouting slogans of '*Gaura* Mata Kee Jai' in cold and dry voice, bereft of emotions, as they were bidding adieu one of their beloved. Interestingly, their emotions turned into cheerfulness once the caravan crossed the village boundary.

All along the path to Devalgarh people were waiting for a glimpse of *Gaura*. Most of them joined the caravan and before reaching at Devalgarh the caravan had enlarged many folds spanned over many km on the serpent mountain trail.

The size of crowd at Devalgarh had broken all past records. Every person in the crowd seemed to be highly enthusiastic for touching the *Gaura*'s palanquin. The amount of energy flowing in the crowd was unbelievable. Everyone was struggling hard to reach close to the *Gaura*'s palanquin to touch her feet and got her blessings. It was a matter of great surprise that despite such great efforts and struggle there was no clash, no fight and no conflict. Sometime it was too difficult to move further in the crowd. The caravan had to move ahead and it kept on moving though snail's pace. Finally, the *Gaura* was placed on her throne at Devalgarh temple with chanting hymns.

With all efforts and energy, I entered the *Gaura*'s temple to offer prayers before to begin my return journey back to Sumadi. As the late setting sun casted an eerie shadow over the village, I arrived at my home. I gazed at the *Gaura*'s temple that was completely calm. A gloom descended over the temple like a thick canopy reflecting my mood due to bidding adieu to my beloved *Gaura*.

Sumadi - A wonderful village in Uttarakhand

6.0

Aunty

It took me only twenty five minutes to reach Balodi from my village Sumadi. The day I reached at Balodi, sky was clear that helped me to see a panoramic view of the snow laden mountains. The Chowkhamba and many other peaks seemed to be covered with a fresh quilt of snow far away at the horizon. The fine cool breeze blowing here had made Balodi cooler than Sumadi. Though, both the villages had similar elevation, there was marked differences in the climate. The sun exposed mountain slopes had made Sumadi relatively warmer whereas Balodi was located at sun shade mountain slope. There was severe scarcity of water in Sumadi, especially during summer. Balodi had plenty of water round the year.

Besides these benefits, I liked to visit Balodi to see my sister, who lived here. She had a cute baby – Shailu - who was two yrs old then and I often saw him sleeping on a small cot. I spent night listening future plans of my sister, and set off to return Sumadi, next day. I had not yet gone far from her residence the rain began. I stopped beneath a lone Salix tree attempting to avoid soaking in the rains. Salix was quite rare in my village forest and the adjacent areas. There were only three places, all humid, where I had encountered only two to three Salix trees. This tree was always our first preference to make cricket bat. I don't remember when and who told us its use to make bat. Fortunately, people never harm these trees.

Once rain stopped I started homewards. Walking few steps uphill, I arrived at the perennial water spring of Dhinsiri. Close to this spring, there was an old sacred fig tree locally called as peepal. I had heard, from the village elders, many mysterious stories associated with both peepal and the Dhinsiri's water spring. Whenever, I used to pass through this spring I had quite mixed feelings. This place was abode of both God and Ghost together, which was generally not common in the hills.

The spring and the peepal tree were worshipped by the villagers. But the pond just beneath the spring was believed to be haunted by an evil spirit. Many women of the nearby villages were tracked and made frighten by the pond devil. People avoided passing through this pond even in the day time. The only hope and source of courage for passerby was peepal tree that they believed the abode of God. 'Ashwastham cha brikchhanam' (Of all trees I am peepal tree), as mentioned by the Lord Krishna – the incarnation of Lord Vishnu - in 'Geeta' gave them courage while passing through. Peepal was highly venerated by the villagers. Water is also worshipped by Hindus and so that the villagers did. 'Vishnur vishnur harir hari,' I heard priest always chanting whenever he performed any ritual.

I was confused on the pond's association with ghost. If the spring, the source of pond, belonged to the Lord Krishna then how come ghost haunted the pond. But if people had such opinion then it was hard to dispose of. I gazed uphill at the beautiful mountain – Gaulakchheswar that was the source of legendary tales. Villagers believed that Lord Krishna still lived in this mountain with his thousands of cows. The cow urine seeped out at three localities in the form of springs and Dhinsiri spring was one of them. They felt that these springs had peculiar cow urine smell.

I drank some water of spring and tried to feel its smell and taste. The water was no doubt very sweet. Despite many attempts I could not make out the smell. I walked further and entered the territory of Sumadi just after crossing a ridge that decided the climate between Sumadi and Balodi.

There was no primary health care centre in Balodi, so my sister very on and off visited Sumadi with Shailu for treatments. After couple of years I could hear Shailu expressing his feelings and views. Unfortunately, his father had been lost somewhere in the crowds of Calcutta, where he was posted as a Govt. employee. This incident had severely affected my sister's family life. Money Order was then the major part of hill's economy. Every month villagers who had somebody in job outside the village waited for postman to drop their Money Order.

The sudden loss of her money orders economy had shaken her family's livelihood. Though, she had a small family but she did not have any other source of income. A once joyful and delighted family had become impoverished. They had to learn the hard facts and reality of life, how to survive.

One day Shailu visited us at Sumadi with his mother. We all loved him and he had also mixed up with us, especially his aunt (younger sister of his mother). While chatting, his aunt took out two rupees from his pocket and refused to give him back. Shailu became extremely upset and he pleaded his aunt to return his money. It seemed that two rupees was a very big amount for him. He did not leave any stone to turn for getting back his wealth.

'Please return my rupees. We came here to buy some wheat. Don't deprive us to buy wheat. Please return my money,' he said with deep agony when nothing worked out.

The life had taught him the real lesson of bread and butter and a boy of merely five yrs old had grown up to adult. When his fellow children were enjoying happy-go-lucky life, crying out and demanding for range of toys, Shailu was worried about his both ends meets. He was worried on his economic condition, which could not afford his mother to arrange proper food. Rather than normal babyish behavior of crying for chocolate and sweets he was deeply concerned for wheat. His childhood was lost somewhere in realizing money's values. He suddenly seemed to be a very mature and old person. Tears rolled down from his aunt's eyes. She hugged him so tightly to never ever leave him in this risky world, which made his father to disappear.

7.0

Nagrasani

Monsoon had brought the most exquisite expression in myriad enchanting ways in Sumadi. The green shades had embraced the hills and valleys, everywhere. The gentle murmur of seasonal springs was heard along the serpent paths leading out of the village into the tranquil forest glades and groves. Clouds shrouded me quite on and off while weeding in my farms close to pine groves at the Nagrasani.

My farms were carved on the hilltop. Being at the top of the hill, they formed the most favorite vantage points to see the wide view of majestic mighty mountains and deep valleys of the Himalaya. I wished to spend here my maximum time just watching this natural scenic beauty. Even wherever I had fast on Janmastami and Mahashivratri I used to visit here to forget my day-long fast or to kill my appetite by watching this splendid natural beauty.

My mother, Kamladevi, had joined me in weeding. I could see many people in downhill terraced farms whenever the patches of clouds moved away from the farms. To the right side of my farms there was a small yet beautiful temple of a deity, which was called as Nagrasani devi. Being located on the top of the hill, the temple and temple site both were extremely attractive. Like all other villagers my mother had high reverence to Nagrasani devi.

I was always curious to know about the temple of Nagrasani devi. I asked my mother if she could tell me something. And she narrated an interesting story to me.

Once upon a time, there was a bold and muscular man in a nearby village, Jaletha. While bathing, he found an idol in the river Alaknanda at Kirtinagar. He decided to carry it to his village. He lifted the idol, placed it on his shoulder, and set off to his village. He climbed on and on, and arrived at the hilltop of Nagrasani without any problem. On the hilltop he thought to take rest for a while and hence he kept the idol on the ground.

After a brief rest, he got up to proceed further, as his village was still two km away. He leaned upon the idol to pick it up and to place on this shoulder, but failed to do so. He tried again and again to lift the idol but all his attempts were in vain. He was highly surprised on the fact that the idol had become so heavy and he was unable to even shake it, which he had just carried over on the ten km sheer uphill trails.

Since the dark had prevailed over the mountains, he was forced to move his home without idol. At home he discussed about the idol and the incident took place on the hilltop. Next day, the villagers came to Nagrasani and tried to lift the idol but even all together they could not do so.

Finally, they decided to drop the idea of carrying the idol to village. In due course of time, three villages, Sumadi, Harkandi and Jaletha collectively constructed a temple around the idol. Since then the idol has been worshipped as the Nagrasani devi and the temple has been called as the Nagrasani temple.

'How come the idol had become too heavy to pick up?' I asked my mother.

'The deity had liked the site and its natural beauty. She did not want to leave such an attractive and wonderful place,' replied my mother.

It is a hard fact that the faiths and subsequent myths interwoven around them cannot be analyzed in the light of scientific rigors; nonetheless the locality of Nagrasani was really awesome and extremely rare.

8.0

A Killer in the Clouds

Durgee woke up early in the morning. She had many things to do. She sat on the rounded wall of her courtyard, and thought for a moment from where to begin. She was in her fifteen and like any other hill girl she executed most of the work at home. A day when her school was off she decided to finish her pending work of weeding at the farms. But before that she had to arrange drinking water for breakfast.

She took a rounded container and walked downhill to 'nawn' (pit of water). The 'nawn' was about a km away from her house. While coming back with head-load of water her energy burnt fast due to continuous climb on the hill-trail. Pushing up on the hill she stopped at about hundred steps interval to recoup some energy. This interval had reduced to eighty to sixty steps at the end of her climb before reaching at home.

After unloading the container she sat on the doorstep breathing deeply. Drops of sweating slipped down from her forehead, though it was a relatively cool cloudy day of August. Her younger sister Guddi had just awakened and she was watching the downhill village houses sitting on the rounded wall of courtyard.

Durgee, after a brief rest, entered the kitchen. She cooked maduwa's chapattis, bottle guard's vegetable and snacks of pumpkin's flower. She ate two chapattis, and rest two chapattis she wrapped in a piece of clean cloth for eating at farms. She plucked two leaves of pumpkin in which she wrapped some vegetables and snacks.

Guddi was brushing her teeth at a corner of courtyard. Durgee while collecting a hoe asked Guddi, 'I am going to Maldaru. Chapattis are kept for you in the basket. After breakfast do join me for weeding at Maldaru's farm'.

Guddi nodded her head accepting Durgee's command.

Durgee walked ups and down on the terraced farms trail leading out of the village. Maldaru, the place where Durgee had eight small terraced farms was at three km away from her house at Sumadi.

Some women in the groups of two to five had reached before her in their farms. While working some were singing Garhwali songs. The melodious songs seemed to be coming out from their heart. Durgee had covered about two and half km. The clouds moving up on the terraced farms from the valley had weakened visibility. She could still hear the songs of women folks but she was not able to see the singers.

Reaching at farm, she kept her chapattis and food items on a safer side, which she had wrapped in the pumpkin's leaves. Once she bent down on the ground for weeding she lost in her work. The clouds had shrouded her farms. A thick sheet of grayish clouds passed before her. She was hardly bothered of clouds rather she was busy in indentifying and uprooting the unwanted plants from her terraced farms.

All of a sudden, she saw a goat running frenzied towards her. The goat almost adhered at her. Durgee was amused to see the goat and her unusual behavior. She had never seen this goat before. She was surprised on the fact that why the goad had suddenly fallen in love to her.

She was about to touch the goat's face but before this her attention was caught by a gnarling big cat just in front of her. The leopard was staring hard with ferocious eyes at Durgee who stood between the goat and him, the prey and the predator and the hunt and the hunter. Her breath had stopped in lungs. Her brain stopped thinking. And rather than touching the goat with love she pushed the goat towards leopard.

The goat resisted Durgee's act with full strength. All three – goat, leopard and Durgee were in extreme shocks. God knows what leopard was thinking but certainly leopard hesitated to grab his prey from a girl. Durgee had the only way to safe her by offering goat to the predator.

In this terrific situation, the shepherd's sound of calling his herd from the hill top, coming through the clouds, had brought a great amount of relief to Durgee to scream who had became mum. Her high-pitched yelling alerted the women folks working adjacent to Durgee's farms. They all started calling, 'Durgee, Durgee, Durgeeeeee…. What happened? What happened? Are you ok?'

This made to scream Durgee with extreme pitch, 'Baag, Baag, Baag, Baaaag….' All women started shouting loudly running towards Durgee shrouded with thick clouds.

Leopard smelt the danger and turned to hide away in the clouds. He left his prey with Durgee. The women folk gathered around Durgee consoling and patting her. The goat had recovered from her pain and agony, and had started browsing mild leaves of a nearby shrub. Durgee had realized the fact that had brought the goat from the clouds to her feet. She knew that goat had won the battle of life over death with a natural intuition.

9.0

A Bull in the Leopard's Monarchy

Having exhausted playing cricket for hours in a small ground of Sumadi village I sat on the temple stairs attached with right side of the lone playground. Sampu, Patori, Manoj and Tunna with couple of other teammates joined me to rest for a while before we dispersed for our respective homes.

'Tomorrow I may take my cows to Kwiloun jungle,' Tunna said. 'Is there anybody interested to join me?'

'I wish to join you,' Manoj said thinking for a while. 'Let's have fun in the Jungle.'

'Well, I am also interested to join you. I shall cook some nice food. Let's enjoy,' Tunna said.

The conversation on picnic in jungle also attracted me to join them and finally four of us approved the proposal.

Next day morning, we gathered our cattle and set off to Kwiloun jungle of Sumadi with cooking and other picnic materials. Every family in Sumadi had two to three cows, and a pair of bulls. We passed through the terraced agricultural land perched on a hillside immediately after the cluster of houses.

Having walked over two and half km away from the village we arrived in the Kwiloun jungle. Pine trees, small and big, were scattered all along the hills, under which tussocks of grasses were flourishing on the ground. We stopped chasing our herds and made them free to graze. We selected a hillock to rest and also to keep eyes on our herds while enjoying picnic.

Sitting here under a grove of pine, I gazed across the valley and undulating terrain to presume the area where cows might have moved in next three to four hours while grazing.

'Let's play card,' Sampu said taking out cards from his shirt's pocket. I turned to form a circle for playing cards with Sampu. Tunna and Manoj joined us for two consecutive games and thereafter they got up to collect dried firewood for making tea.

'Hey, we forgot to bring milk,' Manoj said while placing firewood between two stones.

'No problem, we have several cows here,' Patori said.

'Come on. Are you kidding? Don't you know their calves are at home? No cow gives milk without calf,' Manoj said.

'You are wrong and I shall prove it right here,' Sampu said. 'I challenge you.'

'This is not possible,' Manoj remained firmed.

'It is very much possible. Let's follow me,' Sampu said picking two glasses, one empty and other half-filled with water.

Sampu walked downhill staring a group of cows trying to identify the one which could give some milk without her calf. Manoj and I followed him. He stopped before a cow that was mine. Without any delay and discussion he sat down before the cow and sprinkled water three times on the cow's teats before to grip them for drawing milk. Within couple of minutes he had collected enough milk for making five to six cups of tea.

'Hey, this is very bad,' I said. 'You people draw milk from my cow in the jungle only, and that's why we don't get milk at home. Her calf also remains weak.'

'Come on, everybody knows it in the village. I am not alone to know this fact. I am surprised how come you don't know. Look, I am not your archenemy,' Sampu said.

'Don't you realize it is unfair?' I asked Sampu.

'Sorry, I agree with you. Please calm down,' Sampu requested.

The matter was settled down after brief arguments and interruptions made by Tunna and Patori. Sampu had won the challenge which he betted with Manoj, but he had bitter taste of his victory with me.

Reaching back at the picnic point, we had tea with potato snacks and began to cook rice and dal for lunch. Tunna being a knowledgeable cook was only capable among us to fix optimum quantity of salt, spices and chilies to be mixed with dal. The lunch was ready to serve around two o'clock. I plucked some leaves of mountain ebony and Tunna had beautifully spread rice and dal with some salad of radish on the leaves. We all enjoyed our feast on the hillock in a pine grove while listening to the ripple of rivulets flowing down and the jingling of bells tied around the neck of cows and bulls. Once everybody finished the meal, we washed the cooking utensils in the rivulet and sat down once more for playing cards.

When the game reached on the peak and every team was quite concerned to win, all of a sudden I noticed a stampede in a group of cattle to my left. We began to stand up one by one to understand the reason of sudden panic among the cattle. When every cattle was running madly, I surprised to notice a bull bellowing ferociously. Within a couple of minutes the stampede calmed down with a panic sound of a cow to my left, little above the valley.

We all ran fast toward the panic sound. I saw the same bull that was bellowing fiercely running toward the direction of sound we were following, too. Reaching closure to the sound, I shocked to see a leopard sitting over a cow near a lantana bush. Before we reacted and shouted, the ferocious bull had attacked the leopard. The leopard stuck between the bull's strong horns. Before the leopard could react to this sudden attack, the bull pushed him and pressed hard against the mountain slope. Meantime, the injured cow ran away frantically.

The leopard gnarled and struggled hard to get rid of from the bull's strong horns but failed. Earlier, I wanted to cry for the safety of the cow but now I was shouting for the leopard's safety. But the bull was not ready to pay attention to my crying. I had never ever thought that a leopard would have become so helpless while hunting cattle. The bull only released the leopard on our reaching at the spot and shouting repeatedly.

The leopard till then had become extremely scary. Once released, he jumped away in the jungle aimlessly perhaps with a strong lesson not to take prey lightly in future. After all, the local people of Garhwal have been worshipping bulls, as the symbols of warrior Nandi, the loved one's of *Neelkanth*, for centuries definitely for some strong reasons.

At half past three we began calling and gathering our cattle. During stampede they had run to different directions. Some of them had rushed further deep into the jungle while others had rushed home. It was difficult to count their exact number as we were in dark on the number of cattle went back home.

While striding on the base of the hillock, I saw a white cow lying on the ground. I called the cow to stand up but she remained motionless. I walked closure and found her dead. Manoj being nearby to me busy with gathering cows I called him.

'I think, in stampede this cow fell down from the cliff and died,' I said once he reached at the site.

'I think so,' Manoj said. 'We saved one but lost other.'

Sampu and Tunna, by the time, had joined us to look at the dead cow.

'Oh, my God! This is my …..,' Tunna cried.

'This is yours, I am so sorry,' Sampu said.

'What to do? This was my favorite cow. She was very kind and lovely. My parents will also beat me…..,' Tunna said with extreme grief and sorrow. He became too tense.

We all began consoling Tunna. 'We shall come with you to intimate your parents. After all it is not your fault,' Manoj said while examining the dead cow.

'I think this is bitten by some poisonous animal,' Manoj said with confidence.

'What!! How do you say this?' I asked.

'Look at her nose and mouth. They are filled with froth,' he said.

'I see. You are right,' I said while looking at the froth oozing out from the nose and mouth of the dead cow.

'Look at her belly, too. It has also inflated. I think a Harela (green snake) has bitten her and thereafter she fell from the cliff,' Manoj said.

We gathered our cattle and walked back home consoling Tunna for his loss in the jungle and possible rebuke of parents ahead at home. When we informed his parents about the entire incident of leopard attack to snake bite, they became upset of losing their beloved cow. Nonetheless in contrary to Tunna's dilemma, they thanked God for the safe return of their child back home.

10.0

The Tip of the Tail

Panting and prodding, I continued to climb the sheer hilly trail in an evening of October 1989 to return home from the college. Though, there was motorable road between the college, HNB Garhwal University, Srinagar and my village Sumadi, the bus service was quite irregular and limited. Being a hilly area, the pedestrian route was about 18 km to and fro, whereas the motorable road distance was 22 km one way. I used to get up and leave home early in the morning to attend my class at 8.00 am and generally return home late in the evening. Because of the arduous hill route and the entire day activities, which included outdoor games, the return journey was always quite exhausting.

Just like any other evening, the sun was shining on the western hill top and I was quite tired. I looked up at the mountain top – Shoudu hoping to conquer it in another 20-25 minutes. The trek from Shoudu to Sumadi was relatively flat. To recoup some energy for the rest of the journey I sat down under a 'peepal' tree. At every 1 km interval on the trail there was a tree planted by villagers for providing shade to the pedestrians. Whenever, I got tired I used to sit down for some moments in the shade of these trees, which provided immense pleasure, peace and a panoramic view of river Alaknanda.

I regained some energy after taking rest under the peepal tree and moved on in the scattered pine forest towards my village. Within an hour I was expecting to reach the agricultural fields of my village. As soon as I had crossed a small hill top, I saw a strong bull standing still but quite cautious at the corner of the trail and gazing in a bush on the mountain slope. The bull did not pay any attention to the sound of my steps, and kept on gazing towards the bush. I was surprised at this unusual behaviour and, therefore, I turned my eyes in the direction this bull was gazing. I saw nothing unusual; only a bush of Indian barberry about 15 m away, which had become yellowish brown due to senescence. I repeatedly looked at the bull and the bush and for a couple of minutes I did not see anything unusual in the bush, and between the bull and bush. Since the trail was narrow either the bull or I could have walked at one time, I had to drive or disturb the bull to move further ahead.

While planning to drive the bull from the trail I peeped into the bush once again and this time I noticed some movement. At first, it seemed to me like a yellowish brown snake coming out from one side of the bush, but within a fraction of second I saw a white tip to this snake like structure. At once, I realized that it was a tail of some animal. Again I looked in the bush very carefully and I was totally surprised to see a large cat in the bush. The colour of bush matched with the yellowish colour of cat's body and that's why it was difficult to locate and identify the cat easily.

I was alone and was quite afraid on realizing the presence of the large cat in the isolated mountain trail. I quickly gazed upon the entire trail and the mountain in the hope of somebody's presence for help. Unfortunately, there was no one. I stopped still and waited for the next move of the cat in the bush. A flurry of emotions ran through me; I was afraid, surprised, anxious, curious, ... Despite the distance of 15 m between cat and me, the cat did not look at me even once and that added to the sea of surprises. I realized that the cat had been watching the bull and the bull watching the cat before my arrival.

In those circumstances, the presence of the bull was the last hope for me, too. I could not have walked ahead without attracting their attention as the bull was blocking the trail and there was no other trail on the mountain slope to move further. I had to indicate my presence. I made a sound like cleaning throat and that suddenly got the cat's attention. My sudden appearance seemed to surprise the cat. The cat gazed at me, stood up slowly, turned and walked up graciously on the mountain slope. Now I saw the cat very clearly as there were a few pine trees and cat was moving up the mountain slope frequently looking back at me. The body size of cat was quite 'big'. There were numerous black stripes on the yellowish body and the 'tip of the tail' was white. The cat climbed up and disappeared from the scene within 7-8 minutes. I drove the bull to the village and narrated this encounter to my friends in the village and college.

In many folklores of Garhwal, there are descriptions and opinions on tiger. As per folklore, tiger says if he does not have a tail he may hide behind the leaves of 'Saknya' – local name of a perennial herbaceous plant having very small leaves. Interestingly, I was able to locate the tiger from its tail only. Later on, I joined Wildlife Institute of India (WII) where researchers frequently discussed their experiences and encounter with wildlife at the dining table, hostel premises, and library - the frequent meeting places of researchers.

I once discussed this story with my colleagues at WII and when I said that it was a tiger, I saw some of them were not convinced about the occurrence of tiger at an elevation of about 1300 m in the Uttarakhand hills. I described the external appearance and features of the cat to them, such as, stripes on the body, large body size, and white tip of the tail. To verify the description made by me we referred to Prator's book that contained illustrations of respective species. The tiger description in the book matched my description, which included the distinctive white 'tip of the tail'.

I consulted some more literature and in one of the articles, the presence of tiger was reported from the high hills of Uttarakhand. The article further clarified that though presence of tiger at such an elevation is unusual, during the migration of Gujjars with their cattle and Palsi's with their sheep and goats to the high altitude areas in the summer season the tiger may follow some of the herds and reach the high hilly areas.

During my 20 years stay in the village I also had noticed the sudden and seasonal increase of livestock predation by large cats for a couple of weeks, annually. When I inquired of our elders regarding the seasonal spike in predation they said "*baag kee daad khul gayee hai*" (the molar teeth of cat have emerged). It was difficult to understand the real sense of this statement. It may be argued that migration of predatory large cat along with Gujjars or Palsis, the local livestock, being easy prey, might have been attacked and killed. The predation of livestock, otherwise, should have been uniform throughout the year as the area is generally known for the occurrence of common leopard.

The Bhabar belt of the Himalaya is well known habitat of tiger and Corbett National Park is one of the best areas for existing tiger population. It is indeed intriguing and a point of investigation as to determine what compels these large cats to move and redraw their home range characteristics. Obviously, resource crunch and availability of food may be one of the major factors which may influence the home range of such large cats.

While working in the Pin Valley National Park of Himachal Pradesh, I saw a radio collared Himalayan ibex on the mountain top to the right side of Paraiho river. My one of the colleagues who had radio-collared that ibex pointed out that during his study period he never saw his collared ibex in the locality that I mentioned. The locality, which I mentioned, was quite away from the recorded home range of that collared ibex.

Again it may be argued that the home range of both prey and predator species may vary with varying circumstances and specific locality driven factors. I also came across an unusual presence of the Himalayan black bear in the pine forests of my village Sumadi, which did not support and have any historical evidence of bear occurrence. The bear was encountered only once in early 1980s when he mauled a person at the village boundary but after that there was no direct and indirect evidence of its presence.

What we may regard as stray incidences could very well turn out to be range extension, newer habitat and niche occupancies of animals, we think, are well studied. I personally feel that understanding nature and natural phenomenon is not so easy, and whatever we know may only be the tip of a huge iceberg or the 'tip of the tail' in this case.

11.0

The Heavenly Leaf

Traversing the deciduous forests in the Kipling's land at Pachmarhi hill station in 2008 I got to know a tree that bears wonderful leaves. The tree, locally called as tendu, infact is famed for its valuable leaves, which are used in making 'bidi'. Bidi is one such product that is quite common across the width and length of India irrespective of metros, cities, towns, villages and even a hut at quite high altitude areas of the Himalaya.

I had not seen any tendu tree before, as it does not grow in the Himalayan hills - my native place. Nonetheless, I knew the importance of its leaf even at my tender age, merely five years age. My old neighbor, who had retired from his Govt. job, quite on and off asked me to bring his favorite 'ghoda chhap' bidi from the village shop. That old uncle did not hesitate even to instruct me to gather the leftover of bidi from the all possible areas used by smokers.

In the dense shade of banyan tree at my village Sumadi, being a meeting place of villagers, a couple of chairs made of stones had placed to rest here. People smoked here while playing card and discussing burning political and social issues. My neighbor did not forget to request me to visit such places for gathering bidi's leftover.

Later on, at school, I noticed some of my classmates accustomed of bidi. They used to wait eagerly for interval to have some bidi's puffs. Even the permission granted by class teacher for going toilet they used to drag couple of puffs quickly. My parents always cautioned me not to make friendship with those boys who smoked. Despite severe restrictions, they were unable to give up their smoking habits. A few of them after meticulous efforts had been able to give up this bad habit but many of them were not so lucky.

Smoking might have been considered a bad habit since antiquity. But it still attracts people from all walks of life. It easily brings together the people of same wave length. It does not know and differentiate between national and international borders. It also does not differentiate between religion, cast and creeds. It has its own importance, which is not limited to particular age and sex. I saw a carpenter, in my childhood, whose best friend was 'bidi'. He frequently took rest and when someone asked him to continue the work he replied very authoritatively, 'you even don't spare a few minutes to smoke.'

The smoker's society, which is impossible to divide into religion and territory, unfortunately, is not escaped from the rich and poor. The poor prefers bidi, as he cannot afford costly smoking. As soon as he becomes rich his taste switches over to cigarette, which reflects not only his status symbol but also the sign of transforming his penniless and impecunious days. But the habits of both rich and poor smokers more or less remains unaltered. 'Bidi yaishi mohini .... Lakh takke ka aadmi jaaya pasare bheekh' (Bidi is so attractive that even a millionaire may behave like a beggar, if he needs it).

One night of June while having dinner, I received a call. From other side I heard a very familiar voice of my friend Abhishek. 'Kalaji, I just now met an accident.'

'How, where, how are you?' I exclaimed.

'I was driving home after shopping in New Market. Suddenly, a speedy bike hit at my scooty. I was dragged for a while on the road with my scooty and injured terribly. My hands and legs are severely injured,' he said.

'I am sorry. It is so sad,' I said.

'I was taken to a nearby hospital by some unknown gentleman. The doctor has done some preliminary dressing and asked me to come tomorrow for some surgery. Will you give me a favour to drop me at hospital?' he said.

'Oh, yes, certainly, what time?' I replied.

'Doctor has asked to reach his chamber at 9 am. Is it ok for you?' he said.

'Well, no problem at all, I shall drop you at 9 am sharp,' I assured him.

Since his residence was not far away, I walked him to see his injuries. He was lying on bed and his wife was washing blood stains from his left hand. I gazed at his erupted skin on legs and hands. The major injuries were dressed up. One of his toes had tilted straightly to one side but surprisingly there was no visible outer injury on the very same toe. On my inquiry, Abhishek informed me that it was dislocated. I had also learnt from vaidyas that none or less number of visible injuries on the body did not reflect the intensity of accident. If the outer injuries are less, the internal injuries may be more, after any accident. I was really surprised when I saw his x-ray report of dislocated toe, which did not show any injury on the skin.

The other day I took him to hospital. Naturally, he was upset, as his leg had to go under surgery. He wanted me to stay with him in the operation theatre but the team of doctors, as usual, did not allow me to stay in. I waited outside for half an hour. While coming out from the operation theatre his face was glowing. After completing the necessary formalities at hospital, I drove him back home.

'Kalaji, if you don't mind may I ask for one more favour,' Abhishek asked me within couple of minutes of driving back home.

'Yes, why not, please go ahead,' I said.

'Please stop just for a few minutes at any general store. I have to smoke,' I said.

I gazed at him and smiled. He smiled back and said, 'last night was really quite painful. I could not sleep properly for a moment because of continuous and unbearable pain. Moreover, I was worried of surgical operations. The whole night I consoled myself with the hope that once the surgery would be over I must have some deep drag of cigarette in heavenly peace of mind and tranquility of thoughts. This optimism, cheerfulness and feeling of having cigarette made me to conquer the horrible pain of previous night.'

Listening him quietly I could guess and feel why the *Lord Neelkanth* – the God of Gods, the Mahadev - had fallen in love of Marijuana.

12.0

The Forgotten Healers

Passing through a dusty trail leading out of Sumadi, a village in Uttarakhand, I followed my sister to gather cattle. I must have been six then. Suddenly, I saw a herd of horses coming from the opposite direction. Leaving the trail was not possible - on the right was a steep slope and on the left a stone wall. I tried sticking to the wall. As the horses came close, I lost balance and fell. The first horse in the row suddenly stopped and started sniffing me. This broke the momentum of the other horses and they started pushing each other. The sniffer had no choice but to move. The herd jumped over my body, trying not to hurt me, but a horse stepped on my left hand.

I now, while penning down this episode, don't remember whether the joint got dislocated, but I remember my mother taking me to a vaidya – Ratanmani - who after inspection applied a herbal paste to the injury and covered it with cloth. I could not sleep properly for few nights, which troubled my mother a lot, who could not sleep as well. It pained for a few days but soon the injury healed. The vaidya had cured me without charging any fee.

Today, there is no sign of that accident in my hand. Since then decades have been passed and I probably have forgotten many incidences took place in my childhood but I still remember Ratanmani who had given his services and cured my hand free of cost without any expectation from me and my family.

Another incident which I still remember took place twenty years ago when I was a young lad. A young person of my age had bitten by a snake. He was initially brought to a primary health care centre for treatment, as the base hospital was far away from the village. Since there was no improvement in his health due to scarcity of proper medicines, his relatives brought him to a traditional healer of my village, Kirtiram, who used to treat such patients, traditionally. Professionally, he was a teacher in a government primary school. Fortunately, the moment patient was dropped down at his house he was at home.

Looking at the critical condition of patient, Kirtiram's son, who was then doing his master of science, had advised all people gathered around the patient to carry him to the hospital. He also forced Kirtiram not to checkup the patient, as in his views, it was wastage of time which was vital for the moment. And also in case patient was not cured his father would have been blamed. But the patient's relatives were not agreed upon his remark and had pleaded repeatedly folding their hands to checkup the patient.

Realizing the impossibilities of convincing patient's relatives, Kirtiram's son had no option but to allow his father to look after the patient. Kirtiram observed patient's eyes, tongue and body for couple of minutes. He seemed optimistic and without wasting anymore time he began the treatment.

After couple of hour's treatment, amazingly, the patient recovered and opened his eyes. All his relatives felt obliged to Kirtiram and hence they wished to offer the cost of treatment. Despite their repeated pledges Kirtiram refused candidly to accept even a single penny. Next day, the patient's father came to offer some sweets to Kirtiram, which he refused again to accept, humbly. Later on, Kirtiram happened to be in that lad's village whom he had cured. Knowing about Kirtiram's presence in the village, the lad with his family ran to see him. Kirtiram met them all very cordially but again refused to drink even a cup of tea at their home.

As a child, my parents used to give me a decoction of chirayita to cure fever. Later on, I came to know the fact that the chirayita I was administered was actually a substitute— Swertia angustifolia. Swertia chirayita is difficult to find in the wild. In the absence of the required plant species, vaidyas switch to substitutes, which are ineffective in many cases. Another incident which infused my trust in the herbal medicine took place at Bhopal. Once I suffered with the dengue fever. My platelet counts had gone down. Luckily, I remembered a vaidya's advice that juice of papaya leaf treats dengue. Having three bowls of leaf juice of papaya, my platelet counts increased within twenty four hours.

In due course of time, while meeting many traditional healers of Uttarakhand, I learnt some issues of traditional health care systems. One of the notions was to avoid any offer from the patients on behalf of curing some specific diseases, which included curing of snakebite. Traditionally, every practitioner of health care had to take an oath before his mentor to cure patient in all circumstances. The traditional healers used to select and pass on his or her knowledge to genuine and legitimate pupils only who can follow such norms. Such rules were made in the interest of society so that the poor are not deprived of health services.

By virtue, the health care profession traditionally being placed in the category of philanthropy and humanity. Unfortunately, in the era of commercial interest, the traditional system of therapy is in the state of decline.

13.0

Kafal Lore

After four-and-a-half hours of arduous trekking on the hill slopes from Srinagar town in early May, I reached the temperate forest of Khirsu, an eye- catching yet lesser known hill station in Uttarakhand's Pauri district. From here, I saw a number of villages scattered across the downhill slopes in the pine and oak forests. Trekking further, I encountered a variety of colourful pheasants, including khaleej and koklass.

The next morning, I set off to explore the oak and rhododendron forests of Khirsu. Besides being ecologically important, these forests provide some peculiar services, which include delicious fruits. To my delight I saw some kafal (Box Myrtle) trees laden with berries. I cast my eyes around for kafal trees that had branches low enough to pluck fruits. Failing to find one, I picked up my pair of binoculars to soak in the beauty of the hills. I saw a girl swiftly climbing a tree to pluck kafals. Three women standing beneath were gathering fruits in baskets made of bamboo. I learnt from them that the fruit is part of folklore.

One such story is about a woman who plucked a basketful of kafal fruits from the nearby forest and brought them home. The scorching summer heat had parched her throat. She asked her beautiful daughter for water. But there was no water at home. So the woman went to the spring nearby to quench her thirst and asked her daughter to watch over the basket, giving strict instructions not to eat the fruits.

When she returned, the fruits looked fewer. Not realizing that the fruits had shrunk because of loss of water, the woman slapped her daughter hard. The girl died on the spot and turned into a cuckoo. Ever since, every year in May and early June, the cuckoo sings, "kafal pako min nee chakho (kafal has ripened, but I have not tasted it yet)".

The popularity of this wild fruit is also reflected in a song famous in Uttarakhand: 'Bedu pako baarah maasa, narayni kafal pako chait (bedu ripens every month, but kafal only in April-May)'. This is also a representative song of the Garhwal Rifles.

Savitri Devi, one of the three women gathering the fruits I had met in the Khirsu's forest, offered me some fruits. They were delicious, as the name itself reflects—ka + fal, meaning 'what a fruit'.

'All trees of kafal do not bear fruits,' she said. 'People prefer fruit bearing trees. Non fruit bearing trees are generally used as fuelwood.' This made me to understand that kafal was dioecious tree in which male and female plants are different.

Savitri also told me that people collect kafal for their own consumption and for sale. Looking at the tree and its high fruit-bearing branches, I noticed that collection was not an easy task. On many occasions, people slashed down its branches and spread them on the ground to collect sweet tasty fruits. The fruit's maturity was confirmed when its colour changed from green to dark or blackish red. I was told that the fruits were gathered mostly by the women folk.

'Since kafal grows in a specific altitudinal range, people living beyond it eagerly wait for kafal sellers. Earlier, people would exchange two bowls of pulses like gahath, masoor and urad for a bowlful of kafal,' Savitri added further.

On returning to Srinagar, I arrived in Balodi, a village that had almost no kafal tree. But I did see a woman selling kafal. She had walked down from a village close to Khirsu. She told me that one full glass of kafal cost about rupees fifteen in rural areas. Vendors used to sell kafal in local markets where the cost fluctuates, depending upon the availability of the fruit. At Srinagar, the cost of kafal was higher.

While surveying the vaidyas in different rural and urban areas of Uttarakhand, I was informed that almost all parts of the kafal tree were used in one way or the other. The bark was used to cure a number of diseases, including mental illnesses. It was known to have anti-allergic property. The fruit itself was said to possess anti-asthmatic property. Traditionally, the fruit and bark together were used for making red and yellow dye. The oil extracted from kafal flowers and seeds were used as a tonic. Its leaves formed a good fodder for cattle. The delicious fruits were also used for making squash, syrup and jam.

Later on, I leant that the Kafal trees have declined several folds in the forests. It is needless to say that such an important tree species must be saved for posterity.

14.0

A Job Hunter

Like any other hilly village, my village Sumadi was peaceful and full of natural beauty. It was surrounded by beautiful terraced agricultural land, which was subsequently surrounded by dense chir pine forests. The natural beauty was stretched all along to far and wide but there were very few to see it. The scenic beauty was unmatchable but these hills could not meet and afford the desires of its inhabitants, as a result there has been a continuous migration of Sumadi's inhabitants to the plains.

I took my education till tenth standard at Sumadi only. The school was about one km away from the village so generally we walked to school in groups. There were dense shrubs of small flowered poison sumac on way to school, which formed some good habitats for wildlife, especially leopard. Though this shrub provided us tasty edible fruits but as they also provided shelter and place to hide leopard, we had mixed feelings for its thickets. Being afraid of leopard attack, we walked on the school way in groups. Once the classes started at school it was not easy to walk in the trail till the closing of school, as it was hard to find out any person walking on school's trail. The trail remained deserted most of the time.

For higher studies I went to a nearby town, Srinagar. Walking in Srinagar had given relief from the fear of wildlife. But I felt uncomfortable to give space quite on and off for moving vehicles on the road. There was no problem with passerby as they were low in number.

After completing my Master in Science, I joined Wildlife Institute to pursue PhD at Dehradun in early 1990s. In Dehradun, though some roads were comfortable to walk but some market places, Paltan Bazaar (main shopping centre) and Chakrata road (famous for picture halls) had enough crowds and were not comfortable to walk freely.

Since I did not get proper job in Dehradun after completing PhD my journey continued for hunting job elsewhere and I arrived at New Delhi. Staying in New Delhi, I came across the realization of a true crowd. Here I realized that India is really the second largest populated country. It was really difficult to properly walk on the roads. Even it was worse when I thought to cross such roads. Uncertainty always prevailed in my mind while walking in Delhi. I always kept my mind on alert and alarm mode the moment I am on road. I could not think other than walking safely, and keeping myself away from speedy vehicles and busy crowds.

Though Delhi was considered to have sea of jobs, and thousands of people from hills used to migrate to Delhi, my search for a good, stable and contented job was continued. And I could not get one such job here. My search made me to visit Mumbai in late 90s, as I got a call for interview at Piramal Health Care Ltd.

I had a cousin in Mumbai, who had assured me to receive at railway station. He had given me several instructions and one of them was a strict warning not to move away anywhere else from the station. He instructed me to wait near the bench whenever I got down at the station. Mobile phone was not so common at that time and I did not have any mobile. Mukul, my cousin, had to locate me at the station without any such instrument's help.

I got down at railway station at 3 am and as instructed by Mukul I sat on the nearest bench. He explored me after half an hour and then I felt relaxed. All of a sudden, I saw a frantic teen moving on the roof of a train. A group of people shouting loudly had gathered just on the ground beneath the train. I could not understand whether he was unable to get down or he wanted to get rid of the crowd. 'It is as usual incident here at railway stations. This is a pick-pocket trying to run away from the crowd,' Mukul said.

He took me in his Kholi (residence). After a brief rest I set off for interview at Mulund. Mukul came along with me at the railway station. Now the scene at station had completely changed as what I had seen in the early morning. There was crowd and only crowd all around me. People were running to catch their trains. The crowd was so much that I had to struggle to walk ahead. Mukul had read my face so he consoled me not to worry.

'You have to just stand facing toward train, in which you have to step in, rest the crowd will do. They will carry and push you in. Only you have to be careful at the last step otherwise you may fall down on the railway line,' Mukul said.

'I see, this is interesting,' I replied with surprise.

'That's why I said don't worry, there are so many interesting things. It is your very first day in Mumbai. Once your journey is over and you arrive at your destination and you want to get down, you have to just turn towards the entrance. No need to waste energy in walking. The crowd will bring you out from the train. But please be careful from pick pockets,' he said.

'In the train or at station,' I asked.

'Generally, everywhere, but mostly in train. The crowd is so packed that even if you know somebody is taking your belongings from your pocket you cannot save it,' Mukul said.

'Why? You think me so stupid,' I frowned. 'I shall catch him red handed if I feel somebody's hand in my pocket.'

'No, you cannot. Because you will be pressed by crowd so much that you cannot move an inch. You cannot move your fingers, forget about hands,' Mukul said confidently. 'These pick-pockets are really amazing. Even though it is a quite risky task, they don't give up it. When a pick-pocket is caught, everyone around him will beat and kick him. Even the smallest, feeblest guy turns into a vigilante, judge, and executioner.'

Once my journey to Mulund came to an end I realized that he was right.

I came back to New Delhi and felt a great relief realizing the hard fact that Delhi had lesser crowds than Mumbai.

I thought that I remained frightened at my village because of not finding people on trails, and here in Mumbai and Delhi I was afraid because it was packed with people.

15.0

My First Job

After a month long exam at Srinagar, which was reeling under extreme heat wave, it was time to relax and enjoy with friends at Sumadi. Soon, the monotonous life for consecutive two weeks at Sumadi had made things boring. I was desperate for some change. In a day of last week of June, I picked up two pairs of trouser and shirt, a tooth paste with brush, and some undergarments to pack in a reddish cotton handbag. I checked my pocket where I found two hundred rupees. I picked up my bag and walked down to Srinagar.

While walking on the Kala Road at Srinagar I happened to meet Prafull, one of my friends at Sumadi. He was in hurry to catch bus to Dehradun.

'Where are you going?' Prafull asked me.

'I don't know,' I replied. 'I have not yet decided where to go.'

'So, you are just straying. Don't have any work,' he commented.

'You know my exams are over. There is sufficient time for results to be declared. It may take more than a month,' I said.

'I think not before September. Will you continue straying like this? Why don't you join me?' he asked.

'But I don't have enough money to stay in Dehradun.'

'Come on. I am there. I invite you to stay with me. I have a room on rent. I am alone and I shall be happy to have a company,' he insisted.

'I have only two hundred rupees. It cannot afford food even for a week. What is the one way bus fare?' I asked.

'It is roughly fifty rupees. I think two hundred is manageable. I shall take care of your food and accommodation,' he assured.

I agreed upon his arrangements and assurances. Soon, we were in a roadways bus to Dehradun.

We got down at Mussoorie bus station at Dehradun. Bus station was attached to the railway station. We walked hundred meters over a linked road before to arrive at a circle on the Saharanpur road. The road was busy. Pedestrians were struggling hard to find their way ahead. Prafull waved his hand for the auto rickshaws. As soon as an auto rickshaw slowed down, we got into it, as there was some space left for passengers.

'Thank god. Today we got seat easily. It is really difficult to get vikram at this place,' Prafull said. 'Otherwise one has to hire auto which is expensive.'

'Is there difference between auto and vikram? Both seemed to be same,' I asked.

'Yes in colour both are yellow and black but vikram is more spacious than auto. Auto accommodates three or maximum four passengers but vikram accommodates about ten passengers. Auto ferries passengers on booking only. The auto's rates are negotiable. Generally, auto drivers don't use meter to calculate exact fare. Vikram runs to definite places as per the allotted number. Their rates are fixed from one place to other,' Prafull explained.

'How far is your room?' I asked him.

'It is in Panditwadi. We shall reach there in another half an hour,' he said.

We drove though a busy road. All along roadside was decorated with small to big shops. 'Look at your right,' Prafull said.

I peeped out through the vikram's window. There was a huge gate through which a broad road was ended at a splendor monument.

'This is FRI,' he said.

'Incredible!! I wish to visit it,' I said.

'I shall take you there either tomorrow or day after tomorrow,' he said.

'But this gate is closed,' I asked.

'This is main gate. It remains closed. It is only opened when some VIP visits here.'

'Then, how to go in.'

'There are three other gates. This institute spans over a very large area. One entry point is from Panditwadi side.'

Within couple of minutes we reached at Panditwadi. We stepped out from the vikram and about five minutes walk brought us in his room. The room was attached with a small kitchen and a washroom was outside at some distance in the kitchen garden. There was a cot, a chair and a table in the room along with an iron box. I took bath and sat on the string cot to relax. At one corner of the room I saw an Almirah. It was the single locked item in the room.

'What is there in the Almirah?' I asked.

'Of course not jewelry but it is not less than jewelry. In fact it is more than jewelry,' he said unlocking the Almirah, which was full of musical instruments.

I got up and picked up a pair of drum and sat down on the floor. I began to play drum. Prafull picked up Veena and began to fix its strings. 'Well, there are sufficient reasons and objects to enjoy here,' I said.

He laughed while playing with Veena. But music was not enough to dissolve our appetite. We went out to purchase some vegetables and ration. But reaching at market being tired we decided to have dinner. I had an extremely sound sleep over the night in the only cot half shared by Prafull.

Next day, Prafull went to attend his classes in Polytechnique and I began playing with his musical instruments. Long hours of rehearsal in the closed room became uninteresting. On Prafull's return I asked him, 'it is boring. Is there any job outside for me? This way I shall earn some money, also.'

'I understand. Let's go to see FRI,' he said.

We walked to FRI gate at Panditwadi. It was opened. Vehicles were moving in and out but pedestrians were only one or two. A couple of persons in uniform were sitting at the gate side. We hesitated to enter the gate being unknown and outsider. Prafull came forward and asked the security person, 'may we visit in?'

'Whom do you want to visit?' he asked.

Since he knew no one in the FRI he became mum.

'Why do you want to visit in?' he questioned.

'We are students and have keen interest in forestry,' I said.

He looked at us for a moment and allowed us to move in. The road further ushered us to the extensive lawns. The experience of watching the grand building of FRI in the middle of extensive lawns was really captivating. We sat on the grass and remained sitting for long. Being M.Sc. final year botany student I dreamt to pursue my further study in this historical institute. With thick inspirations and dreams I came back with Prafull to our lone room.

With every passing day my desire to get some job kept on inflating. I shared the same feeling frequently with Prafull, which he was helpless to fulfill. A day I requested him to help me out in finding any private school looking for a teacher. He agreed and we set off to find out one such school. We visited couple of schools but did not get any positive response. I was even prepared to teach in primary school. Though, Prafull refused to allow me to do so, we did not even get any such school, too. The whole day exercise could not turn up useful and we had no choice but to return to our room.

Sitting on the string cot, I heard someone knocking the room's wooden door. Before I respond, he entered the room without any hesitation calling Prafull. He was about five feet, fair and well-dressed person in his late thirties. He hugged Prafull and they both smiled meeting with each other. After introducing me to him Prafull said, 'This is Deepak, this house owner. He is principal in an English school.' And they began chatting non-stop.

Next day morning Prafull asked me, 'I have searched a job for you.'

I jumped with surprise and said, 'Really!!'

'Yes, but it is not in Dehradun. If you are interested you have to go to Gajrola.'

'Gajrola, where is it?'

'It is in Uttar Pradesh only, nearby to Muzaffarnagar.'

'I heard it is an unsafe and risky place to live.'

'It is not that much of risky, as people of Garhwal think and believe. Look, Deepak lives there. He is looking for a biology teacher to his school. I think this is a good opportunity.'

'But, I cannot live in fear. That area, I heard, is not good for people like me.'

'Come on, I have been there and I had taught in the very same school. I did not face there any problem.'

'Is there no vacancy for Mathematics and other subjects?'

'Math's teacher post is also lying vacant.'

'That's fantastic. Let us go together. I shall go if you agree to give me company,' I said enthusiastically.

'But I have to attend classes here though the course is over.'

'Do something. Explore some ways so that we can go together,' I insisted Prafull.

'Well, give me some time to think. I shall talk to my teacher.'

'Please do that.'

In afternoon, when Prafull came back from his college he had a good news to share. We both gave our consent to join Deepak shortly and started planning to join his school at Jhanakpuri. Next day, we set off to catch train to Gajrola. On reaching at Dehradun's railway station, Prafull walked to collect ticket from the ticket counter and I stood at a side taking care of baggage. A tall and well built policeman came to me and whispered, 'Where are you going?'

'Gajrola,' I said.

'Call back your companion,' he instructed.

'He is getting ticket,' I said.

'Don't take ticket. I shall take you there,' he insisted.

I could not understand the state of affairs, as I was about to travel first time in the train. I went to Prafull and informed him about the policeman. Prafull wanted to say something but looking at policeman coming closure to us he kept quite.

Policeman repeated his words, 'I shall take you in just half of the fare to Gajrola. No need to buy ticket.'

Prafull refused his proposal immediately without any second thought and returned to ticket counter. The policeman began to negotiate with me. I made him to understand my position by saying that it was hard for me to convince my companion. Prafull came with two tickets and we walked further inside the station.

'You did not pay any heed to his words. We would have saved half of the fare,' I asked Prafull.

'You don't know. It is a big racket. Rather saving half we may lose more. Don't you know it is a punishable offence to travel without ticket?' Prafull asked.

'He was a policeman, an official who always abide by law. He is duty bound to make sure that no one can violate the law. There would be some mechanism or reservation for policeman to ferry people in the train,' I said.

'To the best of my knowledge no such rule exists. I know these people. They stray in the station for easy prey. Sometime they have setting with TT but not all the time. In case TT does not fall in their trap, they run away and passenger is caught red handed. Be careful always from these burglars in khaki,' Prafull advised.

The train drew into the station and we stepped in the general carriage. Twenty minutes later, the train blew whistle. With hissing of train's engine, the carriage shuddered and jolted forward leaving behind the railway station. Once TT had checked our tickets we laid down peacefully on our berths.

I could not sleep properly due to continuous shuddering and jolting of trains. In mid night, the TT got off the train much before Gajrola. He was replaced by another TT. Shortly, the new TT started rechecking tickets. Unexpectedly, the panic began to spread in the carriage. Many passengers got up to see the policeman on duty but he was absconded. TT shouted over couple of passengers, 'How dare you have to travel without ticket. You don't know it is a crime.'

'Sorry sir. Please help us. Please do something,' passengers pleaded.

'Come with me,' he ordered.

TT took them to a dark corner. God knows what happened there in the dark. Since hullabaloo had disturbed Prafull, he heard and smelt the situation, too.

'Have you got the message?' Prafull asked lying on the berth above me.

'My God! We are saved. You are great Prafull. I appreciate your decision. But where is that policeman?' I asked.

'His duty is also over. He would have got down with previous TT. They were the birds of a feather flock together. Look these passengers. A vice is the root of all evils. Greed breeds crime and finally invites trouble. As you sow, so shall you reap,' Prafull grinned.

The train stopped at Gajrola. We took our baggage and stepped out from the carriage. Since we had reached before dawn, the station was dimly lit. There was couple of tea stalls and fruit vendors and some stray dogs. I had a cup of tea in the faint light of dawn and began to wait for sunrise.

'How far is that school?' I asked Prafull as he had taught in the school, earlier.

'Exactly, I don't remember but not far. It is on the Grand Trunk Road,' he said.

'The one that was built by Shershah Suri,' I said.

'Yes, it is a historical road. It remains busy nevertheless it is quite difficult to get vehicle to drop at Jhanakpuri where we have the school. Most of the vehicles run on GT Road are long route one and hence do not stop at Jhanakpuri,' Prafull explained.

When sun was about to rise we walked out of the station and looked for a vehicle. Luckily, we managed to get some space in a truck. After twenty minutes drive on the GT Road we were dropped before the school gate. Entering the school premises I saw the students standing in rows were performing morning prayers. Deepak smiled on us and indicated to keep baggage on a side and stand facing student's rows. Students sung 'Jan Gan Man Adhinayak Jai Hai ……. …Jai Ho', and dispersed to enter the class rooms.

Deepak introduced us to the teachers. I was quite tired due to overnight journey but Deepak wanted me to take couple of classes. So after light breakfast I walked into a class of ninth standard. Though, I had taught boys and girls earlier at my village and Srinagar, I was not experienced enough to deliver formal lectures in the class. Luckily, my subject knowledge helped me a lot.

There was no staff room for teachers. I was given the key of laboratory as I had to teach Chemistry and Biology and both subjects demanded laboratory work. Once the school time was over, Deepak took me to a room in the first floor where teachers used to stay overnight, if required. It was a sort of dormitory wherein five string cots were placed. The room was deprived of table and chairs. A couple of old iron boxes were placed near to some of the cots, showing they were occupied.

I pushed my only bag beneath an unoccupied cot. Prafull had placed his bag in the same room before me. Being known to the teachers he was busy chatting with two fellow teachers whom we had to share the dormitory. Half of the left side of first floor was used as hostel for resident students. All the classes were run in the ground floor.

Being tired I wanted to take bed rest, as early as possible. I had early dinner and slipped into my bed.

Next day, I was bit nervous when I entered the classroom packed with students. Majority of students had better physique and height than me. Being a new teacher, everyone seemed to be keen to hear me. After a brief introduction I began to deliver lecture, which they, fortunately, heard silently. After marathon lectures for next four consecutive periods I got break to rest in the laboratory. A fortnight passed with almost similar routine.

A day at breakfast, which we had together generally with the hostel students, a student came to me and offered a spoon of ghee.

'One spoon is enough,' I said while accepting his offer.

'Sir, you should eat, at least, four to five spoon of ghee,' he said.

'But it is hard for me to digest, even one,' I said.

'I see. That's why you are so thin. I finish one kg in a week,' he said.

'One kg! And you don't face any health problem. I mean you digest all you eat. Are you kidding?' I asked.

'Every student here in hostel has his own ghee container. Some of them eat more than me every week,' he said.

'How do you manage to get so much of ghee every week?' I asked.

'We have our own cows and buffaloes. Every week my father drops a box of ghee in my room, here and takes back empty boxes to fill again,' he explained.

I had got the secret of student's health. They ate well and preferred to play kushti and kabbaddi.

To take a break from the routine life, a Sunday Prafull, I and a teacher, who also hailed from Dehradun, planned to watch a movie. We drove to Amroha in a bus as we wanted to avoid being seen by our students at Gajrola. After watching the movie Ghayal, we walked out from theatre to catch bus. We waited and waited for long but did not get bus. We, finally, landed into a truck which was overloaded with crops residues. Five passengers, apart from driver and conductor, were travelling in the same truck.

'Where are you going?' a fellow passenger asked me.

'Jhanakpuri,' I replied.

He looked at me and asked again, 'Do you have relative over there?'

'No, I am a teacher in school,' I said.

Suddenly, he became quite polite and offered some better space to sit on the sacks of hay. The moment we stepped out from the truck at the school gate it had become dark.

'Always you forgot advices,' Prafull said while we were entering the school gate.

'What do you mean? What happened?' I asked.

'You disclose our identity. Those people in truck could have kidnapped or killed us. This is not a peaceful mountain village. They may tell students about our travel in truck and watching movie. Be careful, and don't reveal your identity to every unknown person,' Prafull said. The teacher who visited with us was fully agreed with Prafull's opinion.

I was about to complete a month at the school. A day when I was in the class, I heard a sound of cracker in the principal's office. I advised students to keep silence in the class and walked fast to Deepak's room. I saw Ombeer, one of the fellow teachers, holding a boy of about fifteen years and trying to overpower him. Deepak was trying hard to grab away a revolver from his hand. By the time Prafull had also reached on the spot. Looking around many persons, the boy loosened his grip in fear and ran away from the room leaving the revolver and shouting ills to Deepak.

'What is this? Who is he? What happened?' voices raised in the room.

'You all please go to attend your classes. This is not the time to discuss. Please don't let the students know about the incidence,' Deepak said.

All the teachers walked back to class rooms. Though, I was in class physically but my mind was in the principal's room. I was unable to concentrate on teaching so I assigned some work to the students and came out to know about the incidence. The boy who fired at Deepak was at the school's gate with his two companions. I went to ask Ombeer about the incidence, as he was known as Deepak's right hand.

'Everything is quite normal. Why are you so upset? We have informed the student's guardians,' Ombeer informed me on my asking about the incident.

'The last period is over yet the students are still in the school,' I said.

'This is just for precautionary purpose, nothing else. That fellow is still on the gate and he may kidnap any student. We have to hand over the students to their guardians. That's it,' Ombeer said.

'Is he mad? Why is he doing all this?' I asked.

'He is our former student. Recently, he is expelled due to continuous absence from the classes. He wanted the principal to take him back,' Ombeer said.

'This is ridiculous. How dare he cherish such an unethical wish?' I said.

'His father belongs to a sitting state minister's party hence he believes he can do whatever he wishes,' Ombeer said.

I went back to class. Since the school ran classes from first to twelve standards, there were small kids below six years age. They were asked to stay back till their parents come to receive them. Many of them started crying as they were asked to stay back even after the last period had become over. The poor landline phone facility was also hampering in conveying the message. Two school peons were deployed to visit door to door to convey the message. It had consumed lot of time. The poor students remained locked in the school till evening.

On reaching at school and after knowing about the facts the guardians had become extremely angry. They wanted to shoot out the boy who had paralyzed the school functioning and had made to suffer their beloved ones.

'It is hard to run this school in this area,' Deepak said to the guardians.

'Sorry sir. Tell us what to do. We all are with you,' a guardian pleaded.

'We should catch that nonsense boy and hand over to cops,' another guardian said.

'Trounce him to death. How dare he? Tit for tat,' voices came out from the crowd.

'See, such incidences will force us to close down the school. I cannot take risk. You know how hard I am working to run this school. It is difficult to get good teachers. I am literally pleading people to join here. I have arranged well qualified teachers and even brought teachers from Dehradun. You ask anyone how hard it is to retain good teachers. These teachers have come all the way from Dehradun and I am now afraid of their security,' Deepak shouted spewing out his day long anger.

'We assure you for your safety. This sort of incident will never repeat. Please don't think to close down the school. It has a grave concern of student's future,' a guardian said.

'But tell me how to retain teachers in this circumstances,' Deepak asked frowningly.

'Sir, please bear with us. It is our collective responsibility to take care of you and all the teachers,' a guardian said. 'Let's go to police station and demand there for teacher's security,' he said the fellow guardians.

'We assure you all for your safety,' they said to us while striding to the police station.

Around eight o'clock in the night two cops reached at school for patrolling. They assured us for our safety. However, the day episode had created ample panic in the lonely room for night stay.

As the school had become unsafe I talked to Prafull. We both agreed to return Dehradun. Though, we did not share our planning to Deepak, our conduct perhaps had made him to guess something fishy. He called us and assured us for our safety. The panic and fear continued in the school premises for next two days, and third day we chalked out our plan to run away from the school.

After dinner we both pretended to be slept. Around mid night we got up, picked up our baggage and walked out silently from the school to catch train to Dehradun.

'Will Deepak pay our remuneration? What do you think?' I asked Prafull.

'Let's first reach Dehradun. He is a nice man and I think he will pay,' Prafull said.

'Even if he does not pay we have stayed free of cost,' I said.

'It is no use crying over spilt milk,' Prafull said.

We reached at Gajrola railway station and sat on a bench for a while with deep contentment even after not getting our wages. We looked at each other. With smiling faces we got up and strolled to the inquiry counter to know about train's schedule. Before we reached on the counter, I was stunned to see Ombeer gazing at us from the counter. We both were shocked.

'You are strange people running like thieves. You are …. …. ..' Ombeer kept on saying. I heard few of his words but soon my mind began to think more than my ears to hear.

'Look Ombeer, I have completed the entire syllabus. There is no valid reason to stay back now. My task is over,' I said.

'It is not the issue of syllabus. You are our guests. How can you go and leave us like this? What will it convey to the students? See, I am native of this place. I assure you nothing wrong will happen. You please don't generalize everything with a single incidence. I make sure to take care of you at any cost. Let's go back. Don't make a mountain of mob hill. Deepak sent me to bring you back. Even if you would have reached Dehradun I would have taken you back from there, too,' Ombeer said.

'See, I have some urgent work at Dehradun,' Prafull said. 'I have to go anyhow.'

'If it is so important you go tomorrow. But I am sorry you have to come with me this time, please. You cannot go like this,' Ombeer said.

'Please try to understand. I have to go. I have an urgent meeting,' Prafull pleaded.

'I understand. You may go tomorrow or day after tomorrow,' Ombeer said.

'See Ombeer, it is tough to stay here,' I said.

'Come on. Let the past bury the dead. Innocents have nothing to fear,' Ombeer said.

'I am sorry, but where the buffalos fight the crops suffer,' I said.

'Pure gold does not fear the flame. You are building castle in the air. Please trust at me. I am not Hanuman to show you inside my chest,' Ombeer grinned.

We tried to persuade Ombeer by all means but he remained adamant. To convince him was a hard nut to crack. We had no choice other than to follow him. We strolled out from the railway station. He made us to sit on his scooter. While driving back to Jhanakpuri Ombeer said, 'Fortune favors the brave. Do good and cast in the river.' And I was thinking 'Man proposes and god disposes.'

Next day, the last night episode had become a popular gossip point in the school. Prafull and I had decided to get rid of the school at any cost. We met Deepak and tried to convince him. He was another hard nut to crack. A day after meeting him was Rakshabandhan and hence we requested him to let us go for Rakshabandhan, which he agreed fortunately.

'I shall pay your salary on your return only,' Deepak said.

'It is all right,' I said.

In the day light we bade adieu to the students and our fellow teachers and stepped out from the school, gracefully. We were so desperate that we did not even wait for a train to Dehradun and got into a crowded bus to Meerut so that Ombeer could not chase us. Reaching at Dehradun I took a deep breath of fresh air.

Three months later Prafull handed over one thousand five hundred rupees to me. It was my first salary. I requested

Prafull to convey my sincere thanks to Deepak who gave me opportunity to learn, earn and above all for his sincerity for keeping his promises to pay my wages. It was just killing two birds with one stone to me, as I had been introduced to the world far away from my native place as well as I was rewarded for visiting and gaining firsthand experience of such an interesting world and the 'first job'.

16.0

The Bear's Trail

A narrow twisted path led downhill in the Valley of Flowers through birch and rhododendron over a ridge where wild strawberries got hold the ground. At the bottom of the hill, in the dale, the path led on to an open slope through a bridge over Pushpawati river, which was tumbling over small to big pebbles on its way to downhill valley.

I walked on this path almost every day in the morning while climbing to the Valley of Flowers for exploring blooms and coming back to my base camp at Ghangaria in the evening for night halt. Walking through the forest, I had occasionally encountered langur, Himalayan weasel and red fox whereas mouse hare and colourful birds were encountered frequently.

Once when I was getting home late, the heavy showers had slowed down my speed. Generally, I wore hunter shoes but that fortunate day I was in slipper, which had added in the problem of trekking down in the soaked mountain slopes. Close to a ridge, my sight was caught by some fresh droppings of a wild animal under a birch tree. By crouching down, I was able to identify the droppings, which were of a bear. I gazed around in the forest and stood still trying to hear the sound of bear's movement. Some twenty feet away from me a monal pheasant went gliding down the other side of the Pushpawati.

As I had walked few steps downhill I saw a well grown Himalayan black bear sniffing in the air, some thirty feet away from me, standing under a fir tree. I became thrilled and stunned, as well. I looked around nervously for some helping hand but no one was seen. I could hear the rushing torrent of Pushpawati just beneath me in the mountain gorge. I paused and waited for the next move of bear. Being unable to predict his move, I took shelter behind a boulder. Luckily, bear did not notice my presence and walked away in the fir-birch forest and disappeared. I gathered my lost patience and walked silently but alertly to my base camp at Ghangaria.

Quite often I had heard the people of Gurudwara Management Committee complaining about the bear's menace in the Hemkund sahib situated at fourteen thousand five hundred feet above mean sea level. Every year the Gurudwara at Hemkund was closed down during winter for five to six months due to heavy snowfall. The abandoned place of worship that was visited by about six lakhs pilgrims annually during season was used as a home by bears during shivering cold winters.

The food material stored in Gurudwara was then eaten by bears. The Akal Takht, the supreme seat of the Sikhs had expressed their anguish on this unwanted act of bears and was worried about the possible damage to Sri Gurugramth Sahib or other religious books by bears in future. Bears used to stay in Gurudwara building not only for food but also for giving birth to cubs in the winter. I was also informed by the villagers about the presence of brown bear around Hemkund.

Close to my canvas tent there was a small tea-stall where I sat down quite often in the cool dusk for enjoying wood's fire. Since there was no means of electronic communication, like mobile, telephone, internet etc, the tea-stall was the best place that connected me to the outside world. The tourists and pilgrims to the Hemkund sahib made me aware of major happenings outside of Ghangaria. Having dropped my field bag in the tent, I went to tea-stall and sat down as usual before the wood's fire. The tea-stall's owner, Chauhan, was so much kind enough that he always made some space for me to sit down close to the furnace.

Soon after me Bharat – a known photographer in the Bhyundar valley – entered the tea-stall. He sat close to me. 'It is quite cold,' he said stretching his hands close to the fire. I informed him about the bear's sighting. This made him to recollect and share his memories of bears in the valley.

He informed me that once a bear had broken down a house during winter when the inhabitants of Bhyundar generally moved down to lower valleys in their winter settlements at Pulna. He was in Bhyundar for some work and saw that intoxicated bear who had smelled the available food material stored in the house.

'The bear reached to the food material after dismantling house where he found some fermented barley and a wine canister. On consuming both he became drunk and then smashed whatever came on his way. My father - Bachan Singh, has once been mauled terribly by a bear while he was camping in the valley. His face and head was seriously injured by the sudden attack of that beast and the signs of that attack are still on his face,' Bharat informed me.

Due to severe cold at Ghangaria, even before onset of winter, I allowed my hairs to grow. I rarely combed my long curly hairs and beard. While enjoying the camp fire with Bharat, I met a young couple who came to visit the Valley of Flowers and was staying in Chauhan's hut. The couple got involved in chatting with me.

'Where are you from?' I asked.

'Kanpur,' he said. 'Have you heard about Kanpur?'

His question made me to surprise and think.

'No,' I said.

'Well do you know Dehradun?'

On my denial now it was his turn to surprise.

'You even don't know Dehradun!! So sad!'

'What do you do in Kanpur?' I asked.

'I work in a factory. It is a big factory having over one thousand employees. You know, the cloth you wear is made in our factory. You people's life is quite miserable. You have not even heard Kanpur. You are spoiling your life in these mountains. One must know about his country. It is unbelievable; you even do not know Kanpur. What a kind of people you are,' he muttered.

His wife saw me as she had seen a yati - a snowman or a Himalayan black bear. She said nothing just kept on staring at my long hairs and beard with amused eyes, as she had seen a bear as I had encountered one a couple of hours back in the evening. With tremendous surprise they got up and walked away to their night stay.

17.0

A Non-vegetarian in the Holy Hills

Quaffing tea at the Ghangaria's base camp, I rose up to climb the Valley of Flowers. Vikram – my field assistant had kept some snacks, toasts and a water bottle in my knapsack for lunch while walking in the valley. With new energy of the day I walked uphill through the giant fir forests. On entering the edge of the forest, I was still thinking about the Himalayan black bear that I had encountered a day before.

After crossing the metal bridge over Pushpawati river and walking one km further uphill I reached on an open mountain ridge dotted with blue gentians, dwarf pinkish and whitish rhododendrons, violet thymes, yellow and pink pedicularis, saxifragas, wild strawberries, androsaces and lilies.

A group of six tourists had reached before me at the edge of a huge snow debris lying over the Pushpawati flowing in a deep gorge between two giant mountains. The continuous skidding of snow from the high mountains and its accumulation in the dale had made a snow bridge over the Pushpawati.

On reaching to them I came to know that they were frightened of walking over this natural snow bridge. I encouraged them to walk over it but I could not succeed to bring them out of their fear. Leaving them behind with their fear and serious discussions on risky mountain trails, I walked over the snow bridge to explore the beauty of alpine flowers.

I walked through the lush green meadows, full of flowers. Many life saving herbs including sacred flowers and colourful ground orchids having high medicinal properties passed through my eyes. By the evening after the full day excursion I returned to my base camp at Ghangaria.

At base camp, Kalyan – my second field assistant handed over an envelope to me. Sitting on my string cot in the canvas tent I opened the letter which informed me that within couple of days a forest officer from China could join me.

'There is breaking news. Soon a Chinese will join us,' I informed Kalyan and Vikram. Vikram was Kalyan's elder brother. Both carried same designation – field assistants, and were my best companion in the lonely mountains.

'How will he come?' Vikram asked. 'I mean when will he join us?'

'He will be dropped by a taxi at Govindghat,' I said.

'Shall I go to see him at Govindghat?' Vikram asked. Govindghat was at thirteen km downhill from our base camp.

'I don't think so. He will be accompanied and guided by forest guards from Govindghat,' I suggested.

'Well, we don't have enough rations to feed him. What does he eat? Will he eat whatever we eat?' Vikram seemed to be overloaded with burdens. 'I have to go to Joshimath for ration,' he said decisively.

'Come on Vikram. Don't worry. Let him come first,' I tried to calm him down.

'But, I think tomorrow I should go for rations. It takes, at least, three days to go and come back from Joshimath. It is over thirteen km trek from here to Govindghat, and sometime it is hard to get bus at Govindghat to Joshimath. All seats in the buses are mainly preoccupied at Badrinath itself and the drivers, on many occasions, do not stop at Govindghat for locals to ferry,' Vikram continued explaining his problems.

'Well, I understand. Here Kalyan will take care. You may go tomorrow as per your plan,' I said accepting his words, finally, as there was no other choice.

I stepped out of the tent to stand straight for a brief time. I stretched my body. The sacred Laxman Ganga was murmuring at the bottom of sacred mountains, the dwelling places of gods and goddesses. The bright moonlight had flooded the grassland stretched before me and the forests on the slopes. The peace and tranquility of mountains were frequently broken by the shouting slogans of pilgrims - 'bole sonihaal sat sri akal' - who were still on way to their destination in the pitch dark.

The red carpet was being rolled out for our new guest. His name was Jiang fu Quan. Vikram and Kalyan were restless but excited to meet and assist him. On a fateful evening Jiang arrived at our base camp after a week long wait. Jiang seemed to be a muscular and sturdy person who was comparatively taller than average Chinese man.

I put an extra cot for Jiang in my tent as I did not have extra tents. I had only two tents. One we used for cooking in which Vikram and Kalyan unfolded their cots to rest after dinner, and second tent I used for reading, sleeping and as reception for guests and visitors.

Jiang was a trainee in India learning about the wildlife management. Staying with me for two weeks was the part of his training component. For me, the first and foremost thing was to make his stay comfortable. After formal introduction, I inquired about his food habits and his likings and dislikes.

'I have brought enough food from Dehradun itself for two weeks,' Jiang said realizing my feelings.

'I was wondering had you been choosy for food,' I asked.

'It is a matter of two weeks only. It is manageable. I take my dinner early before sun set,' he informed me. Being stayed in Dehradun for nine months he had been acquainted with Indian food habits and choices. 'What about you?' he asked.

'Here I am forced to take dinner early because I do not have any facility that could keep me awake. We don't have electricity and reading for long hours is also uncomfortable in the dim lamp's light. No light means no TV, no serial and no movies. I usually take my dinner at twenty hours and then go to bed,' I disclosed my problems.

There were some wooden boxes in Jinag's luggage. He got up and dragged one of the wooden boxes near to his cot and opened it. It was full of dry bread packets. He was told that the breads might get fungus if not dried. He picked up a packet and kept it on cot. Again he pulled a bag which had couple of vinegar's bottles and different types of sauces.

'I wish to cook my food,' he pointed out.

'Vikram will cook for you. You just tell him what you want to eat,' I said.

'It is all right. It is easy and won't consume much time,' he said opening a sack of potatoes.

Jiang walked to Vikram's tent with the raw material taken out from the bags and began cooking his food on the stove. He had prepared dinner hardly within ten minutes. Shortly, I saw his dinner plate was ready having some slices of breads and few drops of sauce along with a bowl full of half boiled potatoes soaked in some liquid. He added a few drops of vinegar in his potato bowl and started enjoying his dinner.

'Would you like to eat some?' he offered me.

'Yes, I wish to taste the dish in bowl,' I said.

Jiang took an empty bowl and poured some potato dish in it. Pushing the bowl to me he said, 'Hope, you like it.'

'It is different,' I said sipping some soup.

'Did you like it?'

'Of course, it is tasty.'

We went to bed after chatting about Dehradun, and colleagues at the institute apart from the different dishes we used to eat in different restaurants of Dehradun.

Next day, Jiang prepared similar dishes for breakfast except the addition of some cabbage and tomato in the potato soup.

About eight O'clock we walked to the Valley of Flowers. I showed him many flowering plants, their usual and unusual habitats and mouse hare. I also disclosed him various useful properties of useful alpine flowers. He admired most of the edible, medicinal and aromatic plants.

'This tall and broadleaf herb is used for digestive disorders,' I said raising my finger towards the Himalayan rhubarb, locally called as dolu, growing in the stony area. Jiang looked towards the direction of my finger. As soon as he located dolu I noticed a broad glow in his small eyes.

'What sort of digestive disorder?' he asked me with elevated curiosity.

'It cures constipation and internal injuries, as well,' I said.

'You mean the whole plant is used.'

'Oh, yes. Its leaf, stem, and flowers, all are used. It is sour in taste.'

Jiang plucked a leaf of dolu and chewed it. 'It is vinegary,' he said trusting my words.

The whole day, we walked in the different localities of the valley and reached back at Ghangaria just before the sun set. Jiang wanted to cook his food on his own. He prepared the same dish for dinner and ate it just after sun set. And again the next day he ate the same dish, at the breakfast, lunch and dinner. I advised Jinag to take some chapattis and dal but he ignored my advice.

Whenever, we walked in the Valley of Flowers, quite often, I noticed Jiang standing before dolu herb chewing its vinegary leaf and stem. This made me to believe that he had become fond of dolu's taste, as it was vinegary, and he never forgot to add some drops of vinegar in his half boiled potato dish.

Eating unchanged dishes continuously for a week had made Jinag to drop his weight and temper, as well. He started counting his remaining days with me at the Ghangaria. Even being a non-vegetarian his destiny had forced him to survive on veg only. A day he asked me, 'Is there any way to get non-vegetarian dish?'

'Sorry Jiang, no chance. No one is allowed to have non-veg in this area. You know we have here Hemkund sahib, which is visited by millions of pilgrims just within four months. Pilgrims ....'

'Yes, I got to know it at Dehradun itself. That is why I did not bring any packed non-veg food,' Jiang interrupted before I complete.

'Smoking is also prohibited, though I have noticed few people smoking deceptively. A day I was walking up to Hemkund sahib to record the different stages of plant forms on the way. I saw a poor weary labour sitting against a rock and smoking a bidi to recoup his breath. A pilgrim saw him and became so ferocious that he pulled out his sword and hit on that labour's head. The sword slipped away through the labour's shoulder as he had swiftly jumped downhill. The labour ran hysterically on the mountain slope, and I was shocked looking the whole episode. I heard pilgrim shouting loudly cursing the labour. He meant to say that no one can smoke on the way of his Guru. Hemkund is the spot on which Guru Govind Singh had mediated in his previous birth,' I said narrating a past event.

Jiang heard me calmly and said, 'I can understand it. One should not hurt other's feeling.'

Next day, Jiang saw a stray dog near to my tent. He called me and whispered, 'this is very tasty. May I catch it to cook?' His mouth had become watery and his small eyes were shinning like anything in hope.

'No, no, Jiang. This is not a good idea,' I scared.

'But, this is just a stray dog,' he defended his position.

'Non-veg is not allowed here. You know it Jiang,' I reminded him.

His face though faded, he nodded his head in agreement and pushed himself in the tent with utmost failure. He wanted to control his feelings by maintaining some distance from the prey. After an hour we both were striding once again to the Valley of Flowers through the birch-rhododendron forests after crossing fir forests.

To complete Jiang's work on time or even before schedule so that he could go back to Dehradun to have proper food, we planned to stay for next two days in the upper reaches of the valley. After reaching at Ghangaria in the evening, I asked Vikram to arrange for next two days stay in the valley. Vikram started packing up necessary food and cooking items, including breads and sauces for Jiang.

Next day, we pitched our tent at the high altitude grassy mountain slope of the Valley of Flowers on a small flat area. In the evening just after sun set, we sat down on the grassy slope close to our tent. Vikram prepared an attractive spread for both of us in the moonlight. I washed my hands and asked Jinag to begin eating food. But soon I saw Jiang smelling his toast rather than eating. Within a few seconds he threw away his bread one by one and started shouting.

'What happened?' I asked Jiang shockingly.

'I cannot eat it.'

'Why?'

'It is ridiculous. Even no one can eat it.'

'For god shake, will you please tell me, what has happened?'

'It is stinking.'

'Stinking!'

'Yes, by all means.'

'May I have a slice,' I asked Vikram.

Biting a piece of toast I felt some bad smell. Soon I realized it was really difficult to chew. It had strong smell of kerosene oil.

The peaceful environment of the valley had turned into chaos. I asked Vikram the reason of bread having kerosene smell.

'The kerosene bottle broke somewhere on the way in my rucksack. And the bread soaked the same,' Vikram said in low voice with deep sorrow.

'I am sorry Jiang, it is really unfortunate,' I tried to bring Jiang to his natural calm. 'Please eat some chapattis.'

The day long work in the valley had exhausted him. He was hungry too and his breads had soaked the kerosene. I felt guilty but it could not have calmed down his hunger. I got up and walked away from the tent. I came back with some leaves and stems of dolu and requested him to eat some chapattis with his favorite dolu. Fortunately, Jiang realized the situation and calmed down while eating chapattis with delicious vinegary dolu.

After going back to Dehradun, he wrote an excellent report on his painful survey. And within one and half month he flew away to his motherland. After two years of his departure from Dehradun, I heard the very sad news of his demise. I was told that Jiang had intestinal ulcer. This fact, finally, disclosed the mystery why he liked dolu all the time, even in his worst moments of his life with me.

18.0

His Confession

The canter loaded with iron rods and bundles of barbed wire were unloaded at Benakuli – a small roadside helmet on way to Badrinath. Since there was no motorable road from Benakuli onwards to the Khiron valley, the unloaded material had to be carried either by labours or by mules.

I walked in the village to find out any mode of such transportation. A lad around 22 years old peeping out from a small window of his moderate house saw me on the village trail and came out to know my whereabouts. On my request for help he was anxious to know the purpose of carrying the construction material to such a desolate land. I informed him my motive of establishing 10×10 m fenced areas at 11,500 feet in the Khiron valley for setting a comparison between freely grazed and controlled areas. He assured me to all possible support for the purpose I explained him.

He was very friendly and took me in his house where I learnt his name – Gopal. Within short span of time, he served me a cup of tea with some sattu. Before I finished the nutritious dish, Gopal had made up his mind to arrange labour for erecting enclosures. I offered him the entire contract of putting 6 enclosures of 10×10 m in the Khiron valley on 3 different landscape units – undulating land areas, steep slopes and gentle slopes. I stayed overnight with him and decided to go Khiron valley next day so that I could show him the land and the proper sites for putting enclosures.

Gopal had arranged necessary logistics for trekking to the Khiron valley from dawn to dusk. It was third week of May and I was feeling a severe cold in the morning at Benakuli. After having 'Alu-Parathas' in breakfast I set off with Gopal to Khiron valley. Some 50 m downhill from motorable road I saw a small but quite beautiful temple. I bowed my head with respect and in desire of seeking blessings for fruitful journey. On my inquiry about the deity living in this temple Gopal rather narrated an interesting story.

Once upon a time, a cow in Benakuli had a newly born calf. A day, on her return from the jungle when her owner went her to draw milk he could not get a single drop of milk. He thought that some naughty person might have taken her milk in the jungle. Next day, he got no milk again and subsequently the problem remained constant every day. Her calf had begun weaker and weaker day by day due to unavailability of milk. Hence, a day her owner decided to follow her in the jungle to find out the reason.

Cow kept grazing in the jungle as usual. While returning home she stopped near a big boulder and began to pour her milk over it. Looking at this unusual fact the cow owner had been surprised and he disclosed the entire story to the villagers. Since then villagers believed that the boulder was not an ordinary boulder but the symbol of the *Lord*

Neelkanth. Subsequently, they had constructed this temple around the *Neelkanth*.

Walking further 100 m down I crossed a bridge over Alaknanda, and entered the mixed forest of Himalayan fir, wild hazel, rhododendrons and horse chestnut. I noticed some open patches in the forest, which appeared to be under severe anthropogenic pressures mainly in terms of heavy grazing. In some of these open patches there was good growth of relatively less disturbed palatable herbs but interestingly all plants of wild marjoram were deprived of leaves and flowers. I learnt from Gopal that people of nearby villages such as Patudi, Benakuli, Pandukeshwar, and Lambagad collect its leaf and flower for selling to the pilgrims visiting Badrinath. Wild marjoram, locally called as ban tulsi, had been the most preferred offerings to the Lord Badrinath from time immemorial.

After 3 km ups and down trekking in the broadleaf and coniferous forests I reached in a village – Khiron. This was the first and last village in the Khiron valley. The village had about 15 houses with a small temple of Goddess Unaini. Coming across the sightings of temples frequently in my wanderings across the high hills of Garhwal was not a surprise to me, as I was walking in the land where every stone, dale and mountain has been associated with god and goddesses. The Khiron village was located on relatively flat area. There were some agricultural fields in one side of the village.

Strolling further up in the Khiron valley I gazed on the mountain slope rising from the village was deprived of tree species. A few women were gathering some herbs on these slopes. For a close view of these herbs I picked up my binocular. I could see the women selectively collecting a herb with whitish flowers, which was Allium humile locally called as 'faran'. 'The faran of this valley is not only highly fragrant and delicious but quite well-known in these hills, and therefore people from remote and far away areas trickle down here to collect this spicy herb', Gopal said.

After agricultural land, the way to Khiron valley led along the continuous steep climb, which was covered by birch-rhododendron community. After crossing this patch of forest I arrived in the alpine meadows of Khiron valley. Panting and prodding I walked further to find out the suitable site for erecting enclosures.

Looking around the landscape my sight was caught by a colourful object on a big boulder. Initially, for a moment I thought it was a woman in bright colourful cloths. But in the next moment I was compelled to review my opinion on the presence of a woman in such a desolate area. Moving a few steps toward the boulder created disturbances to the object hence it all of a sudden flew away and landed on the downhill valley. When it glided down the hills I identified the object. It was an extremely beautiful and colourful pheasant of the Himalaya – the Himalayan monal.

I zeroed my investigations in the valley and finally showed the site to Gopal for establishing barbed wire enclosures, and returned to my camp at Pandukeshwar – a roadside village on way to Badrinath at the bank of Alaknanda. Within two weeks Gopal erected all the six enclosures the way I had instructed him to put on place. Now my experiment had started and at every 15 days interval I had to sample the vegetation in and outside the enclosures.

I used to climb to Khiron valley with my assistant Prem – who hails from Reni village, to collect aboveground live plant biomass. I brought the collected plant biomass to my camp at Pandukeshwar and segregated it by species. I measured the fresh weight of plant biomass and then packed all individuals of each species in a separate paper bag. Since I did not have oven at my camp I drove to Tapovan – a village on way to Reni and Malari via Joshimath - for drying the plant biomass, as I had a friend at Tapovan who had an oven.

I collected the aboveground plant biomass twice in a month – 15th and 30th day of each month. Once on a schedule day of plant biomass collection I had severe fever. I could not make out to visit the Khiron valley for collection of standing biomass. I requested Prem to go Khiron for this purpose as he had learnt the methods of live plant biomass collection. I also asked him to tag each bag for identification of enclosure number and site. Before sun-set he returned with biomass which I decided to examine once I felt better. Next day, I opened the bags and as usual started segregating the species. While doing so I became unconvinced on the composition and occurrence of some unusual plant species in the collected lots. The dilemma deepened with opening of every new bag.

I stopped examining the species further. I called up Prem to share my doubts. I asked him whether he had done any mistake in tagging the bags or inadvertently he would have collected biomass from some other sites. Prem firmly refuted my doubts and assured me that he had collected the biomass from the enclosures only following the earlier methodology. I reopened the bags and once again started segregating and examining the species but my doubts remained. Finally, I decided to go Khiron valley next morning for biomass collection on my own and informed the same to Prem.

Next morning, I saw Prem standing before me in a diffident and apologetic manner. He confessed the fact that because of continuous rainfall he gathered biomass at the lower elevation only. I took a deep breath and set off for biomass collection to the Khiron valley. Any person acquainted with the Himalayan ecology can guess the elevation range of the Himalaya with the help of plant species and vice-versa, as the vegetation distribution is governed by the altitudes in the Himalaya. My continuous observations and trekking across the mountains of the Himalaya had made me to learn this fact and had ultimately warned me from wrong data collection and its subsequent interpretations.

19.0

On His Wishes

Loved by all and revered by Hindus, the Himalaya, the world loftiest mountain remained to be known the dwelling place of almighty – *Neelkanth*. Apart from the Kailash Mansarovar, the Kedarnath weaves its spell and showers His blessings over all pilgrims who come to see and luckily enough to feel *Neelkanth*'s presence here in Kedarnath amid the lofty snow-laden mountains. Perhaps it was this realization that always attracted me to visit here, at least once in the life time.

I shared my feelings with Shekhar who stayed at Reni village about ten km away from Joshimath. Since Shekhar had a Rajdoot bike, we decided to use it for travelling to Kedarnath upto Gaurikund, the last town connected with motorable road. We set off on the pilgrimage in the next morning from the Reni. Driving through Joshimath, Helung, Pipalkoti and Chamoli we reached at Gopeshwar – the district headquarters of Chamoli.

At Gopeshwar I asked Shekhar to be seated behind me with the rucksack and I took over the driving responsibility. Since I did not have a good command on bike driving, Shekhar kept on making me cautious to drive on the risky hilly road. He pressed me hard and finally persuaded me to wear a helmet. I drove about six km, which brought in more confidence in my bike driving skill. We crossed some small hilly villages and thereafter we reached on a narrow road having sharps turns quite on and off.

On one such sharp U turn, the moment I was turning the bike along the turn suddenly a jeep came running against me. The turn was sharp with downhill slope and there was almost no space to cross the running jeep. Moreover, my left side had a deep gorge of indefinite length. To save us sliding in the deep mountain gorge I turned the bike to my right before pressing down the break. While doing so I could not control the bike fully. This made me to collide with the jeep.

The sudden jolt bumped me and my head hit hard on the jeep's headlight. And the next push had thrown me on the jeep's right side, and my helmet had slipped under the jeep. Before lying on the roadside, I had become unconscious. But somewhere in my mind still I was thinking about Shekhar whether he was alive or passed away. My mind had assured me that I was no more part of this world. I could hear some voices but I was unable to guess who they were.

I tried to stand up in my state of unconsciousness. Meantime, I kept on analyzing whether I was dead or alive. I was even unable to realize whether I had got up or was still lying on the roadside. After couple of minutes, among the different voices, I recognized a sound saying, 'Kala, Kala are you ok?' This seemed to be Shekhar's voice. And I realized that probably he was not hurt and was still alive. But I was not sure of my own status, whether I had become dead, was going to be dead shortly or would remain alive. It was useless to me whether my eyes were closed or open because I was unable to see anything.

After sometime, I tried to look around and I found myself encircled by a group of people. I began to identify them but failed to make out one. I thought probably I was alive but I had lost my memory. Feeling a touch on my shoulder by someone behind me made me to look behind. He was Shekhar.

'Are you ok?' he asked with twinkling eyes.

'Yes, I am,' I replied identifying Shekhar, which made me to realize that I could recollect my past.

'Thanks. Please leave us alone. We are ok,' Shekhar requested the crowd.

'Well, but first you have to compensate for the headlight,' the jeep's driver came forward to ask us showing the broken headlight.

'How much?' Shekhar said.

'Hundred rupees only,' he replied.

Shekhar without any inquiry and delay handed over him hundred rupees. The jeep driver moved on his way with his passengers, and the remaining part of the crowd walked to their way. Shekhar began to test the bike's condition. He noticed some problem in the bike's handle. It was not turning to left side and had fixed to right side only.

The nearest workshop to repair the bike was about five km away at Gopeshwar. Being a relatively heavy bike, pushing and pulling of Rajdoot on up and down mountain road was a very tedious task. Shekhar checked the handle again to find out if there was any possibility to make it movable for the time being. By checking again and again he found that the lower part of handle was obstructed by the front part of the silencer.

'We have to detach the silencer. It may help to move the handle to left side, too,' Shekar suggested.

'Let's see,' I agreed.

We detached the silencer and it worked out. We turned to Gopeshwar for repairing the bike. Being the evening hours, people were returning home from their works, and many had come on the roads for evening walks and for shopping. While driving, the high pitched noise of our Rajdoot had become the subject of people's attention all along the road. A few people even came out from their houses to find out what kind of vehicle it was. Our bike was airing horrible ghastly sound that increased with its speed. Such a terrific sound had brought me back to my complete consciousness and I wrapped my towel around my ears to protect my eardrum. Though, Shekhar slowed down the bike's speed but while driving uphill he could not control the sound.

At Gopeshwar, soon we came to know that workshop was further three hundred meter away on the uphill. Being a district headquarters and more vigilant by police we felt Gopeshwar unsafe for us with our bike. Chamoli was ten km away from Gopeshwar but the continuous downhill drive was its advantage. Shekhar switched off the bike's engine and slipped it on the downhill road in newton to Chamoli rather than workshop at Gopeshwar.

We handed over the bike to mechanic at Chamoli's workshop, and stepped into a hotel for night stay. The moment we set off to visit the Kedarnath we were extremely delighted and inquisitive but now the moment we were stepping into the hotel's room we were saddened and distressed. Amazingly, despite the cruel mishap on the deadly mountain road my body had not succumbed even to a minor scratch. And I was forced to realize the fact that one could not reach to Him, dead or alive, against His wishes.

I dared again to visit Kedarnath only after a year passed away. And again I shared my bravery with Shekhar. I found him braver than me, as he immediately accepted the proposal. Riding on the same Rajdoot we drove via same route. This time we managed to cross Mandal after Gopeshwar and reached at Chopta.

Chopta was a small hill station on the hill top. The famous Tungnath temple, one of the five sacred Kedars, was just three km away from here. The other sacred Kedars are Rudranath, Madmaheshwar, Kalpeshwar and Kedarnath. Interestingly, all five Kedars and five Badris are located in Garhwal, which had made Garhwal the land of Gods.

Chopta was a quite attractive vantage point. I could see layers of rolling mountains to the horizon dotted with terraced fields perched on the hills. The wind sweeping down from the Himalayan snows, time and again, hurried over the hills of Chopta hummed and moaned in the huge deodars. All such attractions of this tiny hill station had made us to camp here for the night.

Next day, we set off to continue our journey. We passed through Okhimath, Guptkashi and many villages dotted in the forests and hills before finally reaching at Gaurikund via Sonprayag. On the way, we were lucky enough to see some dense oak-mixed forests but unfortunately no wild animal. Shekhar being fond of tea stopped the bike at a tea-stall a few km before Gaurikund. Seeing a local person sitting leisurely in the tea-stall I, casually, asked him, 'did you see any wild animal in these forests?'

'Yes, I have seen,' he replied. 'Quite often I have encountered black bear, wild pig, and barking deer adjacent to my village.' 'Why are you asking all this?' he questioned.

'I like to see wildlife. Did you see leopard here?' I asked.

'Do you like leopard also,' he quizzed rather answering.

'Of course yes,' I said.

'Would you wish to see leopard?' he asked.

'Is it possible?' I asked.

'Yes, I can show you leopard's skin. 'Would you wish to have some skins?' he asked.

'Do you have a one?'

'I have many.'

'How many?'

'How many you wish to have, four, five, six…'

'Six, you have six such skins. But how did you manage to get that much?' I asked.

'From these forests only, as they are rich in wildlife,' he disclosed.

Though, he did not show me a single skin, he was confident enough to sell me as much as I wished to buy. This made me to think that if he was right then God knows the fate of …

We stayed overnight at Gaurikund. Next day, we set off to walk on the hills to our destination in the early morning hours before sunrise. Thousands of pilgrims were walking on the way chanting 'Har Har Mahadev'. A few rich pilgrims were in palanquin and many others rode on horses and mules. A few, mainly children but some adults also, were half in and half out in the baskets of porters back.

It took us about four hours from Gaurikund to reach at the legendary historical temple of Kedarnath. The temple site was snowy and freezing that made us to shiver. I offered puja and bowed my head before the Kedar baba – the *Neelkanth*-recollecting the century's old realization that nobody could reach to *Him*, dead or alive, against *His* wishes.

20.0

Seers of Pandukeshwar

A foggy day of July, wrapped in thoughts with hands in raincoat's pocket I entered the lone Alaknanda Gramin Bank of Pandukeshwar. Rakesh, the bank manager knew about me staying at Pandukeshwar, as a few days before, I had opened an account in his bank. In the one room bank two customers were chatting sitting on chairs before the bank manager's table.

After Namaste, Rakesh indicated me to sit on the only chair left unoccupied. Since there was a very narrow space to reach the chair, I struggled hard cris-crossing my body to catch the chair. The gentlemen resumed their chatting once I sat on the chair.

'Well, swamiji you were talking about a plum tree,' Rakesh said staring at the dark skinned, clean shaved, fine haircut person wearing white dhoti and kurta, seemed to be in his late fifties.

'About five years ago I went to a horticulture nursery at Joshimath to buy some fruit tree's seedlings. I asked them to give me some plantlets of apple, which I brought at my hut. I planted them around my hut and took all necessary care to grow them and flourish,' swami pointed out.

'Now you would be enjoying the fruits of your hard work and long-sufferings,' a person sitting beside the swami interrupted.

'You are right, now they bear fruits. But unfortunately they bear plum rather than apples,' swami said.

This made me to laugh.

'Look, somebody is laughing,' swami said. My unexpected laughs had hurt his feelings.

'Sorry swamiji, I did not mean to hurt you. I laugh on your saying that apple tree bears plum fruits,' I explained my position.

'Oh, yes, don't you trust me. I mean it only. I planted apple trees and now they bear plums,' he stressed on his point.

I became silent rather than explaining further that at seedling stage the identity of plum and apple plants might be mistaken.

To cheer up the heavy environment Rakesh came forward to introduce me, 'swamiji, this is Chandra, doing research in the Valley of Flowers. Here he has rented a quarter in Kalpeshwar's house.'

'That's nice. I like research. Whenever I do research I forget even my own existence,' swami said, which brought back the soothing environment.

This was my first meeting with swamiji. Once swami left the bank's room, Rakesh briefed me about swami's charismatic character and powers.

'This swami is very powerful and popular, too. His name is Om. Last year in August, here we had a very heavy downpour, which brought a huge flood in the Alaknanda basin. All sadhus huts washed away in Alaknanda, except this Om swami. He is a charismatic, enigmatic and extremely spiritual person. He knows how to cure even the deadly and chronic diseases.'

'The Himalaya is well-known for having miraculous medicinal herbs. He would have learnt the uses of such herbs from some vaidya,' I pointed out.

'No, he does not use herbs rather than he uses stones for curing ailments and even any problem at home and in life,' he disclosed another mystery of Om.

'Stones!'

'Yes, stones. He is an expert of curing any sort of disease, even any psychological disorder. He has a great skill of removing stones from kidney and gallbladder by using stones.'

'Interesting!'

Rakesh continued, 'it is a miracle. He has some supernatural powers. Two months back, the District Magistrate of Chamoli came to see him.'

'Was he sick?' I asked.

'No, his son remained sick for many years. The DM approached to many well-known MBBS doctors for curing his son but nothing worked out. He had become hopeless. A fortunate day, looking him gloomy one of his employees advised him to approach Om. Initially, DM showed his reluctance but later he thought to try at least once. He approached to Om with his son and within three weeks his son's health had improved a lot. Since then DM has become Om's pupil. Now his son is completely fine,' Rakesh narrated the story in brief.

'How did he cure DM's son?' I asked.

'He treats patients by giving them colourful stones as symbol of good luck and wealth. The colourful stones, also called as gems, have healing powers, positive energy waves and other mystical powers, which bestow multiple benefits on its wearers if worn under an expert's guidance,' Rakesh said.

'It is hard to believe. How is it possible?' I questioned again.

'See, our body is made up of five cosmic elements and each of which is influenced by the position of planets. Every gem stone is believed to draw certain power of beams from its respective planet and channelize it into the wearer's body. Since the composition and genetic makeup of human body vary, the potential impact of gem differs individually, as per the birth planetary chart,' Rakesh explained.

'You seem to be well educated on stone therapy,' I said.

'I learn it from Om Swami only,' Rakesh said.

'What else have you learnt?' I asked.

'There are nine types of precious gems. Rests are substitute's adding upto eighty four. The real gem has a better impact on its wearer than a substitute. Blue sapphire is most important gem. If it suits to somebody he or she will definitely have bright future. The stone should be worn with similar colour metal, as yellow sapphire is advised to wear with gold and pearl with silver. The weight specifications of gem to be worn vary with gender, which is suggested five plus ratti for male and three plus ratti for female,' Rakesh elucidated.

'You are well-versed with gem's knowledge,' I said.

'It is not even a tip of iceberg. Om swami has a fair knowledge I don't. He says that each gem has specific life cycle. The wearer must know the gem's life cycle from the astrologers as its potential impact declines or expires after the due date. One should also ensure four Cs – colour, carat, clarity, and cut - for beneficial effects of the chosen gem. It is really difficult to find out good quality gems. Due to lot of demand, at present, the market floods with fake gems,' Rakesh enlightened me.

Hearing about gems and Om swami from Rakesh had changed my initial perceptions about Om swami. Though, first impression always remained for long, as said. Since the first meeting with Om swami weeks passed by, as I had become busy with my tasks.

A day of October, Harish Chandola, a known journalist came to see me from Joshimath. While talking with Harish soon I realized that he came to see Om swami rather than me. I took him to Om swami's hut at the bank of Alaknanda. Before entering the hut, I saw a signboard placed before the hut on the ground inscribed 'Consultation Fee 100,000'. Having read this I was amused for a moment.

'Look at this,' I asked Harish showing the board.

'This is incredible. Who pay this much in this desolate wilderness area. What this swami is doing here with the poor villagers. He should suppose to be in some metros,' he said with extreme surprise.

'But I met him once in the bank without paying any fee,' I said.

'So you have saved one lakh,' Harish whispered. 'Is there any other sadhu whom I can meet?'

'Unfortunately, I know here Om only. But I heard many sadhus live here. Let's have a chance. You stay back and I go to take permission from him,' I said.

Harish agreed upon my idea. I stepped further toward the hut. On reaching the door I peeped into the hut. Om was squatted on a carpet behind a small block of wooden. A thick book placing on the block was opened before him. There was couple of cabinets in the hut packed with books. Om was staring at his left side cabinet.

'Namaste swamiji,' I greeted Om with folded hands.

'Namaste,' he turned his head to look at me trying to recognize.

'We met once in the bank at Pandukeshwar,' I tried to remind him. 'Rakesh had introduced us.'

He was sharp enough to identify me and said, 'oh, you are a researcher.'

'Yes swamiji,' I said expecting that he might agree to meet Harish.

'Come in,' he invited me cordially.

'Swamiji, actually I have a friend waiting outside to meet you. He came all the way from Joshimath,' I explained.

'Well, you know my fee is ……. Have you read the board?' he asked.

'Yes, we both have seen. But it is beyond his capacity to pay such a huge amount,' I said hesitantly.

'I am sorry. He has to, if he wishes to see me,' he said firmly.

I had no choice so I greeted Om swami and came back. Till then Harish had got upset over the hike and mystery of consultation fee. In expectation of meeting to some other swami we moved away from the Om's hut. Walking about hundred meters we saw a hut on a knoll. We reached on the hut's gate and stared in locating if there was any board hanging on consultation charges. A young sadhu saw us and when I informed him our desire to see some sadhu he allowed us to enter the gate.

We sat down on the hut's grassy lawns. A tall person with white hairs, long beard, broad shining eyes, and lower half of the body wrapped in saffron dhoti came out from the hut. He squatted on a boulder close to us in the grassy lawn. He appeared to be in his sixties. He looked at me without saying anything but his calm and broad eyes seemed to have several questions, including the reason of our visit to him.

'Swamiji I live here in Pandukeshwar and this is my friend,' I briefly introduced us to sadhu. 'He came to see you all the way from Joshimath.'

The sadhu started staring at Harish.

'Swamiji, I am getting old but I have been always deprived of spirituality. I hardly worship God but now I wish to learn about the Gods. I wish to wash out my sins committed throughout my life. I am a brainless stupid duffer,' Harish shared his feelings to the sadhu.

'My child, don't use such words, which have no productive meanings. Don't pronounce such terms, which don't deserve to be used. Don't be so hard on yourself. You are not dropped from the heaven knowing everything. It is enough to remember Him. It is more than enough to nurture the wishes of knowing Him. He is omnipotent, and omnipresence. His altruism is boundless and He knows your remorse and your feelings,' the sadhu preached retaining his calmness.

I guessed that sadhu's intension was more on the use of term 'sin' by Harish, which he wished not to be used. He meant to convey us that such terms circulate negative feelings and energy in our body. He even did not wish to use the term negative.

'Swamiji please enlighten me the reality of this world and the spirituality. I wish to worship God. But I am confused from where to begin. We have thirty three crore deities. Please tell me how to start and from where to start,' Harish pleaded, desperately.

'My child, we have over hundred crore gods. God is everywhere in every human being. The God lives even in every molecule,' Swami said.

'Yes, I read it. But swamiji please let me know whom to worship. If I worship one of them others will be disappointed,' Harish explained.

'Look at this tree,' swami raised his finger toward a deodar tree of his lawn. 'Can you count its leaves just now?'

'They are innumerable and untold,' Harish said looking at the vastness of the tree from ground to sky.

'Look at the branches holding all these leaves. They are so many. So my child, don't go to hold each leaf. Don't waste energy in catching each branch. Try to explore the root of this huge tree. Once you hold the root the entire tee is in your hand with all the branches and leaves. Hold the root my child,' swami said philosophically.

In the meantime, a couple arrived before the sadhu. They bowed down to sadhu's feet. Sadhu showered his blessings on them. The husband picked up two notes of five hundred rupees from his pocket and while putting them down on the sadhu's feet said politely, 'swamiji, we came here to visit Lord Badrinath. Today morning only, we came to know about you staying here in the bank of Alaknanda. We could not bring anything for you. Kindly accept our apology and please buy some ration for you and your pupil.'

'No, please don't show me money. Keep this in your pocket and take some fruits to your kids desperately waiting for you at home,' swami said refusing to accept the money.

'Swamiji, please I request you to kindly accept,' both husband and wife pleaded.

'No, I cannot. I don't need it. You need it for your family,' swami refused again.

They both felt quite uncomfortable. Once again with hesitation they pleaded sadhu to accept but he was firmed with his words.

'My child, don't hesitate. I don't need it. It is of no use to me but useful for you and your family. I assure you if I happened to be in your city I shall surely drop at your home for some food. So don't mind. My blessings will remain with you and your family.'

The couple had to step out from the hut's gate to catch the bus, which they did, and I lost somewhere in comparing Om swami with the sadhu sitting before me calm and content. Probably, many questions boiling up in Harish's mind had got their answer yet there remained a few to be answered.

'Swamiji, how can one ensure that has picked up the root not the leaf or the branch?' Harish posed a question bubbling in his mind for long.

'Well, to know this one needs to study this tree. As much as one concentrate studying his/her object he/she knows the object to that extent, deeply. Thoroughly,' sadhu said confidently.

While returning from the hut, we kept silence for long contemplating sadhu's philosophical words. Harish drove back to Joshimath and I entered my quarter with many thoughts to analyze in my lonely hours.

A day Kalpeshwar, the house owner at Pandukeshwar where I had rented a room, came home for a week. He had a shop at Ghangaria. He was fond of wine, which he loved to enjoy almost every evening. Since he was on leave, he began to consume wise since morning only. In the afternoon, he came to my quarter and asked me to go on outing. Being a hilly village Pandukeshwar became too cold to walk in the evening hours in case of rains, especially during winter.

We walked on the road leading to Badrinath for an hour, and then decided to go downhill towards the bank of Alaknanda.

'Would you like to eat fish?' Kalpeshwar quizzed.

'Will you catch fish in the Alaknanda?' I asked rather replying.

'Sometime I catch but not now. It consumes lot of time, and we also don't have net. But if you wish I can arrange,' he said.

'Well, I don't mind to have fish. But how will you arrange?' I asked.

'You just wait and watch,' he assured.

We walked along the Alaknanda for half an hour. I kept on following Kalpeshwar who had reached close to Om swami's hut.

'Where are you going? Look, here we have Om swami's hut. His onetime fee for meeting is one lakh,' I informed Kalpeshwar.

'What rubbish? Who told you?' he asked frowningly.

'I read it.'

'Where?'

'On a board placed before his hut,' I said.

'Nonsense, this fellow is sitting on our land free of cost and putting such signboard without our notice,' he said contemptuously.

Having said this he entered Om swami's gate yelling, 'Hey Om, Om…'

Stepping further inside the gate he saw the signboard of consultation fee. He pulled up the board and threw it away calling again, 'Om Swami, where are you?'

Om swami came out from his hut silently like a ghost and said very politely, 'Namaste.'

'Are you here for business? What is this?' Kalpeshwar said raising his finger towards the board he threw away. 'You have put such board without my notice.'

Om swami remained frozen and did not reply.

'I came for fish. Give me some fresh good quality fishes, and stop all this business in my land,' Kalpeshwar once again warned Om swami.

'Sorry Kalpeshwar, for past few days I could not make out to catch fishes,' Om said in a low voice.

'Why, what happened to you? Now even you don't wish to share your catches,' Kalpeshwar asked.

'No. Please don't take it otherwise. Actually, the water level has increased suddenly in the river and it is risky to catch fishes,' Om explained.

I was astounded hearing their conversation and thinking that how come a sadhu catching and eating fishes. For me sadhu supposed to be non-vegetarian. What kind of sadhu is this, I thought.

'What about this signboard and fee business?' Kalpeshwar asked.

'No, no, it is nothing,' Om said.

'Ok, but give me some fishes. I cannot take your words granted. Let me check in your hut. Are you double-dealing with me?' Kalpeshwar asked.

'Please trust me. I am not lying. There is no fish in my hut. You can test out anywhere,' Om said.

'Well, this time I am going but next time I won't go without having my share,' Kalpeshwar said almost in threatening voice.

'Yes, I promise,' Om said.

We walked from the Om swami's territory. While walking uphill back home, I asked Kalpeshwar, 'well, finally I got to know that Om swami was the person who stocks and supplies fish to you.'

'Whenever, I visit him he himself offers me fishes. But unluckily today he does not have one. He is a very kind person and never hides anything from me,' Kalpeshwar said.

The very next day Rakesh met me in a shop at Pandukeshwar. I shared my experiences on Om with him. Rakesh again defended Om like anything.

'Well, I agree with you. It may be a matter of sentiments and beliefs to you but please tell me one thing. Does it suit to a sadhu of his stature to charge fee from people desperate to see him?' I asked Rakesh.

'Look, you cannot understand it. He put that board simply to keep away crowd from his hut. He is here to meditate. He is here to think about God, and to understand the God. He is here to go closure to the God. He is here to know the reality of life. If people keep on visiting his hut to see him he will be disturbed again and again, which harm his meditation. He is a very popular sadhu and people come from far and wide to see him which interrupt his day to day activities and meditation,' Rakesh explained some hard facts of Om's life.

Days, weeks and months passed by, and I had reached in the last phase of data collection from the Valley of Flowers, Khiron valley, Badrinath valley and adjacent alpine meadows. A day I went to see SDM Joshimath to thank him for his support, as and when required for my research during my stay in Pandukeshwar and Ghangaria. Below his residence was the main road to Badrinath. A narrow short cut road twisted its way down connected SDM residence to the main road.

While walking down to the main road, I saw a well built gentleman wearing black spectacle and blue suit with bright red tie. He was walking straight on the main road holding a small black handbag. I looked at him, again and again, trying to recollect something. I was asking myself, I have seen this person but where. Looking at his gesture and posture I thought I might have seen him in some high level seminar or conference. As he approached closure, he seemed more familiar.

'Hi, how are you?' I threw an arrow in the dark.

'I am fine, thank you,' as soon as his last word completed I flabbergasted and exclaimed in deep surprise. 'Oh, my God! You!'

'What happened? Why are you so surprised? Is there any problem?' he asked looking at me and my conduct.

I could not stop my sight to look at him and his costumes, and finally exclaimed, 'no, it is all right swamiji.'

He had got my emotions and said, 'you seem to be surprised on my look and dress. You think a sadhu does not deserve to wear decent suits. Please come out from that traditional belief and way of thinking. You know I am not like those ordinary sadhus. I am different.'

I was compelled to agree upon his words that he was a very different sadhu. It was difficult to an ordinary person like me to catch his extraordinary character.

21.0

Nanda's Neelkanth

Summiting an unknown mountain peak above Bruz Khal at 15,000 feet, I cast my eyes round for a convenient spot to take rest for a while and recoup my energy. Inhaling deeply I unloaded my backpack and sat on a rocky outcrop. Unloaded rucksack made me to feel extremely relaxed but my lungs were struggling still hard to normalize my breathing. I opened mouth to help my lungs along but not enough air flowed in.

I gazed at the sky, which was painted at horizon with the layers of deep orange to light orange colours. Some thick pieces of clouds hovering above dales and mountains were interrupting the continuity of extensive landscape beauty. In couple of minutes my breathing had reached to the normal course. I looked right where a part of clouds had just blown above in the sky revealing hidden beauty of a snow laden mountain.

At the snail's pace, the clouds had dispersed from a mountain peak facing me. I became mesmerized when I saw the peculiar peak of the *Nanda* Devi – first half horizontal and second half vertical. I picked up my Pentax SLR camera and before I got ready to click some photographs the *Nanda* Devi had camouflaged in the dark clouds.

The fine cool breeze had kept on passing over the rocky outcrop I was sitting. Being the month of September, only a few relict stands of annul herbs, mostly in senescence phase, peeping out from the boulders and rocks were visible. The elevation had become one of the reasons for poor growth and availability of plants, but because of marginal ecological and stressful conditions such plants accumulate great medicinal properties.

I had decided to capture a view of the *Nanda* Devi in my camera. For this I was on the mercy of clouds to unveil this majestic peak to me. I recollected a day when I along with two of my colleagues climbed above 14,000 feet at Kunth Khal, which forms the eastern part of the Valley of Flowers National Park. A few minutes before my companions I had reached then at the summit and saw the picturesque peak of the *Nanda* Devi. Before their arrival at the spot to see the same magic, the *Nanda* Devi had shrouded all around by thick clouds. Our waiting for half an hour for a glance of *Nanda* Devi had reaped no fruits.

I fumbled my rucksack to pull out the water bottle. Having quenched my thirst, I gazed at the downhill slope where a boulder was tenanted by couple of mouse hares or Pyca. When I had seen mouse hare first time in the Himalayas I was unable to differentiate between a mouse and a mouse hare. Later on I got to know the fact that the major difference lies in the tail, which is almost absent in the mouse hare.

These mouse hares have seldom been the subject of hot debates at the present day wildlife conservation programmes, which is mainly revolve around a few large animals such as tiger, elephant, rhinos and loins. We seldom have any idea on their population size and major role in maintaining the health of an ecosystem.

The time had been running at its usual speed. The needle of my wrist watch had crossed the 5th line indicating me to find out the suitable place for pitching the tent. I had recouped sufficient energy to move further yet I was desperate to have a look of the *Nanda* Devi peak. The clouds, for some time, had dispersed just from the peak but continued to encircle the *Nanda* Devi. The long waiting had come to an end. This time without any delay I captured such a beautiful scene in my camera.

Having seen such a miraculous heavenly manifestation on the earth symbolized as the goddess *Nanda* – the consort of the *Lord Neelkanth* - I got up and walked some 400 m downhill where the rolling land was laden with brahmakamal – a sacred flower of Hindus. The air was filled with the fragrance of these yellowish white blooms. Here a small patch of land about 20 m^2 was relatively flat and less windy due to presence of a few big boulders. I pitched my tent aside a boulder for the night stay in the garden of brahmakamal.

Dinesh and Manoj – my assistants who hailed from Chai village near Joshimath – had started arranging things to prepare food. Dinesh infact was the person who had chalked out our entire trek from Joshimath to Badrinath via Chai-Thai village, Chinap valley, Bruz Khal, Khiron valley and the base of the *Neelkanth*. He had got this idea from the shepherds who lived on move in this area during the summer and rainy seasons.

The land around my tent carpeted with brahmakamal was soggy, so I sat on the boulder. Most of the clouds in the sky and on the mountains had dissolved in the universe and I could see the wide-ranging magnificent view of insurmountable gigantic mountains and gorgeous valleys. The entire landscape beauty had augmented after some moments when the sun reached just above the mountain top in the west and the silvery peaks started turning golden.

I was fortunate enough to see such a brilliant sunset in the great Himalayan mountain range. It had made me to forget the past four day tedious trek. I sipped tea while standing in the moon light that had some unique flavor. On my enquiry of such a distinct flavor of tea Dinesh enlightened me about an important aromatic as well as medicinal herb. It was locally called as 'tagar'. Botanically it is called as *Pleurospermum candolii*, a plant belongs to family Umbelliferae and grows in the high altitude areas.

Next day after breakfast, our entourage set off for the upper Khiron valley – a valley at the base of the *Neelkanth*. I marched downhill and after about two hours I reached a place where several small trails led to downhill valley. I decided to walk one seemed to be shortest that had descended sharply to the river valley. Walking along soon I realized my choice was wrong once I entered the birch-rhododendron forest. Here we had a different species of rhododendron botanically called as *Rhododendron campanulatum*. It bears whitish blooms in contrast to one that grows at low elevations with reddish blooms – *R. arboreum* locally known as 'buransh'.

It was quite difficult to walk in the grove of birch and rhododendron. Birch trees were less problematic though they had curved and strong branches creating hurdle to move ahead. Passing through rhododendron was really awful. It had curved as well as highly flexible branches leaned close to the ground. It was almost not possible to escape from walking on these branches. A step rested on any of its branch made to bend it further down on the ground. But while releasing the same branch with another step it disturbed the entire rhythm due to its flexibility, which either hit back anywhere or made one to tumble. The curved branches of birch and rhododendron were indicating that the area received heavy snowfall in winter. Rhododendron had developed an additional feature in the form of flexible branches for adaptation in the area remained under heavy snowfall for almost half of the year.

After six and half hours of arduous but adventurous trek in which almost 2 hours taken by birch-rhododendron grove I reached in the valley at the bank of river Kheer Ganga. I followed the river course for some distance to locate the possible place to cross it. Soon I got a bridge made of a single log placed over the river. It was quite risky to walk on the log. Here Manoj came forward to walk on the log. After crossing the river he entered the nearby forest and brought one more log, which he positioned along the log placed over the river. He lifted the log to his shoulder and instructed Dinesh to do the same at another side of the river. Now the bridge had one more support system to hold while walking on the log.

I started walking on the log with the support of holding the one by left hand lifted by Manoj and Dinesh. After crossing this small but turbulent river the way led to *Neelkanth* base was a continuous climb. The bridge I had just crossed was at 10,500 feet, and after climbing 2000 feet further uphill I saw a hut in the undulating alpine meadow. Before I made up my mind for next move, suddenly two repeatedly barking dogs came flooding to me. I stopped moving and became soundless. For couple of minutes they glared and sniffed me and my companions. I took a deep breath only when a stiff call coming out from the hut calmed down both the dogs.

I stared towards the hut with hope in the wilderness. For past five days I had not seen any person other than Dinesh and Manoj. I walked to speak the man standing outside the hut. Both the dogs had become almost friendly now and followed me too. Meantime, the man standing near the hut had stretched a woolen carpet on the ground. On reaching the hut I saw two men - one about 20 year old lad and second middle aged person. They draped white handmade woolen cloths. Both had medium size height and seemed quite sturdy.

The middle aged person named Ganesh had caught a 'chillum' in his left hand, and from his right hand he was scratching his shaggy beard. He brought the chillum to his lips and took in a deep drag before responding to my formal Namaste. He took another puff from the chillum while gazing at me. I noticed a sea of surprises and numerous questions in his small black eyes, probably due to our arrival in a desolate mountain area. He passed on the chillum to me and on my polite refusal he took one last deep drag from the chillum before making it empty by slipping out the ash and flinging it into his hut.

The hut's wall was made by simply placing stones over stones without using any plaster. And its roof was made of sacred 'bhojpatra' (birch) wood and barks. Being an alpine meadow situated above 11,000 feet, it was difficult to get here tree species except a few relict stands of bhojpatra depending on the slopes facing or not facing sun. The papery bark of bhojpatra covering their hut has been well known since antiquity for writing historical scripts. A strong breeze rushed over the hut to rustle the bhojpatra's bark on the roof and by the side of doors. I bent my head and shoulder to enter the hut and found it difficult to stand upright even in the middle.

'I have to stay back in this hut for another three weeks to graze my 3400 sheep and goats'. Ganesh said calmly. The later conversation and his gesture had indicated the hardship of the area and feelings of living away from family for nearly half of the year.

Unlike previous night, in Khiron valley there was ample flatland to pitch tent. I pitched my tent near the Ganesh's hut. After a brief rest on the unfolded white mattresses in the tent I stepped out and walked in the lush green valley with Ganesh.

'This valley ends at the base of the snow capped mountain where we have a beautiful lake – Unaini,' Ganesh said stretching out his right hand toward a snowy mountain. He showed me some important herbs used by him for curing fever, headache and wounds. I was surprised to notice the hard fact that Himalayan marsh orchid locally called as 'hathajadi' and used as tonic was nowhere seen in the area wherever we had walked in the valley. Because of its tuber, which looked like a kid's palm, it was also known as 'salampanja' in Hindi and 'angbolakpa' in Tibet. 'People are much aware of 'hathajadi' and its values and therefore they visit all possible areas of its occurrence for collection. Its tuber fetches good cost and also people eat it raw as tonic', Ganesh said when inquired by me.

I noticed some marked differences in the land halted overnight by sheep and goats around the hut and the area away from the hut visited by me and grazed by sheep and goats throughout the day. The ground upto 100 m away from hut, mostly in eastern side, was impoverished of plants and covered by droppings of sheep and goats. After 100 m away from the hut, for another 100 m Nepal dock locally called as 'khukhuiyan' had dominated in patches on the flatland but the slopes had diverse alpine plants. The vegetation within

200 m radius of hut had been severely damaged by herd's activities. Beyond this limit Ganesh's herd pressure seemed to be declined and dispersed.

The dark had loomed large along the clouds stretching across the valley. After having dinner, I sat with Ganesh who had engaged with his chillum sitting close to hut's door. The soothing breeze coming from hut's entrance fanned his long hairs. I heard dogs barking now and then from two different directions guarding the herds. 'My both bhotiya dogs are capable to fight even leopard and bear. The herd is safe and I sleep without fear because of my dogs', said Ganesh before dragging another puff from his chillum.

Next morning while unzipping my tent's entrance, Dinesh's words came flooding to me. 'What a beautiful mountains. Yesterday we could not see it. Today sky is clear'. I pushed me out from the narrow entrance of my tent. The exquisite nature's beauty was scattered before me. The entire range of snowy mountains had submerged in the golden sun rise. The sight that I witnessed of the nearest mountain stood before me was truly breathtaking both in its grandness and majesty. It was the *Neelkanth* who stood like the Mahadev – the God of the Gods, and above all the spouse of the goddess *Nanda*.

After breakfast I bade adieu to both cheerful Ganesh and his companion, and set-off to complete my rest of the journey. I strolled in the lap of the great *Neelkanth*. The meadows had been intermingling with the stony deserts on the upper reaches of the Khiron valley. Here pointing towards a unique fungus profusely growing on the ground Dinesh whispered, 'It is a very nutritious fungus and after consuming it by horses and cattle they become quite healthy and strong'. I looked down for a moment at the fungus, which was about 5 cm white strand above the ground, and walked ahead. At that point of time I took his words lightly because of my ignorance to the destiny of this fungus, which had made to be much larger than the fungus itself. Later on, after a decade the same fungus had overshadowed the entire market of medicinal plants coming from the Himalaya. And I learned the values of this less known fungus - *Cordyseps sinensis* locally called as 'kira-jadi' or 'yarsha-gumba' – which costs in millions.

In the lap of the '*Nanda's Neelkanth*', walking downhill to the Badrinath I looked down the stony desert. While strolling on the sharp stones in the cold desert I followed a narrow gorge under which I heard rippling of a stream. Marching continuously for one and half hours I had arrived at a stable meadow from where I could see the extensive Badrinath valley. Before entering the valley I had destined not only to talk with a saint but also had a cup of herbal tea in his hut constructed close to a rivulet. In the valley of lord Badrinath, I could see the holy river Alaknanda had embraced this heavenly land and the Saraswati river before continued her journey to the sea.

Having bowed before the Lord Badrinath, I thanked Him from the core of my heart, for making my journey safe and sound. In the beginning of my expedition before summiting the peak above the Bruz Khal, one time an incident had shaken me deep to my soul when I had lost all hopes to breathe again. Climbing up continuously via Marwadi bridge over Alaknanda and then Chi-Thai villages, I reached in the Chinap valley where I saw five lads staying in a cave.

'Excuse me, what brings you here?' I asked reaching close to their cave.

'Please stay away. Don't enter the cave,' they ordered.

'What happened?' I said stepping back from the cave's entrance.

'We are on religious tour and going back with the baskets of bramakamal's blooms. Nobody is allowed to touch us before we offer these blooms to the goddess *Nanda* in our village temple,' they informed.

'Well, I understand. I shall stay away from you,' I said and walked away from the cave.

Chinap being an undulating alpine meadow had adequate plain land to pitch the tent for night halt. Next day morning, I surprised when I saw all the lads bathing in severe cold water. During conversation they advised me not to climb further.

'We strongly belief that once this religious journey to gather and offer brahmakamals to the *Nanda* Devi is over, nobody should follow and enter the brahmakamal's areas via the same route. You should abandon your journey right here and go back,' they advised.

'I have full faith in *Nanda* and *Her Neelkanth* and will not do anything against of their wishes. But, it is not possible for me to go back at this stage,' I said.

'Well, if it is so important for you don't forget to follow the law of nature and never try to spoil the sanctity of area beyond the tree line,' the lad draped in saffron advised.

There was no trail further up on the grassy mountain above one km from Chinap. I pushed up holding bunches of tussock grasses hanging from the precipitous rocky mountains. After crossing the rocky mountain slope, Manoj cooked khichdi (a local dish) and due to scarcity of water he kept unwashed utensils in the rucksack.

As informed at Chinap valley by the lads carrying brahmakamal, there was a temple dedicated to the *Nanda* Devi at Sona Shikhar, around 4,700 m altitude. I made up my mind to visit the temple first and then move further. Before 100 m down from the temple, all of a sudden, I felt extremely cold. Within a very short span of time, I was shrouded with thick clouds. And suddenly snowfall was in progress.

I gazed around and realized that I was in a cold stony desert. The bitter wind drove at me, sheeting my cloth with snow and chilling me to the bone. The entire area had worn thick veil of clouds, and being uncertain to the route I stopped to walk further. The sudden and swift severe cold had numbed me to the bones. In such unpleasant situation, my wandering gaze was arrested by unexpected thunder strikes. The deadly lightning running through the ghastly clouds, on many occasion, was an inch away from me, and I was designed to watch my death in the lightning with full of brutal thunders.

I fumbled my portable tent and pushed in with Dinesh and Manoj, as it was horrifying to watch the electric flash in the clouds. By the time, Dinesh got to recollect the suggestions of lads at Chinap valley 'not to spoil the sanctity of nature'. He felt that we had committed a mistake, as we were carrying the unwashed utensils. He quickly lighted an 'agarbattii' and begged the pardon from the invisible goddess *Nanda*. To my surprise, within few minutes clouds completely camouflaged in the space, and the landscape covered under the fresh shower of snow seemed to be as somebody had scattered his innumerable pearls. Standing on the top of the mountain, I witnessed many surrounding mountains being at low heights were giving way to the spectacular scenic beauty.

Whether the incident I faced was merely an accident or it was the reaction of disobeying the rules framed by the *Nanda* and *Her Neelkanth* to maintain their celestial home or it was a well-known feature of the high altitude ecosystem, but I realized and learned that one must take adequate precautions while wondering in the Himalaya.

Neelkanth

22.0

My Maiden Visit to Penn State

Sitting alone on the bed in the hostel room at Kosi I was extremely glad holding an opened envelop. Ultimately, my dream was about to take some shape. It was almost unbelievable. To confirm and make it believable I once again began to examine the letter, which read: 'You are invited to deliver a lecture on the medicinal plants of Uttarakhand in the forthcoming International conference going to be held in Pennsylvania State University during 18-25 May 2005. Your to and fro economic class air fare will be reimbursed by the Conference Organizers.'

In past, though I had applied several occasions to participate in the conference organized in abroad and on many occasions organizers had agreed to invite me to deliver lectures, yet it was first occasion when I was assured to reimburse my travel expenses and waived off my registration fees fully.

I thought to share my feelings and happiness with my hostel mates but the second thought immediately stopped me to do so. I had to arrange so many things, including visa and tickets. In case I was not given visa, which had fair chances, my colleagues might have laughed at me. I had now mixed feelings of anxiety to visit United States of America and tension of arranging things. I could not sleep overnight. Next day, I wrote to organizers thanking them for their kind invitation and also conveying my keen interest to attend the same.

I began to arrange all the necessary documents for applying visa. In the weekend, I went to Srinagar Garhwal for collection of my post graduate degree from the University office. Though, I had passed out from the University in 1992, the degree certificate was never required. A copy of marks-sheet was enough proof to apply for any vacant post, including registration for PhD. I had a remote relative in University office and he helped me in issuing my degrees, both graduate and post graduate.

On my return to Kosi I applied for visa through online. A date was allotted to me to present physically at US Consulate at New Delhi. I, then, started finding out the place of my stay in Penn State. Sitting hours on computers I surfed many hotels and motels in and around the State College of Pennsylvania. I got to know that many Indians had settled in US and they had shops in Pennsylvania, as well but none of them was running hotel.

A family from my village Sumadi had settled in Washington and so that I tried to get their contact but could not succeed. Finally, I decided to contact Rahul, one of my friends who lived in Florida. Rahul and I stayed together at the Wildlife Institute's hostel at Dehradun. He was always ready to help me. I wrote to him about my possible visit. He assured to arrange some cheap accommodation for me.

I was keen to see and understand how a developed country looked like, especially the country which was most powerful. I wanted to see the country's reality on ground, its inhabitants, hotels, roads, shops, vehicles, homes, forests. If I was just landed at Pennsylvania, I could not get the essence of ground realities so I planned to land at New York and travel by road to State College. I shared my wish with Rahul. He suggested me to take bus or train to State College as soon as I arrived at New York because accommodation at New York was quite expensive.

I had an American friend, Eric who lived in Los Angelis. I wrote to him expecting if he could do something for me. Eric provided me a contact of his friend, David Shank, at New York, which I noted down in my diary for the purpose of any unforeseen requirement. Rahul further suggested me in his next mail to keep some general medicine, as cost of treatment in USA was quite expensive.

Next week, I went to New Delhi to submit my documents at the American Consulate. I was told that one should reach early in the Consulate so I reached at Consulate before 7.30 am. I was surprised to see two long queues before the Consulate as I was expecting to be the first person driving to Consulate in the early morning hours. Before reaching to stand in the queue a person called me.

'You are too late. Your turn may not come today,' he said.

'So what to do,' I asked.

'If you wish I can help you. I can arrange your meeting today itself in five hundred rupees only.'

'How will you do that?'

'You don't worry, sit on my bike. I shall take you to a café and from there I shall fix date for you.'

'The date is already allotted to me.'

'So what! Look at the queue. I don't think your turn will come before the closing time.' Having said this without waiting for my response he moved on to trap another person.

Luckily, I got my turn. The officer behind window inquired my whereabouts and after being satisfied he stamped on my passport.

'Well Dr Kala your passport with visa will be dispatched by currier to your address,' he said.

Before returning to Kosi I booked my to and fro air tickets to New York at Connaught Place.

Being a research scholar on contract basis, I was exempted to take permissions from concerned Ministries. I had made up my mind to take two weeks leave from my employer. I was entitled to get one month leave per year and I had not yet taken a single leave so I was quite satisfied and tension free. Almost everything was in order and settled down.

I had ten days in hand to catch flight for New York. I applied for leave to my office. The head of the office, who also hailed from hills, by chance met me in the institute's corridor. I greeted him but before I convey him about my tour he walked away. I went to his office room to just let him know about my leave application.

He thought for a moment and then said decisively, 'you cannot go to attend the conference.' It shocked me. Being a student, I was expecting positive remarks on my hard work and achievements from the head of the Institute but it was just other way round. I had arranged everything on my own and I was also not demanding any funds and help from the office expect leave for about two weeks.

'Sir, but why?' I asked.

'It is a very sensitive issue; especially you cannot say, even you don't deserve to say anything about the biodiversity of our country,' he said.

'Sir, I have been working on the Himalayan biodiversity and its conservation for past one decade. I have written many research papers on the similar aspects,' I said.

'Whatever, I don't permit you to deliver any lecture on biodiversity abroad,' he interrupted before I finished.

My face became rosy. I had never thought for such an embarrassing moment. I had lost my composure and said, 'sir, I shall go by all means. Even if I have to resign I shall do so but I shall go.'

Now it was his turn to be shocked. After some moments of pin dropped silence he shouted, 'are you threatening me?'

'No sir, this is true. I shall resign,' I replied.

'How dare you have to speak all this to me? You know, I am a self-made great scientist. No one helped me out in my carrier. I know the world much better than you. You may go now,' he shouted.

He picked up a cigarette and dragged a deep puff. I got up and walked out leaving him with his cigarette. I was upset but firmed to attend the conference even on the cost of losing my job.

Date to flying for New York was approaching fast, and leave was not yet sanctioned to me. I was making my mind to submit my resignation by the time I was handed over a confidential memo by the administration. Through the memo I was asked to give explanation in writing on one of my research papers published in 'Current Science' – a science journal. The findings of my paper were challenged. Further, I was instructed to make a presentation and defend my findings before a committee one day after the date of my departure to New York.

To get rid of all these hassles I had the only option to hand over my resignation. I typed and kept my resignation in an envelope. I thought to submit it by next day. I had only three days in hand to catch the flight so in the evening I picked up necessary documents and goods to pack up.

Around eight o'clock in the night, someone knocked my door. I peeped out from the window but since it had become dark I saw a shadow.

'Who is there?' I asked.

'I am sir, 'he said'. 'Saheb wanted to see you.'

'Where?'

'In the office.'

'Office! But this is already eight o'clock,' I whispered.

I knew the poor man was only doing his job, so I walked back to office.

The head of the institution was surrounded by couple of scientists. I was asked to wait outside. Soon, the head called me in.

'You have not yet submitted the explanation,' he asked me steering down on a file opened before him.

'Sir, I shall submit tomorrow. There is still time to submit. The deadline is not yet crossed,' I replied.

'Ok, you can go now,' he ordered.

While stepping up home I was highly disappointed on the way I was treated and called up after office hours without any urgency. I was upset on the matter which would have been better answered by the administrative staff. I felt deeply humiliated and so I decided not to submit resignation but to fight with the system.

I prepared a strong note claiming that the work which was questioned by the head's office and published in 'Current Science' was not conducted under the Institute's funding rather I did it on my own. Since it was nothing to do with the Institute's administration and funding sources, there was no reason to give explanation from the author (s).

Since there was no valid reason for not sanctioning leave to me I was granted two weeks leave. After all such unnecessary hassles and struggles the moment of joy had come and I set off to walk one km downhill with my baggage to catch a bus at Kosi's tiny station to New Delhi.

Next day, I board in the Air India flight at Palam airport to New York in the early morning. Of course, I was thrilled, as it was my first international visit. The aircraft was quite big and had capacity of about three hundred passengers. I noticed that many passengers were quite accustomed to the flights being frequent visitors. I had managed to get a window seat. Most of the passengers sitting on the window seat had shut the windows down. Some of them had put pillow on their faces and others had covered their face with towel or handkerchief avoiding light to enter and were attempting to sleep.

I remained busy in watching landscape beneath me through window. The screen before me on the backside of my front seat was very helpful in giving information of direction and places over I was flying. I flew over the Pakistan, Afghanistan and some gulf countries, which seemed to have quite arid lands. Though, I was flying above thirty five thousand feet I could differentiate the barren lands, rivers, human habitations, cities, agriculture lands, forests and mountains. The cities in gulf countries seemed to be quite prosperous, as they had huge buildings and well designed broad roads.

I crossed the aerial boundaries of European countries. While flying over the Germany I noticed that the agricultural land was dotted with windmills. Our flight had to land at Heathrow Airport at London for re-filling fuel. A river was flowing through this historical city. Many ships, small and big, were either on port or were floating on the ocean. I enjoyed the beauty of the huge bluish ocean before landing at London. Miles away from the sky I could smell the city's prosperity. The roofs of houses were, generally, brown and in the courtyard of every house there were couple of cars.

At Heathrow Airport before filling the fuel all the passengers flying to New York were asked to vacate the aircraft. We waited in the Airport for about an hour before boarding again. I was once again in the sky. There was no land beneath me but it was water and water only; even flying miles away from London I could see oceans only dotted with large and small ships. One of the interesting parts of the oceans was its different shades. I saw dark bluish sea meeting with blackish sea and large brownish and light blue water bodies. In the sky, some aircrafts flew against ours and others flew with us at some distance.

Though nineteen hours of continuous day light had passed, still there was no sign of darkness. I had not slept for such a long time and my eyes had become too heavy. However, the sighting of a new world had made me awaken and thrilled. I had noticed sunrise while flying high above Pakistan and after nineteen hours it was still shining in the sky. I had lived the moment and hence realized why people said in history that 'sun never set in the British Raj.'

There was no end of the day but the end of the ocean had come with the beginning of snowy mountains. I was now flying above the hard rocky mountain chains laden with snow. I had started my journey from the great Himalayan mountains, literally stand the abode of snow, and after passing through many mesmerizing landscapes and colourful oceans I had once again arrived above the snowy mountains.

After crossing over the majestic mountains I reached above the New York city, which spanned far and wide with its multistoried buildings. Before landing with the fall of height I could see the grandness of buildings, broadness of roads and the beauty of urban landscapes.

Twenty two hours of air journey had brought me at the John F. Kennedy airport. I collected my luggage and started following the fellow passengers to exit the airport. Since it was a new world for me, I was quite excited and cautious, as well. I hardly opened with fellow passengers. I reached at the immigration counter, where a man in dress was checking the passport and visa before allowing the passengers to go ahead. On reaching the counter when I handed over my passport to him he looked at it and then made some entry in the computer. After waiting for couple of minutes, he asked, 'are you first time in United States of America?'

'Yes,' I replied.

'Well, I beg your pardon, you have to wait,' having said this he called up the passenger next to me in the queue for security check.

Standing a side nervousness had begun to hold back me. I was looking on the passengers anticipating that someone of them might be treated like me. When no passenger left I was called up again. After making some necessary entries in the computer the security asked for my thumb impression, and then stamped on my visa.

'Thank you sir, you may go now,' he said stepping back to clear way for me to enter the United States of America.

I was now free to move. I came out from the airport and reached at taxi stand. Before hiring taxi I ringed to David Shank. I enquired him about the route of Pennsylvania and also informed him about my desire to meet him before to leave New York. He asked me to catch a bus for the city. I stepped in a bus and within thirty minutes I was dropped in the city's centre. I gazed around but could not find out any bus stand.

There were many storied buildings on both sides of the road, and there was no sign of bus station. I became confused and thought that the driver had dropped me on the wrong place even I had explicitly requested him to drop me at the station. I inquired from a person walking down on the street.

'This is bus station only,' he said.

'But there is no bus,' I said.

'Go in,' he said raising finger towards a building in front of me.

I walked into the building. Still there was no bus but many shops, and it appeared to me a busy market centre. Since I had become helpless to locate the bus stand I called up Shank again. He realized my problem and asked me to wait for him and do not move further. On his inquiry I informed him the place to meet, and I started waiting for his arrival.

Security persons armed with modern tools were patrolling at the place I was waiting for Shank. About ten minutes later, a person came to me and asked something. I could not understand his language but he kept on saying. 'Sorry, I did not get you,' I repeated my reply. His behave seemed to be quite suspicious when I gazed on the policemen saying third time, 'I beg your pardon I did not get you.' By chance a policeman walked toward me from some twenty meter. Looking the policeman coming closure he fled, all of a sudden.

Waiting for about forty minutes I saw a man of about forty years old with rounded spectacles, white T-shirt and in Bermuda holding an A-4 size paper. Quite often he lifted the paper possibly showing the words written on it to the people standing here and there. On coming closure to me I read the words 'CP Kala'.

'Hi Shank,' I exclaimed with joy.

He looked at me and raised his left hand finger toward the paper in his right hand.

I nodded my head in yes.

'Hi CP! You are most welcome in New York,' he said with broad smile.

We hugged each other with great joy though we never met before. I only knew that he was a friend of one of my friends whom I knew from his articles only.

'How was your journey?' Shank asked.

'Very fine, very interesting.'

We chatted for couple of minutes before Shank asked me about my next plan.

'I wish to catch bus to State College, Pennsylvania,' I disclosed my plan.

'Well, do you have tickets?' Shank asked.

'No.'

'I book tickets for you,' walking towards a window he said. 'Shall I pay for your tickets?'

'No, no please, I shall pay my own.'

'I hope you have sufficient money for your expenses. New York is a costly city,' he said.

Since no ticket was available for the same day he asked me if the next day tickets will serve the purpose. On my consent he asked further, 'if you book return ticket as well it becomes cheaper. When will you return?'

'After three days,' I replied.

'So shall I book return ticket too?'

'Oh, yes.'

'Well this work is done. Enjoy your journey to Penn State,' while giving tickets to me he said.

'Thanks, but tonight I have to stay in a hotel. Is there any cheap accommodation?'

He thought for a while and said, 'oh, yes, there is. It is quite cheap. You need not to worry. Just follow me.'

I followed him to subway and soon we were in metro.

'This is the life line of New York. Half of the city is under ground,' Shank informed me. After twenty five minutes the metro dropped us at Manhattan. I could see the sun, at the last prepared to exit in the horizon till next morning after accompanying me for twenty six hours.

'Where is the locality of World Trade Centre?' I asked Shank.

'Oh, yes, everyone is familiar with that tragic incident. I was driving to shopping the moment whole building slipped down. It was really horrific and unbelievable.' Raising his finger towards a multistoried buildings area he said, 'look these grand buildings. The World Trade Centre tower was encircled by all these towers.'

'Anyway, are you vegetarian or non-vegetarian?' he asked.

'I am selective non-veg.'

This made him to laugh. I joined him to laugh and then explained, 'I eat chicken but not mutton. I feel itching if I eat mutton.'

He took me to a restaurant and asked for my choice of food. It was a Japanese restaurant and Shank took me here because I belonged to Asia and he wanted to serve me homely food and environment. I realized it in the restaurant. But looking at Shank's whole hearted hospitalities I was not in the position to inform him that north Indian foods and Japanese food had almost no matching.

I finally narrowed down my choice for roasted chicken, which he asked the shopkeeper to pack and drop at his residence.

'CP, if you don't mind, can you stay tonight at my residence?' Shank asked.

'With great pleasure! Nothing can be better than to stay with you,' I said with joy.

'Actually, I had arranged a room for you at my uncle's residence but he has gone out and you will feel lonely there. Therefore, I decided to take you to my flat.'

'So nice of you, Shank.'

He took me to his flat in a building at Manhattan. It was a beautiful old world house. As I stepped further into the stairs and floor, the wooden flooring creaked beneath my feet. I climbed to third floor with Shank where he pressed a switch. A good looking woman wearing spectacle unbolted the doors. She smiled at me and I introduced myself before Shank spoke out.

'I am Alex,' she introduced herself. 'You are most welcome at our home.'

I entered the room. It was a humble, clean and packed with household items. I sat on a sofa after pushing my baggage to a corner. Till now I had become extremely tired as I had not slept for past twenty seven hours. Shank ringed to someone and started chatting loudly. He used my name couple of times, which kept me on alarm. Soon I realized that he was talking with Eric about my safe arrival. I too talked with Eric and I felt that Eric was also quite happy on my arrival and my staying with Shank. Since Eric was in Los Angelis, there was no chance to see him.

We had superb dinner. Though I had spent couple of hours with Shank but I was still unfamiliar with his profession.

'What do you do Shank?' I asked.

'I am a writer. I have just completed a book project,' having said this he got up and picked a book from the shelf. He signed and offered a copy to me.

'Congratulations!' I said while reading the book title, "The Forgetting: Alzheimer's: Portrait of an Epidemic".

I turned the cover page. The very first page carried information about the book and Shank, as quoted in the New York Times, Washington Post and other prominent magazines and newspapers. Shank was portrayed as a great writer and his book was credited as a great work on forgetting. Reading such remarks I felt deep regard to such a simple and 'down to earth' person.

Alex and Shank could read my eyes, which had become rosy due to unsleeping twenty seven hours and hence they suggested me to take bed rest. I was in sound sleep as soon as I went to bed. I woke up when Alex alarmed me next day not to miss my bus in the morning.

Holding my toothbrush I entered a small room, which Alex had indicated to be a toilet. A beautiful soft carpet was unrolled over its floor. A blue towel was hanging on my left wall. My right side wall had couple of shelves decorated with books and magazines. I became confused whether it was a reading room or a toilet. It was a very different exposure for me. I was taught from the childhood not to touch or carry books into the unholy or impure places such as toilet. Rather I was taught to pay due regard to a book just like the goddess Saraswati. I had to believe that I was very much in a toilet once I saw a commode in front of me.

A roll of tissue paper was hanging close to the commode. I looked for water but I could not find out it. I knew that until I did not use water to wash myself I remained uncomfortable. But here I had to use tissue papers only. So quickly I rushed to bathroom to feel comfortable. By the time, Alex had arranged breakfast. Shank and I again started chatting about the books while enjoying the breakfast.

'Do you have any new title in mind for your next book?' I asked Shank.

'Well, I am writing on Chess.'

'Chess!'

'Yes.'

'Interesting! Will you cover its historical aspects?'

'Oh, yes, I shall. Do you have some idea about it?'

'Not exactly on chess but we have a long history of a game called chousar in our country. Even one of the great Maharajas in India lost his kingdom not in the battleground but at home playing chousar,' I revealed indicating Mahabharat's episode on Yudhister's defeat in chousar to Shakuni.

'Really!' Shank exclaimed with broad eyes.

'In past, we had a great writer in India. His name was Vyas. He wrote a great epic – Mahabharat. You know the Hindus most sacred book, GEETA, is taken from the Mahabharat.'

'This is really interesting,' he picked up a notebook and a pen and asked me to narrate the entire story.

The dilemma encircled me, as it was not possible to tell him Mahabharat's story in such a short period. I had to catch bus to Penn State. I convinced Shank that it was a long story and chousar played an important role in this story. I narrated briefly the main chousar part of the epic wherein Yudhister had lost not only his entire kingdom to Duryodhan but also his four brothers and wife Draupati. I informed him that finally, this episode laid the foundation for a deadly battle in Kurukshetra. Fortunately, Alex interfered, 'I think you are getting late.'

Before I bade adieu to Alex, she handed over a bag full of fruits to me, including banana and apples along with a water bottle and some snacks.

'You have eight hours journey to Pennsylvania. You are also not familiar with route and shops and might have difficulty in locating one. Eat fruits and snacks whenever the bus stops at stations and you feel to eat,' Alex guided me with affection.

It was a very touchy moment. This made me to recall my mother who used to keep some paranthas/ chapattis in my bag whenever I went away from home, generally to Dehradun. While travelling to Dehradun, buses were stopped at Byasi, where I used to buy some soup or vegetables to eat chapattis kept in my bag by my mother.

Picking up the bag from Alex's hand, I felt from the core of my heart that humanity and brotherhood forever remain the most powerful treasures and tools in this materialistic and mortal world.

Shank accompanied me till I got into the bus. Before I bade adieu to him he handed over two cards to me. 'CP, I buy this for you to travel in metros and to visit New York city. You can use it once you come back,' he said.

'Thank you Shank.' I hugged him tightly with deep passion before stepping into the bus. Though I thanked Shank for his brotherly passion, I knew that such relations could not be tied in a few formal words.

The bus I stepped in belonged to Greyhound Company. My seat was comfortable yet I felt some uneasiness. While driving out from the station I thought over the reason of awkwardness but I failed to sort out it. My sight was caught again and again by the driver's seat and I sensed that the reason of my uneasiness had some link with the driver. I had deep surprise when I realized that driver's seat was wrong side to me as an Indian.

Bus had slowly caught its speed and I was watching the multistoried buildings coming closure and quickly vanishing away from me. The road was quite broad and smooth. Once the bus had entered the outskirt of the city I saw the well maintained grassy lawns all along the road. After two hours of driving we arrived at a station where some passengers were replaced by others.

The male driver was also replaced by a female driver. She was quite expert in her job and took us with great care and commendable driving to the next stop. Passing through forests, cities, villages, grasslands and cottages, the bus finally dropped me at the State college's bus station. I picked up my baggage and walked out from the station to locate the place of my accommodation. After a few minutes of walk I reached at a busy market centre. Here the numbers of pedestrians were higher compared to the vehicles. My sight was caught by a tall well built man coming apposite to me.

'Excuse me. May I know where is Nittany Motel?' I asked him.

'How will you go there? I mean do you have any means to reach there?' he posed a question rather answering my question.

'If it is far away, I shall hire some taxi,' I replied.

'Are you visiting State College?'

'Yes.'

'But it is closed for summer vacation.'

'I came to attend a conference.'

'I see. Alright. If you don't mind and wait for couple of minutes I may drop you,' he offered to help me.

He was unknown to me nonetheless I thought everyone was unknown to me. I nodded my head in accepting his offer. He walked into a shop and I stood on a roadside with my baggage watching the pedestrians and people on routine jobs. He came within ten minutes and asked me to follow him. Walking some fifty meters on the motorable road he stopped beside a car and asked me to place baggage into it. I sat with him in the front seat. While driving to motel I was obviously cautious being helped by an unknown person.

'Where are you from?' he asked.

'India.'

'I am from Iraq,' he said before I asked.

'What do you think about America's war against Iraq?'

Being unsure about his identity his question perplexed me for a moment. Though his tone and pronunciations were quite different from Americans, I could not take any risk. So I replied bit diplomatically. 'I am always against of any war. No Indian favours war with any country,' I said peeping into his eyes wherein I noticed a ray of hope and faith. His face reflected some expression of delight and satisfaction.

'I know Indians always have good relations with our country. My country is extremely beautiful and prosperous. I love Iraq as much as I love myself, even more than me. What a country. I hate this Bush for dragging my country into this meaningless war. No one should play with the sentiments of citizens of any country. There was nothing to hide but these people were desperate for oil and that's why they intentionally made ifs and buts to destabilize the all Arab countries. I hate this,' he continued appreciating Iraq and blaming Americans and America's Foreign Policy and lust for war.

We arrived at the motel after fifteen minutes drive. I picked up my baggage and thanked him for the help he rendered without any vested interest. He accompanied me to the reception.

'Good afternoon. May I help you sir?' the motel receptionist asked me.

'Well, I am Chandra Prakash Kala. Is there a room booked on this name?' She started turning pages of a register lying before her on the reception.

'Sorry sir, no room is booked on this name,' she said. 'When did you reserve room here?'

'I have a friend in Miami, Florida – Rahul Srivastav. He was supposed to book a room for me,' I said.

She started exploring my name in her computer data. And my Iraqi friend seemed upset just like me.

'I am sorry sir. Please don't mind a room is booked on your name,' she said feeling guilty on her previous remark.

I bade adieu to the Iraqi friend and paid forty five US $ to one night stay, which was quite expensive for me. Completing rests of the necessary formalities at reception, I walked to the lift to reach my room. Since my biological clock had been totally upset, I was feeling extremely tired and sleepy at 6 pm only. After a pleasant shower and a very light dinner I slipped into bed.

Next day, I walked to Conference venue, Penn Conference Centre, which was about two and half km away from my motel. Having completed the formalities of registration, I entered the conference hall packed with participants from various countries. Just after the welcome address, an announcement attracted my attention. 'Participants looking for accommodation may contact to Ms Barbara. The proceeding now breaks for high tea and you all are requested to assemble again here within ten minutes.'

I approached to Ms Barbara and disclosed my willingness for some accommodation, if available, which she had accepted. On my query for the rate of accommodation she informed that for participants it was free of cost. Her words made me happy and relaxed. After all anything free remains the most wonderful thing in this expensive world.

My presentation was scheduled for the next day. I immediately went to check out from the motel and shifted in my new accommodation, which seemed to be someone's residence. On my enquiry about the house Barbara replied, 'you need not to worry about the house and its owner. You can stay here as long as you wish to stay without paying any rent. Only you have to arrange your food on your own. For the time being, breakfast, lunch and dinner are arranged free for you for next three days till the conference continues.'

I came back to conference venue. At reception I was advised to make my social security card. The organizers had arranged a vehicle, which drove me to the office of social security.

'May I help you sir?' a young girl asked me at the reception.

'I came for my social security card.'

'May I have your passport and insurance papers?' she asked.

I was surprised when within couple of minutes she handed over me my social security card. I thanked her. It was interesting to me to note that even in Government offices employees were quite fast and supportive. I recollected the hassles I faced while preparing my domicile and ration card in my native district. It took over two weeks to get my domicile. Moreover, I had to please the concerned employees who made me to wait for hours. I slipped the card into my pocket and returned to conference venue.

The moment I reached the conference venue break for lunch had been announced. I walked straight to get lunch. It was another hall decorated with chairs around a table. Every table was adorned with flowers. Several dishes were placed in the row to the right side connected with a queue of people waiting their turn to grab the food of their choice.

On my turn, my sight was caught on the name plates placed before the dishes. Sahi Paneer, Sahi Chicken, Tandoori Roti, ………. All dishes seemed to be very familiar. I was bit surprised. I took some rice and Sahi Paneer and sat on a chair to eat. The food was quite tasty. Soon I heard an announcement inviting a speaker named Madhu for presentation. Madhu being an Indian name attracted my attention. A lady rose up and started her talk with a power point presentation. Her voice and tone was very similar to her name, 'Madhu' literally means nectar. The way of her presentation was equally sweet and attractive.

I had attended many seminars, meetings and conferences but it was a rarest of rare moment of my life when I had delicious Indian cuisine with equally melodious presentation. Madhu was an Indian who had settled in Pennsylvania. She was a professor in Pennsylvania State University.

'My mother was a housewife and was very particular to her kitchen. She woke up early, relieved, took bath and then washed her kitchen. Kitchen was just like a temple for her. Every day she policed the kitchen floor with reddish soil and cow dung. She cooked each dish with great zeal and interest. She allowed no one in the kitchen till all the dishes were cooked and ready to serve. She served food on her own to each family member with love and great care. First, the youngest member of the family was served food and then rest of the family member,' Madhu explained in her presentation.

Her each statement was very close to my heart, as my childhood had passed through the similar line of exposure and experiences. Her entire talk was quite touchy. Her ever smiling face had added the delicacy in already delicious environment. I felt the impulse to talk her and to congratulate her for such a vibrant presentation. After lunch, I walked to meet her. She was surrounded by a group of people. Interestingly, most of them were speaking Hindi. I was astounded to see many Indians together, suddenly.

I got to know that some of them had settled in USA and Canada and some had come to attend the conference from India like me. Madhu appeared to be quite friendly. She informed me that hundreds of students from India joined Penn University every year. Since summer vacation was on, I could not have chance to meet them.

In the next day forenoon, I delivered my lecture on the Himalayan medicinal plants. God knows whether audience liked it or not but some participants were keen to know the Latin name of 'Sanjeevani' that saved the life of Laxman, the younger brother of the Lord Ram.

After the daylong marathon presentations, cultural programmes were organized for the participants in the evening hours. An African band rocked the evening. The participants were also encouraged to show their acting, dancing and singing talents. Every participant enjoyed the entire cultural evening and many of them participated in dancing and singing. The programme continued till late night.

At the closing ceremony participants were requested to air their views on the conference proceedings. A young lady on her turn started crying out. Initially, I thought that she was not comfortable and afraid of sharing her views. But soon I got to know that she could not control her emotions on the fact of her detachment from the participants and conference. Others hugged each other before final send-off. Next morning, I too got up early to catch bus to New York. Barbara drove me to station.

'Chandra thanks for your visit. I hope you would have had a comfortable stay at my residence,' she finally disclosed the secret.

'Oh, I see, it was your house,' I said with surprise. 'Thanks for your enormous hospitality.'

'It is all right. I thank you, too for giving me company. I stay alone in my entire house apart from my two pets,' she said.

'Why don't you give some rooms on rent?' I advised.

'It is difficult for a lone woman to deal with tenants. I don't have good experience with tenants,' she explained.

We greeted each other before I stepped into the bus. I watched her as the bus station slipped away. She was alone on the station, as she remained at home, looking at me and smiling. I watched her until the buildings hid the station. But I could not rid my mind of her beautiful eyes with full of philanthropy. I stayed awake for entire journey watching out people, forests, roads and environment.

At New Jersey, I had a distant relative, Lalit, whom I had never met. I knew about him from my wife. Before flying to New York, I had dropped a mail to Lalit about my visit. He was kind enough to assure me to extend any sort of help, if required. I thought to meet Lalit rather than disturbing Shank again at New York. As soon as the bus stopped at Pittsburg to exchange passengers and driver, as well, I got down phoning Lalit.

Lalit suggested me to catch train from New York to New Jersey. He educated me the mode and route to catch train. I did exactly what he said. The train rushed over a long bridge and stopped at New Jersey station. As the carriage door opened I stepped off the footboard with my baggage, and walked out from the station. Lalit's residence was close by and I had to walk further.

While walking I wondered to see Indians everywhere. Since I did not have his residence number I asked a person if he knew Lalit. Though, he was not familiar with Lalit, he advised me to make a call and hence asked me for Lalit's landline number. He pressed the numbers in his mobile and pushed it to me. From other side Lalit's wife picked up. I informed her about my arrival just close to her house. She spotted me on the road through her window and came out to receive me.

'Where is Lalit?' she asked me just after my formal namastey.

'Is he not at home?' I quizzed.

'No, he went to see you at New York.'

'New York! But he did not say me so.'

'He said so to pick up you. Anyway, alright, I inform him on his mobile.'

I pushed in and sat on the sofa befriending with Lalit's two kids - a three year old daughter and five year old son. After half an hour Lalit reached at home. He was a tall and handsome person in his late thirties. Within couple of minute's interaction I anticipated that his company would be interesting for next three days in the USA. I could have shared freely my feelings and experiences with him right from my arrival at JF Kennedy airport to my staying in Shank's house, roads, buildings, peoples, and incidences at conference.

Next day, we drove to a mall and I purchased two jeans as the souvenir. To hoard mall's memory Lalit shot up my few photographs. But soon he smelled some off beam in the mall and asked me to leave with camera. He instructed me to wait for him in the car. 'I shall let you know the reason outside. You go I follow you soon,' he carried on before I asked anything.

I with all surprises stepped off the mall. Lalit joined me at the car parking after about ten minutes of wait. 'Actually, two women were whispering suspiciously gazing frequently at us in the mall. As soon as I took your snap I saw a board indicating 'no photographic area'. I suspected they might have called police. If you come in contact with police you will be interrogated, unnecessarily. Your return journey may be delayed because of all these hassles,' Lalit said.

'But, what about you? Police can also interrogate you as I have been staying with you,' I asked.

'I am not going anywhere. I shall deal with them,' Lalit said.

'But the photograph was not taken intentionally. We can ask them to examine the roll or otherwise destroy it. We are not criminals,' I said.

'It is not so simple. After 9/11, the police here have become quite cautious and alert. They suspect foreigners, especially Asian origins in New Jersey, as the perpetrators of 9/11 were believed to have some connection with New Jersey. Some believe that most part of the conspiracy was plotted at New Jersey only. You know, eighty percent of population here is Asians, 'Lalit said while driving back home.

Next day, Lalit took me to New York city. We walked at the World Trade Centre, and thereafter visited the 'Statue of Liberty'. At a corner, I saw people offering flowers, bouquets, and also lighting candles. They used to raise their hands in prayers for some moment. Reaching at the site, I saw a big but dented and one-side broken metal tomb.

'This tomb is the top of damaged world trade tower. People come here to pay tribute to all those who had lost their life to that unforgettable bloody terrorist attack,' Lalit enlightened me.

We also visited the ziro, which was still encircling by many grand historical buildings. There was a spot where the first president, George Washington, had taken oath of the office first time in 1769. Here I made a photograph with the America's greatest person's statue. But before doing so I first looked around to satisfy me if photography was not prohibited at the site.

In the evening, Lalit took me to Madam Tushar's place. Here I saw wax statue of many world famous personalities. The visitors were posing with statue of their choice and were busy in clicking photographs. By twenty-one hours we reached back home at New Jersey. We chatted till late night. 'We cannot hit and punish our kids on their mistakes. The kids are taught even in their very first class at school to press nine one, if anyone, including mother and father, makes them to scare or punish,' Lalit said.

'Why nine one,' I asked.

'It is police helpline number. Once it is pressed, the police act fast. They mainly questions woman or kids about the reason of calls and also to establish truth. It becomes hard to persuade them even there was no reason and the number was pressed unknowingly,' Lalit informed.

My return flight was scheduled to the next day morning. Lalit handed over a packet to me as gift. He wanted to give me some more gifts but I refused politely as I was unable to carry the weight higher than the prescribed limit for passengers. But no one could have stopped me to carry some of the unforgettable moments and memories of Americans and Indians I met during my short visit to America.

Next day, while saying goodbye to America at the John F. Kennedy airport, I recited, 'God Bless America; God Bless India.'

23.0

Battle between the Best

On a cold but clear December day while walking in my Vanika's residence garden at Bhopal my sight was caught by the white creamish blooms of drumstick at a corner. Several honey bees were flying from one bloom to other. The nearest lone but huge tree of mulberry did not appear attractive as drumstick, as most of its leaves had faded and many others had dropped down. I looked down at the huge trunk of mulberry, which had a cavity quite close to the ground. Quite often I had spotted lizards and variety of insects in this cavity. Always, I suspected that snakes could shelter anytime in this cavity. Hence I wanted to get rid of this mulberry tree but the law of land did not permit me to do so.

I peeped into the cavity and noticed some movement. At a first glance, I felt that it was a snake but soon I realized that my imagination was not true. It was a hive deep inside the cavity. Soon I noticed honey bees flying away and entering the cavity with honey bags hanging from their legs. Since then whenever I walked into my garden I often stood near the cavity to watch their activities. They remained busy flying in and out for making honey. They always appeared quite peace loving hard workers.

I was happy enough to see their hive and was expecting to receive some sweet natural honey in days to come. I knew that honey was a very important medicine in Ayurveda, and hence it formed a major ingredient in several Ayurvedic medicines. Unfortunately, it was hard to find out original honey in the market. The honey's importance grew several folds in winter for its use to cure cough and cold. When Shaurya, my son he was then six years old, had cough during the winter I used to apply some honey on his finger, which he liked the most. It was really horrible to make him to swallow the allopathic medicine, which had bitter taste.

I had first tasted honey when I was eleven years old. My neighbor at Sumadi had a beehive in a hole of their house-wall. They used to collect honey from that hole once in four to five years. One such day I was at home and I got opportunity to receive a small piece of hive. Each compartment of the hive was filled with honey. 'One should not speak to anyone about the plan of honey collection. The honeybees understand our language and hence they eat and finish all the honey if you speak out the plan, 'I heard my neighbor informing his labour.

Though I spent many years in the Valley of Flowers watching many beehives en-route hanging from the rocks, I was not fortunate enough to taste it. I was told about its unique taste by the Bhyundar villagers, apart from that one could not eat more than two spoonful honey because of its high concentration and extreme sweetness.

A week passed by. The potato started sprouting and growing up along with spinach, coriander, beans, green peas, and onions in my garden at Vanika. Shaurya sometime walked over the growing potatoes and despite my repeated directives he forgot to follow the instruction. I sat near a potato plant and called up him.

'Do you know? This is quite interesting plant,' I said raising my finger towards a growing up potato.

'Interesting!' he quizzed.

'Yes, very interesting. It makes food on its own.'

His eyes broadened. He asked, 'How come?'

'It absorbs water from the roots and takes energy from the sun and carbon dioxide, which we release from our n….'

'And the food is stored belowground for us in the form of potatoes,' he interrupted before I finish.

'Exactly,' I said.

Before I wanted to tell him that all the carbohydrate (food) was not stored but also used in growth, reproduction etc. Shaurya had run away. After sometime I saw him sitting before a potato plant and exhaling deeply over its leaf. When asked he said, 'I am giving them carbon dioxide, as you give them water.'

In the afternoon, I walked again in the garden for basking as the rooms were cold. I stopped in front of the honeybee's cavity. They were busy as usual. I noticed that some bees were guarding all around the cavity. They hovered over the cavity and along the mulberry's trunk for couple of minutes. I always noticed them calm and peaceful but this time they seemed to be upset.

I leaned over the cavity to have a closure look. There were a few red ants on the trunk. It was difficult to locate them in a first glance, as they matched exactly with the trunk's colour. I had realized the cause of bee's disappointment. I dragged a plastic chair and sat on it to keep a close eye on the next move.

I surprised to see a full battalion of ants in different groups just four inch away from the cavity waiting for the order of their commander-in-chief. Within couple of minutes five ants moved cautiously towards cavity with extremely slow pace. One of them, which had taken lead, moved one side quickly and then all four dispersed in different directions.

By the time a bee patrolling around the cavity had reached closure to one of the ants. As soon as the bee's tentacle touched the ant the battle began. Suddenly all four ants turned to overpower the fighting bee and caught it from all the sides. The ants started dragging the catch away from the cavity. Meantime a hovering bee guard had seen the incident and he started chasing the ants to safe the fellow guard. Soon he had joined by two more bees. But the ants grip was so tight that all was in vain.

One of the bees on patrol realizing the gravity of situation in the battleground flew and entered the cavity to convey the message about the fellow guards. Suddenly, there was a lot of noise in the cavity and bees flooded out ferociously. They attacked on the intruders from land to the air. The peaceful tree trunk had changed into the battleground of Kurukshetra. The fight continued for fifteen minutes between the two extremely laborious and powerful natural forces. Two bees, at the end, lost their life in the fight.

The ants had finally decided to leave the bees territory. Within next couple of minutes the bees settled down calmly in their cavity and moved on their work. I was not sure whether the battle was over forever or the ants left the battleground in order to refine their fighting strategy. I was not sure whether bees would prefer to continue occupy the cavity or leave the place in search of peace. But I was sure that if bees leave I shall be deprived of the sweet original honey.

24.0

The Fragrance of Parijaat

I was one of the residents of Vanika at Bhopal who had Parijaat tree. It was a lone tree in which I saw a small world continues to flourish at various seasons round the year. All leaves from its branches fell down before onset of summer probably to cope up the extreme heat waves. As soon as the first shower of rains began the buds sprouted quickly from entire plant and within a short period of time – less than two weeks – it became verdant.

In a morning of third week of July, I saw a red-vented bulbul picking some grass tillers and putting the collected stuff on a 'V shaped' twig of Parijaat covered with dense foliage. She remained busy in weaving and knitting nest for a week and by the end of July the nest was almost in shape to live. Her nest was quite close to my bedroom's window - at about one and half meter aerial distance - and quite on and off I used to peep out through my window to notice her activities in the nest. In a morning of second week of August, I spotted two eggs in the nest. Since then, whenever I stood behind the window and came out in the courtyard my sight often caught by the bulbul's activities.

Bulbul kept on sitting on the eggs for long hours. Watching bulbul in the nest had become a part of my day-to-day activities and its presence gave me a sense of living a family close to my window. A day when I was in the office Richa informed me on phone about the attack of a predatory bird that swallowed both the eggs. She reiterated that bulbul did her level best to fight but alas ultimately she lost the battle. I calmed myself recollecting the philosophy of nature and principles of ecology that suggest 'one's survival depends on others'. Next day bulbul came frequently to see the nest and sat on a branch of Parijaat close to deserted nest. She watched at broken nest - might be with some hope - but at last she flew away and never turned back.

One generation of bulbul could not succeed to flourish but Parijaat kept on flourishing. Its leaves became thick and branches strong and straight. Within three months, it accumulated sufficient food to produce flowers and fruits in order to continue its population. It began blooming from first week of September and then its fragrance diffused far and wide. Everyday a large number of tiny whitish blooms with an orange red centre opened at the dusk and fell down at the dawn. The flowers remained sensitive to sun. Its soft petals began to curl in the evening. Once dry, the flowers took golden shade.

In Hindu mythology, almost all varieties of flowers have remained best offerings to the Gods and Goddesses from time immemorial. Generally, the fresh blooms are plucked for offerings to the Gods and the flowers once shed down are mostly not used for this purpose. Parijaat has advantage over this tradition, as its dropped flowers on ground are also picked up to offer the God. This may be due to a poplar legend associated with Parijaat that goes back to the period of the Lord Krishna. According to this legend the Krishna brought this tree from the heaven to earth for his beloved queen Satyabhama and planted it in Satyabhama's courtyard in a way that when the tree flowered, the blooms fell in the Rukmini's courtyard – second queen of the Krishna.

Parijaat being a holy tree species, people worship it with a belief that it guards their life and wards off all evils. Kunti – the mother of Pandavas - is believed to offer the blooms of this tree to the *Lord Neelkanth*. Hindus believe that the soul takes countless births on its journey to perfection (Mokchha), and the fragrance of Parijaat possesses so much unexplainable power that a person with pure soul inhaling it may remember events of his past lives. These beliefs embed in rich cultural and spiritual heritage of India, which proliferate several fabulous meanings and also ignite the minds for creativity. Such myths also help to learn the art of love and deep appreciations for every created object that may be useful in the form of food, medicine, condiment and cosmetics. These myths also energize people to protect and propagate such important plant species in view of maintaining the constant supply of their beneficial products.

An auspicious day of Navratra in first week of October I came across the fact its flowers are eaten as snacks. I with my family collected the blooms, which we washed carefully in tap water to remove the small insects hiding in the blooms. We mixed an equal proportion of 'besan' (gram flour) with the blooms and then added some spice, salt and green chillies. This mixture was kneaded with water, and subsequently the finished dough was divided into equal portions - roughly the size of a golf ball. Such small portions of dough were fried in refined oil. It was really a delicious snack, which had a unique taste due to its mild pungency.

The failure in nurturing of her own generation in the previous year had taught bulbul some good lessons not to make nest again into the parijaat of my courtyard. But nature takes its course and now it was the time of sun bird to choose parijaat for flourishing her generation. In second week of next August, I saw a sunbird weaving a nest into the parijaat. Looking at the nest even after many days I was confused to ensure whether the nest was in final shape or still it needed some more work.

Most of the days in August reeled under heavy rainfall at Bhopal. During such heavy rains most of the time sunbird flew away from the nest as the nest soaked the rainwater and gained weight. If the bird remained sitting in the nest it would have detached from the branch. However, she made frequent visits to the nest with some eatables. The environment in and around the nest remained quite calm and mysterious. I could not even hear any sound of chickens in the nest, and the mystery loomed large whether there were chickens in the nest or not.

Sunbird's nest was quite different from the one that made by the bulbul. Rather than hidden inside the dense foliage, as of bulbul, it was in open and easily visible hanging from a branch. The nest was closed all around except from a side where there was a small opening to enter. The upper side of this opening there was a roof which used to check the rain drops to enter the nest.

For a casual visitor the nest could be a broken piece of dried wood hanging from a twig on which a spider had made some web. Though, the nest appeared to be quite disorganized and unattractive, it was constructed in such a way so that, whenever required, it could refuse to go along with the natural risks and disasters.

Vanika received some heavy showers in a late night of September. Next day morning, when the sunbird entered the nest for feeding her chicken, the nest fell down. The bird flew away but her chicken was not able to fly and hence remained in the fallen nest on the ground. This worried us. Shaurya had gone to school and Richa was upset and was muttering in dilemma.

It was difficult to readjust and restore the nest into the same branch from where it had fallen down. The branch was quite away from my reach. I looked for some support to climb into the tree but all the branches were quite flexible and mild. I gazed around for some movable stairs but could not find one. It was about half past nine and I was in hurry to move to office.

Since the branches of parijaat were relatively flexible, I pulled a twig adjacent to the nest side and asked Richa to hold it till I tied the nest with a strong thread on the same. After hanging the nest in the similar way as it was earlier, I looked around for sunbird. She was away from my sight but I could hear her twits inside the bushes of ber. I had doubts on the bird's acceptance of nest's new location. Around eleven o'clock Richa faded away my doubts when she informed me that both male and female sunbird had started feeding the chicken in the nest.

Alas, my contentment could not last for long. The next day, a pair of squirrel entered the nest and they not only destroyed it but they killed the chicken. Sunbirds chirped loudly but it was all useless. I felt guilty of not having adequate knowledge of nature and its ecosystem. I was not aware and also it did not click me that squirrel could play a role of villain in this episode.

Sunbird had better knowledge of nature and its surrounding ecosystem, as evident from her making the nest in such a way so that no squirrel could reach to it. She built her nest hanging from a very thin and tendril branch of parijaat so that snakes and squirrels could not enter it. But alas, she failed to read the erratic pattern in showers.

Apart from bulbul, the generation of sunbird also failed to flourish but Parijaat remained robust. Botanically, it is named as *Nyctanthes arbor-tristis.* The first name *Nyctanthus* indicates its night flowering character hence it is also known as 'night flowering jasmine'. The second or the species name *arbor-tristis* reflects its other name as 'sad tree' or 'tree of sorrow', as its blooms die away at dawn. The blooms begin to shed down from the early morning hours and about eleven o'clock almost all blooms drop down. In different languages and locations it has different names as Harsingar in Hindi, Nishipushpika and Prajakta in Sanskrit, Sefali in Bengali, Pavazhamalli in Tamil, Ganga Shiuli in Oriya, and honoured as a state flower of West Bengal.

Parijaat is a multipurpose species. The courtyard with flowers, in the morning, provides a deep pleasure to eyes and fragrance to the mind, heart and soul. The blooms are known quite nutritious and also used as yellow dye. Bark and leaves are used to cure fever and seeds are used in the treatment of piles. Leaves are used to cure diabetes and also the skin diseases, as it is known to possess the properties that eradicate germs and bacteria due to bitter nature. Its blooms when eaten with milk it cures backache. The centre part of blooms, which had reddish tint, is also used as an adulterant of kesar.

The air passes through the leaves of Parijaat becomes pure as they possess harmful germs and bacteria killing properties. Traditionally, in case of swelling and pain, the leaves have been tied at the infected organs. The leaf juice with honey is used to cure dry cough and with salt is used to cure internal disorders, including harmful parasites. The leaves are also used as sandpaper to polish wood.

The leaves, fruits, flowers and fragrance of Parijaat illustrate some of the finest boons of nature to humans. In general, the numbers of life saving properties of Parijaat exhibit its divine nature and association with heaven, as described in the legends.

25.0

Botanist of Surguja

It was a usual rainy day of August. The moment I entered the thin deciduous forests of Parsa village, I realized what was worse than getting caught in a downpour - mosquitoes. Every uncovered part of me was bitten in seconds. I was in the forests of Surguja district in Chhattisgarh to lay a transect. Transect is basically a path along which one counts the number of times a plant species has occurred to have an idea of its abundance. This was to help me estimate the plant populations that were available and useful to humans for a variety of reasons. But I had to abandon the plan for that day.

While I battled the army of blood suckers, Ramdhan, my field assistant, and a local Baiga man in his 60s, stood calmly with an unperturbed smile. Ramdhan said the mosquito problem was not a big one. I attributed this to his years of growing up in the Central Indian forests. He was used to the menace, obviously. I was born and brought up in the Himalaya. There, the cold keeps mosquitoes away.

The next day, I entered the forests with mosquito repellent cream on my body. The heat and the humidity and the sweat washed away the cream. The only refuge now was to cover my neck and face with a piece of cloth. This became my forest gear.

And one day, I noticed it. Ramdhan was deftly swiping at mosquitoes with a tender branch of leaves in his right hand. I saw some branches of the same plant all around his neck. That aroused my curiosity. The plant was Indian satinwood, locally called as bhirra. I was informed that local people of Surguja have been using this plant as a mosquito repellent for centuries. They rub bhirra leaves on the exposed parts of their body and also wear its twigs on the head and neck.

It was a good start to know the plants of Surguja where forests comprise almost half the land. I continued to explore the forests of the Udaipur block in Surguja district and recorded over seventy plant species which tribal and non-tribal communities used. Considered the secret to good health, they used plants as food, beverages and medicines.

A day in jungle, Sukhnandan, a teenager with some primary education, told me that people here believed in ghosts and spirits. So when someone was ill, he or she would consult a healer. The healing ritual included use of the plant species.

Syamnath, another teenage guide from Parsa village, saved me one day. It was close: I was walking fast and did not notice the two-foot long snake. Nath could not have screamed any sooner. It was a cobra. When inquired Syamnath informed me that snakebite was a common problem. But the healers here had discovered herbal remedy. They made a paste of tendu roots to use as anti-venom. If he did not find tendu, he tries the root of grey downy balsam.

People of Surguja spent most of their time in the forests for rearing livestock and gathering firewood, fodder, medicinal and edible plants. They came in contact of snakes and scorpions frequently while working in the forests but traditional healers helped them out when bitten by such venomous creatures. Likewise snakebite, they had antidote for scorpion bites in the form of a leaf paste of prickly chaff-flower, and juice of Indian squill's tuber.

Having lived in the Himalaya for long, I was familiar with its plants and animals, including the most preferred edible mushroom – morel, which grew in the shady and wet forest floors of the Himalaya. It was a gourmet's delight and expensive too. Himalayan people believed that strong flashes of lightning helped enhance morel mushroom production. In the forests of Surguja, I found the tribal digging for a mushroom, which was purported to be as delicious as morel.

A day I collected about half a kg of Khukri, as the mushroom was called, from the termite dunes. But my cook dulled its taste with too many spices. The next time he managed to get it right. I also recorded over twenty other edible plants. People here relish fruits and vegetables. Tendu's fruits were eaten.

Fishing, a money earner for the tribal, was made easier with a kind of powdered fish poison that was obtained again from the roots, barks and fruits of plants. Tribals used the powder with care. They targeted streams whose water was unfit for drinking. Usually, they plugged the flow of running water with stones before sprinkling the powder. This killed the fishes.

Dinner was never complete without a drink. People had their own brand of liquor: mahua. They collected fruits and flowers of honey tree locally called as mahua and dried it first to prepare the liquor. Some plant species I came across here had been rare and endangered. I also noticed the destructive harvesting practices. Looking into the variety of values in these important species one must save them for posterity. Losing a species would lose a vast knowledge associated with it.

I believe that the customary beliefs and practices, if used wisely, could be a useful tool to save these important plants from fading out. The concept of sacred groves and sacred species was an example, which led to the protection of genetic diversity in natural habitats. Some places in Surguja were considered sacred. Hence the natural resources in these areas remained protected.

Ramdhan was an example among many of the traditional knowledge holders who lived and believed in customs. He knew the local names of most of the woody plant species and identified several herbaceous species. He has had no formal education. I felt that the country needs more taxonomists like him.

26.0

The Childhood Friend

Durga had completed his M.Sc. in Chemistry with distinction. But still it was not a sufficient qualification to get job in his home town. Even it was quite difficult to get job in his native state, Uttarakhand. Uttarakhand then had only a single largest industry – the education industry, which required B.Ed. or B.T.C. Since he was keen to stay back in his state, he took admission in B.Ed. and completed it within the stipulated time – one year.

He was not at all interested to leave his native place. But when it became difficult to get job in his own state, he started applying for all possible posts, anywhere in India. Since he had a professional degree in education, his search remained focused for teaching.

Despite all efforts he could not meet the success. The expectations from family and friends were always high for him due to his hard-working nature. Such inspirations were the major source of energy that ignited his mind to continue hard work and excel the career. His good image in society insisted him not to do anything, knowingly or unknowingly, that was against of his village institutional norms.

His year's long attempt for some respected job when remained unsuccessful, then the same source of inspiration began to transform into source of frustration. He started thinking beyond the reality, and negative thoughts started pouring in his mind. Whether someone said against him or not, he felt discarded within his friend circle and society. Such negative feelings had made him to live in isolation. He had a single wish now, the desire for job.

Any small to big thing or festival, which earlier made him cheerful, had now lost that charisma. The friends, fellow villagers, parties and celebrations, including natural beauty, each one of that was once the source of joy, now appeared to be teasing him. Even the books, which had always been his best companions, seemed to be teasing him to such an extent that he wanted to get rid of them.

There is a ray of light in dawn after every dark night. Durga received an offer letter from a school in central India for teaching post. It was quite far away from Sumadi, but without any second thought he accepted the offer, and started his preparation without any delay. Now, he appeared to be the happiest person of the world. He conveyed this message to his friends and well wishers. Everything was in order now for him, and he could notice the beauty of chir pine forests around his village, the joy in chirping of birds, the warmth in reception of villagers, and the pleasantness in weather.

He set off to Bhopal, to join his duty, as a teacher in the Govt. school. After joining his duty, he met his new friends – the fellow teachers. They helped him to explore a rented two room set close to the school. He purchased all required goods for his comfortable stay. He was fully enjoying his new assignment, friends and environment. It was obvious, as he had got a permanent government job.

Every evening he used to walk down in the New Market, sometime alone yet mostly with his fellow teachers. The first four weeks of stay in Bhopal had made him to enjoy the life to such an extent that he forgot all his past troubles. On getting his first salary, he straight went to the Hanuman temple at New Market to offer his long cherished devotion with a coconut fruit to the 'lord of strength'. He reminded and thanked all his village deities, including his family deity – *Gauradevi* – for their support, affection and blessings. The very same day he posted one thousand rupees Money Order to his mother at Sumadi.

The first two months of Durga at Bhopal had passed quickly with joy and learning new people and environment. A day, one of his fellow teachers informed him about a family that belonged to Garhwal. Durga decided to meet that family, as it resided quite close to his friend's residence. Meeting that family had aroused his feelings to his roots in Garhwal. That night he could not distant himself to memorize his family, childhood friends, and villagers.

Since then every passing day made him to learn by heart his fellow colleagues at Sumadi. In his next letter, he wrote a few lines to his brother at Sumadi about his feelings, who informed Durga in the return letter about Vedu who hailed from Sumadi and lived in Bhopal. Without any delay Durga went to meet Vedu. In Sumadi, Durga seldom talked with Vedu, as he was quite junior to him. But at Bhopal while meeting Vedu he felt as he was meeting his one of the best friends. Both Vedu and Durga talked about their village, villagers, and relatives. Durga enjoyed Vedu's company.

A day of September, Durga saw a large rat snake in his courtyard. He was quite afraid of that dangerous creature.

Though, the snake was chased away from his courtyard, he could not sleep well in that night. Next day, when he informed Vedu about the snake, Vedu said, 'don't worry. Snakes are quite common in Bhopal. I see snakes almost every week. Quite often I have encountered snake in my room itself.'

'Well, it is quite dangerous then,' Durga said.

'Municipality has appointed a snake catcher. Whenever, you see any snake you can call him to take it away. The snake catcher is very smart and keeps his caught either in Van Vihar or drops them in the forests of Pachmarhi,' Vedu informed Durga.

Apart from snakes, Bhopal was the mosquito prone area, which made to restrict Durga's movement, especially walking in the evening and morning. Walking in garden sometime became terrific experience due to heavy influx of mosquitoes. Mosquito net was the only solution, which made to stay in the bed at night, otherwise God knows……..

Durga was not comfortable now. In anticipation of malarial and dengue attack he became worried of his stay. Now quite often he reminded his village and people over there. Home sickness had detained him and his thoughts. There was no more charm in the job, he held after long sufferings. He wanted to get rid of Bhopal. He restarted applying for vacancies at New Delhi, Uttar Pradesh and Uttarakhand.

A day his fellow teachers decided to visit Pachmarhi, a hill station in Madhya Pradesh. It brought back some level of joy to Durga in anticipation of watching some hilly areas just like his village. Before reaching at Pachmarhi town, he saw Denwa river, flowing deep down in the mountain gorge, which reminded Durga his village's landscape. He saw some hills though unmatchable with the Himalaya yet he liked all the landscape beauty.

On reaching in the heart of Pachmarhi town, at the Byson lodge, Durga saw two chir pine trees. His attention was engrossed by both. He went close to the one, and touched it gently. He looked up at its long branches, and needle shaped leaves. He felt standing beneath a pine tree in his village. The long branches of pine appeared to him the large hands of his mother stretching out in love. The sea of emotions flurried through his mind, heart and soul. Tears rolled down in his eyes. He hugged the pine tightly, closing his eyes.

His soul had found the perfect peace, and his spirit had just met his mother, who had nurtured him to grow and flourish. And she was still here stretching her hands to hug her beloved child.

27.0

Ziro

I got down at the bus station of Itanagar after three days journey in train from New Delhi and one night in bus from Guwahati. It was a hot and humid June's morning. Dollo, an Apatani boy of twenty two years old, received me at station. With long lasting smile he dropped me in a lodge situated in the heart of the city. After bathing, I left the room and went in search of breakfast.

Walking few steps down the broad motorable road brought me before a small hotel. I walked in and inquired the available set of choices at the reception.

'Rice with fish curry,' receptionist informed.

'I mean breakfast not lunch,' I said.

'This is for breakfast only,' she said.

'Do you have chapatti?' I asked.

'No.'

'Parantha.'

'No.'

'Anything else.'

'We have rice and fish only.'

I was not used to have rice and fish at breakfast so I left the hotel and continued my search for breakfast.

Walking further two hundred meters brought me before a duplex in which the ground floor appeared to be a restaurant. A woman in her thirty's was sitting on a chair and a man of almost equal age was looking out at restaurant's entrance perhaps for customers.

'Do you serve breakfast?' I asked the person standing at the gate.

'Yes, please come in and have a seat,' he said. 'What do you want? We have chowmin and noodles.'

'Chapatti,' I asked.

He thought for a moment and then talked with the woman sitting on the chair. After some conversations he turned to me and said, 'sorry, we don't serve chapatti. Will noodles do?'

I agreed to have noodles, and they began to do their job. Since their language and tone appeared to be different from common local people, I asked them if they belonged to Arunachal.

'We hailed from Kerala,' while cooking noodles she responded.

'I see. You came all the way from Kerala. How long have you been here?' I asked.

'We have had over fifteen years. We have been running this hotel since beginning,' she said.

'Well, then it will be, of course, profitable,' I said.

'It is the only source of our livelihood,' she said after a brief pause. 'Being outsiders day to day we face many problems. People enter the restaurant forcefully on many occasions and take away our whole day earnings. If we don't have cash or in case we hide it and they become unable to locate it, they simply take away anything whether it is fan or table, chair and any other object. Being outsider, it is tough to deal with them,' she explained her problem.

'Why don't you complain to police?' I asked.

'We complained but it was no use rather it has increased our troubles,' she said.

'How come, police don't want to support you,' I asked.

'It is not like that. Police helped us but they are not available all the times. Once police go away, they come to threaten us the dire consequences if we complain again,' she said.

'Why do they behave like this?' I asked.

'They say being outsider we are earning on their land. So whatever we possess and earn it is not ours but it is their property. It is tough to deal with them,' she said.

'You are in trouble being an outsider, as you explained by all means. I think you should hire a local person who can negotiate and, if require, can also retaliate them,' I suggested a brilliant idea.

'It is of no use,' she said.

'Why?'

'We have already done so. We have hired a person. We pay him some handsome amount for doing nothing. Whenever, those people are about to come in the restaurant he slips away. Being local, he has friendly relationship with intruders. This has increased our trouble. We cannot even dismiss his service now. We have hired a trouble for us,' she said.

'Then it is horrible. Why don't you go back to Kerala?' I said once all of my ideas had exhausted. 'At least you will be there in peace and harmony with your own people.'

'Nothing left in Kerala for us, as we migrated from there long back. We have to struggle and survive here only. This is our only home and line of work now, which we all love. We live and will die with this only,' she said.

I finished my breakfast but I was worried about my lunch. I requested her to arrange chapattis and rice for lunch and dinner, if possible. To my surprise she accepted my request though she made it clear that she was not well versed with cooking chapattis.

I spent three days in Itanagar, and had my food most of the time in her restaurant. During this period I walked and drove in and around Itanagar and interacted with various ethnic communities, including Nyshi and Adi. I came to know that both Nyshi and Adi were the most dominant tribal groups of Arunachal Pradesh who enjoyed major share in the political galleries.

A morning Dollo came to meet me. He was keen to show me other parts of Arunachal, especially the north of Arunachal.

'Can we see Monpas?' I asked Dollo.

'They live in quite interiors of high hilly areas. You have limited days and visiting Monpa tribe demands more days. Being Buddhist they have some nice monasteries, and people from far and wide visit there, nonetheless it consumes time which you don't have. I suggest you to visit Ziro valley. It is a beautiful area and I am sure you will like it,' Dollo said.

'Where is it?' I asked.

'I am native of Ziro. If you wish I take you there,' he offered a cordial invitation.

'I love to see your village,' having said so I got ready to pack up for Ziro.

We got a shared taxi, which drove us through some of the dense rain forests of the world. I saw a hydroelectric dam on the river flowing down through Lower Subansari district. Dollo being a nature lover and conservationist was against of its construction. After about four and half hours drive, we arrived at the Ziro valley.

Ziro valley was simply a dreamland where the agriculture land dotted with villages in queue was surrounded by forests and mountains. This lush green valley appeared to be a most fertile land on earth punctuated with two major rows of bamboo made traditional houses.

'This is the land of Apatani,' Dollo said.

'Fantastic. You are a lucky person inhabiting in such an attractive land. Your land seems to be extremely fertile,' I said.

'We don't purchase grains from outside. We cultivate paddy and fish together.'

'Paddy-fish cultivation!'

'Yes, both need water and our ancestors have developed a technique of raising both paddy and fish together in the same piece of land. That has made us self-reliant and self-contained.'

After sunset Dollo took me to a double storied lodge where we had dinner. He went off his home for night stay and I stayed back in the lodge.

Next morning, Dollo came to pick up me and we walked together in the extensive fields of paddy. In the afternoon he took me to his house where lunch was almost ready. While interacting with his family members his first cousin sister came smiling to me. She opened her closed hands before me and smiled again while saying something in her Apatani dialect. I saw a collection of dragonflies in her hands. I grinned back but could not understand the situation.

'Would you like to enjoy a dish of dragonfly?' Dollo translated her words for me.

'Thank you very much but I have never tasted dragonfly's dish. I am mainly vegetarian,' I replied.

Dollo and his cousin sister chatted for a while. She turned and went off to kitchen. While slipping into the kitchen she appeared to be in different mood. Perhaps she was trying to understand my foolishness of denying for such a delicious dish.

Dollo's house was made up of wood and bamboo. I entered the house and sat on a decorated carpet. The room was neat and clean. Most of the household items were made up of bamboo and canes. Dollo pushed a basket containing some dried red clay like substance towards me and said, 'this is Apatani's salt. We call it tapyo.'

'Is it different from the one which we have in the costal areas?' I asked.

'It is made up of herbs,' Dollo said. 'We prefer to use tapyo in our traditional dishes.'

'How do you make this salt out of plants?' I quizzed.

'It is a long process. About three quintals of base plant material is collected from the nearby areas and then it is dried in the sun for two to three hours. After drying it is immediately burnt to ashes, which is kept in a Sadar - a conical shape bamboo apparatus having a small outlet at the base. Water is poured in gradually until the filtrate starts dripping from the outlet, which is collected in a cauldron. Another earthen pot is placed on the fire filled in starch-laden water of boiled rice. The filtrate is then poured into the boiled rice pot. It is placed on fire for next 5 to 7 hours before cooling it down to the room temperature. On cooling, it turns into solid mass which we rap in the Lolly's leaf before keeping it above a vessel of fermented rice beer. After three days the wet substance, which by now has absorbed the vapours of rice beer, is collected and kept above the fire. This is the final product ready to consume, which weighs roughly one kilo. It resembles to dried red clay,' Dollo explained in detail.

'So finally out of three quintals of plant material you get one kg of tapyo,' I said.

'Though, it is a cumbersome technical process, the delicacy of food because of tapyo compensate the hard labour put behind its making. It also increases the appetite. Eating tapyo always keeps goiter away. It has a great demand in our community. You know one kg of tapyo costs more than three hundred rupees,' Dollo informed me.

While chatting, a woman in her forties entered the room. She had a tattoo on her face. A greenish line of tattoo was running from her forehead to the tip of the nose, and another set of tattoo was on her chin with five vertical lines. Her nose was stuffed with a large nose plugs. Later on, I asked Dollo about her nose plugs, which did not impress me rather it seemed to me spoiling her beauty. He informed me that she had tattooed in order to spoil her beauty purposefully so that males of other neighboring communities could not harm her and took her away.

'Tell me one best festival you like and celebrate with great zeal?' I asked Dollo.

'Myoko,' without a second thought Dollo said. 'We celebrate it with great joy. We believe that on this occasion the gods and goddesses shower their blessings on us and our locality.'

While coming back to Itanagar I appreciated the help and support extended by Dollo as he and his community was very cordial, helpful, simple and supportive.

'I thank you for making me to see such a beautiful area,' I said.

Dollo smiled for a while and said, 'people visiting Arunachal go back with mixed views and judgments depending on the people they come across and interact. Your own colleague Bhagwan's view does not match with yours.'

'What happened with him? Why does he carry second opinion?' I asked.

'One day he hired an Auto rickshaw to attend a seminar some ten km away from the Itanagar. The Auto met an accident on the mid way. Luckily, neither Bhagwan nor the driver succumbed to major injuries. But they could not escape from the conflicts. Bhagwan wanted to get rid of the driver but driver was not ready to let him go. He wanted Bhagwan to pay the damages of his Auto, which Bhagwan refused,' Dollo said.

'Who was driving Auto?' I interrupted.

'Certainly, Auto driver,' he said.

'Then why did Bhagwan to pay?'

'The driver's opinion was different from the one Bhagwan had chipped in,' Dollo said.

'What was that?' I asked being confused.

'In driver's viewpoint the Auto met that unfortunate accident because Bhagwan was sitting in the Auto.'

'So what?'

'In the driver's opinion Bhagwan was unlucky and a bad omen at that point of time and therefore his Auto met the accident. That was the reason of quarrel between both of them,' he explained.

28.0

A City of Biodiversity

Driving towards the meeting venue, on October 11, 2012, I saw a slogan on the back of a city bus running before me. The slogan read 'Biodiversity City'. I had seen and heard a lot about 'green buildings' and 'green city' but 'biodiversity city' was a new term for me then.

On a sharp turn our vehicle was stopped by a group of policemen. They asked me to show my entry pass. On showing a paper, which read 'priority pass' the policeman turned to his colleagues and said, 'delegates, let them go'.

I asked one of them peeping out through the window, 'Where is the CoP-11 conference venue?'

'In High-Tech City,' he replied.

'How far is that?'

'Sir, you are in High Tech City only. The conference venue is two km away from here. Go straight, 'he said.

Now I had three names for a lone city – 'Biodiversity City' and 'High Tech City' apart from its usual name Hyderabad. I passed through a high security before reaching the conference venue. It was a multistory building having many small to large conference halls.

To the right side of building's entrance creamy coloured bags were piled up behind a line of tables. But there was no one to attend the visitors or participants. I called a person who engaged in chatting with a group of people. On my request for a bag as a participant he advised me to collect it next day.

I left the counter and walked in the corridor that was full of stalls depicting biodiversity and the ways to conserve it. I saw number of people in queue at a corner picking and eating some fried snacks. I wanted to get some snacks but I could not see the person selling them. Thinking that it might be free for visitors I stood in the queue. By the time I reached at the pan to pick up some snacks, it had been finished.

I entered one of the halls to learn more about the recent advances in biodiversity. In the hall, unexpectedly, I met one of my old friends, Chandu. On meeting the old friends always increased my excitement and energy levels. He had settled in Bangkok and was working in an international organization. We discussed many things except biodiversity. I learnt that he was staying in the same hotel in which a room was booked for me for next three days by the conference organizers. I was told that it was a five star hotel.

In the evening, we drove together to the hotel, which was at twelve km away from the conference venue. I was hungry, so I asked the driver to drop us in some restaurant. I had heard about the Hyderabadi cuisines, especially biryani from my friends, therefore I decided to have some veg-biryani. We dropped at 'Paradise', which was well known in the city for biryani.

We sat around a table and lost in chatting again on the old days. We both hailed from Uttarakhand and had worked in the *Nanda* Devi Biosphere Reserve for couple of years together. The centre of our discussion remained village life, hills, hill people and old friends. Before leaving the dining table Chandu shared his previous day experience of staying in the hotel, we were going to stay.

'My luggage, after security check in the hotel premises was labeled to drop in my room. After proper check in on the counter, I entered my room. I waited for my baggage but it was not even dropped after half an hour,' Chandu said. 'I lost my patient and so I came out from the room. I saw a boy dragging some luggage on the corridor. The boy stopped close to a nearby door and started knocking it. By the time I had recognized my luggage. When I asked him why he was taking away my baggage he seemed to be surprised. He said that for past half an hour he had been knocking everyone's door to find out the real owner of this luggage.'

On our arrival at the hotel, Chandu's experiences had helped me out and I refused the room service provider to drop my luggage in my room. Being a five star hotel naturally there were five star facilities. The room lock system was digital and one had to touch the card on the door to open it.

One of my colleagues was staying close to my room. Next day morning, I went to ask him if he was ready to move to the conference. He came out of his room. Looking the card in my hand he shouted, 'Oh my God, my room is closed now. I had forgotten to pick up my card'. He came to my room and picked up the phone to inform the receptionist. Even after giving the assurance the receptionist did not turn for long to open his room. He had become fed up and finally he went to reception to collect a new card.

My return flight to Bhopal was in the evening. The trip to Hyderabad was incomplete without to visit the Charminar for which I had deep appreciations from my childhood. This capital city of Andhra Pradesh had rich history and traditions. While driving to Charminar the driver suggested me to visit Salar Jung, which was on our way to Charminar. I had never heard about this museum, yet I thought to see it. After crossing river Musi, we reached at Salar Jung Museum.

The Museum housed over 43,000 objects, 9,000 manuscripts and 50,000 books in 38 rooms as mentioned in the literature provided at the museum. Most of the collection was done by Nawab Mir Yousuf Ali Khan Salar Jung III (1889-1949) who was Prime Minister of the seventh Nizam of Hyderabad. In 1951, under the supervision of Salar Jung Estate Committee, this museum was established. The construction was going on in many rooms so I could not visit them.

The Salar Jung museum was really a great repository of rare objects from Europe to far eastern nations in Asia. The marble statue of a 'veiled lady' in room number twelve was really an art of greatness. This statue was so lovely that a poet had called it as 'the melody in marble'. The Museum was really worth to visit. I rushed into the museum to see maximum objects, as I had less time in hand, and within two hours I set off to see the Charminar.

On reaching beneath this four centuries old magnificent monument, my heart faded down. Charminar was the majestic monument with four graceful minarets of 180 feet but I did not like the way it was valued and managed. Bus, tempo, rickshaw, cycle etc, were moving around this 'symbol of city' freely. I thought that such a great historical monument, which was built in 1591 by Muhamad Quli Qutb Shah as a charm of the city, must have been managed appropriately. Vehicle's entries should be prohibited around it. At least, about 300 to 500 meter area around this magnificent monument must be prohibited for such free entry of vehicles.

The approach as designed and operated for the India Gate in New Delhi should be applied and followed for preservation and management of such a great historical monument. It was not merely a 'charm of the city' but it would remain a charm of the country.

The market close to Charminar was flooded with pearls and lacquer bangles. I wished to purchase some pearls from the Laad Bazaar. Many hawkers chased me one by one and insisted me to buy garlands from them. To get rid off from the hawkers I pushed myself in a shop named Diamond. 'Show me some original pearls,' I asked the shopkeeper.

'You have entered the right place. We are the best manufacturer and wholesale dealer of pearls. You will get best quality pearls here. Even I will give you guarantee card for a year. None of our customer has ever complained us back. You will not regret to purchase from us,' shopkeeper said.

'Please show me both fake and original pearls,' I interrupted.

'Well, let me clear your doubts,' he said showing me both fake and original one.

He took a sharp knife and started scratching both fake and original pearls one by one. 'See, once you scratch the pearls the original will remain as such but the fake one will lose its colour. The fake pearls, as made in the machine, have uniform shape and size but the original are not uniform and have different shapes. Original pearls do not have bright white colour rather they have creamish colour,' he said confidently.

I had become convinced relatively. Though, I knew every potter praised his pots. I purchased two garlands – one with small beads and other one with relatively big beads. I tried to negotiate the prices but the shopkeeper was firmed and claimed that his prices were fixed. I could not convince him and failed to negotiate so I paid as per his demand.

I came out of the shop and again hawkers began to create trouble to walk on the road. I told a hawker that I had already purchased the same but he wanted me to purchase one from him. I asked the cost of a garland seemed to be similar to the one which I had purchased. I noticed marked differences in the prices though seemed same. One that appeared alike to me, the hawker's rate was 90 rupees per garland whereas its rate was rupees 1500 in the shops.

Finally, I consoled myself bearing in mind that whatever I had purchased it was pearls to me. Though the shopkeeper had made a fine demonstration, it was difficult to me to differentiate between the fake and the original pearls. 'It is no use crying over spilt milk,' I thought and walked to step into the vehicle waiting for me to the return journey.

Busy streets of Hyderabad near Charminar

29.0

The Silence of Candolim

The sea shore remains a most fascinating and wonderful land, especially for the residents of the Himalaya. Goa being one of the most popular tourist destinations in the Indian coast, like all my colleagues from my school days, I had been nurturing desire to visit its beaches and historical monuments. I was told that the cooler months (November to March) were the best months to enjoy these beautiful beaches.

On the first week of November I set off to visit Goa from Bhopal via Air India at quarter to twenty hrs with Richa and five yrs old Shaurya. Since there was no direct flight to Goa from Bhopal we had to fly via Mumbai. It took about three hrs to reach Mumbai from Bhopal as the Air India flight took off to Mumbai via Indore where it stopped for about forty minutes. Since there was no Air India flight in the evening to Goa, we hired a taxi from Meru Travel Agency at the Chhatrapati Air Port of Mumbai to reach the place of night stay – 301, Ellora, Vile Parle (East) – the apartment of my colleague David.

Next day, after having a delicious breakfast at David's apartment, we drove back to Air Port. At thirteen hrs we were on board to fly to Goa and within fifty minutes we landed at the Goa Air Port. Since I had already reserved a suit in Phoenix Park Inn, a driver was waiting to receive us at the Air Port. It took about an hour from Air port to the inn, which was at Candolim. On way there were quite nice localities and beautiful scenic places along with forest patches. The road was quite spacious and limited vehicles were running on it. We could see coconut trees along the roadsides. On my query, the driver showed me a cashew tree, which was limited in number.

It was November and still this part of India was warm and humid. I had become wet due to instant sweating. Bhopal remained dried during October and November where I felt itching just before winter due to drying of skin. I thought before flying from Bhopal that itchiness might be stopped in Goa due to high humidity. And I was not wrong.

Phoenix Park Inn was beautiful and attractive not because of its design only but also of its locality. Coconut trees were scattered in its premises. A day while playing in the swimming pool of hotel a coconut just detached from the tree and fell off quite close to Shaurya. He narrowly escaped but the incident had conveyed the message to be careful while walking beneath the groves of coconuts.

Most of the rooms in Park Inn were occupied by foreign tourists. I was told that many chartered planes directly land at Goa from London and other places, and during Christmas the Goa becomes the preeminent destination. Chatting with a tourist – John - who came all the way from London, I came across the fact that it is sometime hard to get reservation in hotels for December and January. John himself was keen to stay in Goa during Christmas but he could not get reservation in hotels for December and that's why he had to arrive here much earlier.

The Candolim beach was only a few steps from the Park Inn and so we walked to see it in the evening. Most beaches in Goa had derived their names from adjoining villages or village where they were situated. Candolim was known as the native village of the famous Abbe Faria, one of the founding fathers of the science of hypnotism. He was also considered to be one of the Goan freedom fighters. The beach was adjacent to Fort Aguada that was built by the Portuguese way back in 1912 for fortification against the Dutch and the Maratha.

The Candolim beach was clean and lined with shacks and bars made of wood and palm leaves. I saw the beach was full of foreign tourists. This white sandy beach was naturally beautified by the scrub-covered dunes.

Since sun was setting, the tourists were packing up their belongings to leave the beach. I took out my slippers and sat down on them but at other side Shaurya was happily playing with sand and turning it into houses, temples etc. I was thinking about the vastness of ocean and Shaurya was playing not at all bother on the presence of such a massive ocean before us.

A few local men and women, seem to be from the poor section of the society, were massaging the legs, fingers and toes of tourists in anticipation to meet their both ends meet. Despite the presence of many tourists on the beach, there was a unique serenity and calmness in the environment, which was unsettling by sea tides. The beauty of golden sun rays impinging and reflecting from the sea tides was miraculous. I enjoyed this incredible natural beauty laid over the clean stretches of sand and in soothing ocean breeze till the sun decided to take a dip in the ocean. Slowly a dark blanket had stretched over the beach through which only the stars were visible advising us to leave.

Walking some two hundred meter away from the beach to the inn I saw the shops in huts lined up in the coconut grove. On my enquiry, a shopkeeper mentioned that Goa was visited by a large number of Russians, and being straightforward they purchased the goods without much negotiation. In the 60's it was mainly visited by American hippies, followed by Englishmen and Germans.

While reading a brochure at the inn I came to know that Goa had over two dozen beaches across 131 km of its coastline. Each beach, fringed by coastal trees and lapped by waters of the Arabian Sea, was unique and made for the perfect picture-postcard. However, a few of them were not safe for swimming. One should read safety and warning boards before entering into these beaches, and must follow the rules and safety guidelines.

As per our tour package, next day we were taken to sight seen. The programme started with visiting the Dolphin centre. Dolphin had become a rare species. At the bank of backwater bodies, I noticed that the roots of trees and shrubs were sprouting up from the mud which was an interesting feature of the marine vegetation and hence such plants are placed in different category called as mangrove. The roots of these plant species come out to take oxygen as there is low oxygen in the water and soil due to high salinity.

There were some cashew trees which constantly added in the economy of this small union territory of India. Cashew tree bore fruits in March therefore I could not see the fleshy and edible nut that hanged from the fruit. There were number of State Govt. approved shops selling cashew in the market, and tourists visiting to Goa did not forget to purchase some cashew for their relatives, as well. Apart from hotels, malls and shops in the market, I saw some Ayurvedic massage parlors.

After visiting Dolphin centre we drove to old Goa city, which was situated not far from Panaji, the Goa's capital.

The remnants of once magnificent Portuguese capital of Goa I could see in the Old Goa in the forms of churches and cathedrals. Some of these buildings had been declared and maintained as archeological museums that provided a fascinating display of Goa's history. The Convent and Church of Saint Francis of Assisi, built in 1521 was one of the most interesting buildings in the Old Goa. Just opposite was the Basilica of Bom Jesus that contained the preserved remains of the body of Saint Frances Xavier, a revered missionary and the patron saint of Goa. As a ritual, the body was shown to the public every ten years. The next exhibition was due in 2014.

These churches and convents had exerted great influence in the 16th - 18th centuries on the development of architecture, sculpture, and painting by spreading forms of Manueline, Mannerist and Baroque art in Asian countries where Catholic missions were established. I could see the beautiful paintings in the church carved on the wooden boards. Most of the statues of the saints, the Virgin Mary, and Jesus were first carved in wood and then painted to adorn the altars. These churches and convents of Old Goa were marked as world heritage site in 1986 by UNESCO.

Our guide was very smart in keeping us always on alarm to follow the time allotted to see the respective church or any sight. His daily experience with tourists made him to learn this art of tackling tourists otherwise it would have been difficult to visit other places. Whenever, I stepped out from the bus I had heavy sweating. This increased my body requirement for water, which I mainly recovered by drinking coconut water. The cost of one water coconut was rupees twenty, which was expensive from other costal belt.

At the lunch time we were drove to a restaurant. The moment we entered the restaurant, there was only one or two customers but within 10-15 minutes there was no seat left and tourists were waiting outside for their turn in the queues. The buses flooded with tourists had started stopping near the restaurants.

The Mangeshi temple was our next destination after lunch. There was a small village – Mangeshi in which this famous temple was located. Mangeshi village being associated with the forefathers of the well-known singer and the Bharat Ratn awardees - Lata Mangeshkar, has become the centre of tourist's attractions. Mangeshi temple was whitish in colour and was very beautiful. There was a long queue of people in the temple premises waiting for their turn to offer puja. The floor of the temple premises was so warm that it was difficult to stand and walk without slippers on it.

After visiting Mangeshi and Durga temples we were taken to Colva beach in south Goa. Unlike the Candolim beach, I noticed a quite less number of foreign tourists and more crowds in the Colva beach. It was bounded along its coast by coconut palms. Some of the visitors were just wetting their feet most probably they were unable to swim, while others soaking up the sun, leisurely sipping *feni* drink, and were taking part in adventure sports through flying up in the sky with the help of inflated balloons. Finally, we drove to enjoy a flavor of evening in the Cruse.

On the way there was an aquarium in which I saw many marine fishes, including crabs, tortoises and some poisonous fishes swimming in the separate glass chambers. We boarded in the cruise at eighteen hrs below the Mandovi Bridge of Panaji. The cruse took us for a beautiful ride down the river Mandovi past Adil Shah's summer place toward the Indian Ocean at Reis Magos Fort. An hour of boarding in cruse gave us an essence of rich culture of Goa. The folk dance as performed in the stage also introduced us the culture of Portuguese who ruled this island for many years until 1961.

The panoramic view of setting sun from the cruse over the vast Indian Ocean was extremely fascinating and added the charming hues to the ocean. After sunset the lighting on the streets as seen from the cruse had a unique look and beauty of the city. There were some casinos which were made attractive with different colours and lights.

The sight seen programme had come to an end at twenty hrs when we were dropped back at Park Inn. The entire programme was organized quite professionally, and thus every customer in the inn seemed to be satisfied with the way it was managed.

Goa, though the smallest state of India, had surprised me with its eye-catching locations, historical monuments, exhilarating coconut groves, magnificent forts and palaces, eternal sea, enticing cultural tradition, lovely beaches, and warm and friendly hospitality. It enriched me something new and something extra on my every step. And the time had come to say 'goodbye Goa' and next day we packed our luggage to fly back to Bhopal.

Shaurya and Richa enjoying sunset at the Candolim

30.0

The Land of Many Shades

Wandering many years in Garhwal and enjoying its sumptuousness, grandness and grandeur, my interest to see beyond these majestic mountains and extensive dales had started growing up with each passing day. One day this long cherished dream came close to the reality when I was assigned a task to roam in Spiti for couple of months in order to comprehend Spitian's home herbal remedy.

I got into a bus at Dehradun to Shimla. I stayed a night at Shimla and resumed my journey to Kaza in another bus, next day. Kaza - the headquarter of Spiti - was located on the bank of beautiful river Spiti that sped down all along the Spiti valley. This major life line river of Spitians was surrounded by gigantic but barren mountains. I had never ever imagined before such a wonderful mesmerizing and unique mountain landscape deprived of forests and meadows. I was surprised to notice some huge mountain like structures of compact soil on the bank of river Spiti.

'These soil mountains, at the bank, will be dissolved in rains,' I educated the fellow traveler without knowing the facts.

'They are there for decades. You are in a rain shadow region,' he said refuting my theory.

'You don't have forest. How do you live without trees?' I said stepping out from the bus at the Kaza bus station.

'Don't you see trees here in Kaza,' he quizzed.

'They are quite few. Are they natural?' I asked.

'They are planted but we do have natural trees of seabuckthorn along the major river valleys,' he clarified.

A man in uniform at station came close to ask me about my whereabouts. Before I spoke out he introduced himself as a forest guard. Since I was associated with an institution of forest and wildlife, my accommodation was booked at the forest guest house. He picked up my rucksack and asked me to follow him.

The rest house seemed to be newly built. I stepped into a room close to its entrance. I found five other rooms of equal sizes; all were interconnected and three of them were well furnished and decorated.

'Which one is booked for me?' I asked the forest guard.

'I don't know. I was asked to drop you here. I go to ask the caretaker,' he said before slipping out of the room.

He came back shortly with an aged person. I repeated my question to him.

'Sir, all rooms are opened for you only. You can stay in any room of your choice. All rooms are allotted to you till your stay at Kaza,' he explained.

For next two days, I stayed back in Kaza to acclimatize my body to work in further high altitude areas. While straying in

Kaza I enjoyed eating some local dishes, including thuppa, chowmine, and noodles. Even being headquarters of Spiti, Kaza was a small town having limited shops and hotels. Its residents were friendly, easy going and peace loving.

The third day's morning I climbed to a narrow hilly path that brought me to the Hikkim monastery. I noticed sparse distribution of plants on way to monastery and its adjoining areas. Arnebia euchroma was one of the dominant plants growing upto fifteen to twenty inches, which was known to have medicinal properties.

The monastery at Hikkim was spanned over a large space. Just after the entrance, I saw a snow leopard's skin hanging from the roof. I rotated the spin wheels and enjoyed the artwork on the walls. Following the same narrow trail I came down to guest house before sunset.

At Kaza, I prepared for the long trek and stay in the Pin Valley national park. The park authorities arranged two assistants for supporting me during my trek cum survey. I packed up my baggage and walked to bus station with the supporting staff. I was told that a single bus ferried passengers twice in a day on the route I had to travel. After over two hours of waiting for bus at the station, a driver informed us about the cancellation of bus for the day. The long hours of waiting for the bus and now its cancellation had crashed my composure and sufferings.

'This is ridiculous. How come they do like this? We have been waiting for past two hours for this bus and now it is cancelled. How will people travel back home?' I whispered in the panic stricken voice.

'No problem sir, we will go tomorrow,' one of my assistants, Dorje, said casually, as nothing uncommon had happened.

Passengers waiting for long at the station started walking back with their baggage. Interestingly, none of them raised voice against the order of bus cancellation. Stress was miles away from their faces. I asked the fellow passenger, 'now there is no bus today to the Pin valley. What will you do?'

'I shall stay back at Kaza. This is only thing that I can do,' he said with smiling face.

'They are tension free people,' I said myself.

The tension-free people and environment full of contentment all around me dropped my anger down and I walked back, just like others, to guest house with by baggage.

Next day, I was fortunate enough to get into bus at the right time. I got down at Sargam – the last village in Pin Valley connected with motorable road. Jang Po- one of my assistants - was native of Sargam. He was kind enough to extend his services by providing free accommodation and hospitality at his home.

Jang Po had two young brothers and two sisters. His mother was in her eighties, and long back he had lost his father. Being the eldest son, he got married to a beautiful local girl some five years back. The brother next to Jang Po had become lama, and the youngest one, who had just seen eighteen springs in his life, helped him in farming and animal husbandry. His one sister was married, who lived with her husband in the neighboring village. Jang Po seemed to be worried as he had not yet found a suitable match for his second sister's marriage. Though, Chhodan had just celebrated her seventeen birth day.

Jang Po was quite active and well informed person. He used to work as guide for tourists visiting Pin Valley national park. He had also worked in a project on Ibex for years. His long association with researchers and tourists had made him to understand the taste of different types of visitors.

'Are you vegetarian?' Jang Po asked me.

'I am selective non-vegetarian. I don't eat mutton,' I replied.

'We are going to prepare yak meat. But I arrange vegetarian for you,' he said.

He passed on the information to his wife working in the kitchen and came back to me.

'This year I expect to have good production of peas,' he said.

'You grow peas, it's wonderful, I like it,' I said.

'We have been growing peas for past six to seven years. It is quite profitable crop,' Jang Po revealed.

'Do you sell it, too?'

'Yes, we do.'

'Interesting! But, where?' I asked as I did not come across any town and city nearby to his village.

'We sell it in Chandigarh and Delhi.'

'You take it to Delhi. But how do you manage….'

'It is simple. We hire trucks to transport and drop our peas packed in sacks in the market centre. The villagers hire trucks collectively depending on the production.'

'That's wonderful. So the people in Delhi are enjoying the peas of Spiti. It seems you have very fertile land,' I said.

'Unfortunately, it is not so much fertile as yours in Ganges floodplains. We make our farms fertile by adding lot of farmyard manure,' he said.

'How much land you possess for farming?' I asked.

'The land is not adequate, especially the land for farming. Most of the land is barren and cannot be used to grow crops. Our forefathers were very visionary and intelligent people. We have many customs and all such traditions, one way or other, are interlinked with our lifestyle, livelihoods, environment, mountains, land and water. The customs,

I presume, would have been made to run the society, smoothly. If such customs would not have been made the society would have been collapsed. The once peace-loving people in the absence of such customs would have been entangled with civil war, at the recent past and the present,' Jang Po explained.

'What is that custom?' I asked being excited to learn about such an important custom which had saved the society.

'We have a traditional custom of polyandry, wherein the eldest brother is, generally, allowed to be married. The girl he married may also consider as the wife of his rest of the brothers. This custom equates with one with Dhropati who had five husbands. If someone does not follow this custom in our society and get married to some other girl, he is, by and large, asked to prepare his own set up or house to live. The right of land ownership remains with the eldest brother, and this arrangement or custom percolates down the line through generations. In this way, the fertile land remained intact with the family, as it is not divided into brothers,' Jang Po explained philosophically.

'Dinner is ready to serve,' Jang Po's wife informed from the kitchen. So he stood up to serve the food. I enjoyed eating chapattis, dal and vegetables having some special Spitians flavor.

After dinner, all the family members gathered in the guest room, which was occupied by me. They squatted on the carpet in a circle. After a brief chatting with each other, they started singing local songs. Though, I could not make out the meanings of chorus they had embedded deeply, I liked its rhythm, the ups and downs, and the emotions on the faces of those natural singers. One by one they started dancing, following each other in a circle. I got up to join their steps, once they insisted me to do so. Meantime, Chhodan brought tea for all, which broke the rhythm for a while.

Dance party geared up again, after tea break. The party continued singing and dancing till midnight. Being exhausted completely from nails to head I threw myself in the bed. Soon I had reached in the state of not realizing whether the party was over or continued.

I got up late in the next day. Jang Po offered me a warm cup of tea. I generally don't take tea hence I denied to enjoy it. I asked Jang Po to show me the place to relieve myself. He filled water in a glass bottle and once handed over the water bottle to me he showed me the way to an upstairs room in his double storied house. I entered the room and latched its wooden door.

It was relatively a big room of four by four meter. There was a fifty by fifty centimeter hole just in the centre of the room, which opened in the room just below it. I bent to see down through the hole. The room below was half filled with human excreta and household waste. I felt bit uncomfortable initially and somehow made me to relieve.

'Your toilet is quite different,' I asked Jang Po after having bath.

'It is difficult to go out in open to relieve during winter when we remained locked in the house for weeks. After all once decomposed, we use that waste as manure. This helps in maintaining the soil fertility. The productions of vegetables remained higher in the farms which received this manure,' Jang Po explained.

At Gechang, six km deep into Pin Valley national park from Sargam, Jang Po had a summer house. I had to also survey the inner part of the Pin Valley hence I asked Jang Po to pack up and move for Gechang. Since it was summer season and Jang Po's family frequently visited Gechang to look after the summer crops, Chhodan and Dorje had also become ready to join us till Gechang.

After breakfast we were about to set off when a forest guard approached me. He was instructed by District Forest Officer to escort me during my explorations in the Pin Valley in order to collect medicinal and aromatic plants under my supervision. One more girl had also joined our caravan to Gechang. Her name was Dolma and she was Chhodan's childhood friend.

The size of our caravan had inflated. We walked all through some of the most xeric cold desert areas and scree slopes. At one moment we reached close to Parahio river but in other moment the trek led us away from it. Finally, we arrived at a spot where we had to cross the Parahio.

There was no bridge, and the violent flow of Parahio was enough to challenge my courage. I did not know how to swim hence I asked Jang Po, 'how will we cross this river? I don't know how to swim. Do you?'

'I also can't swim in this violent rushing water,' he said.

'But there is no bridge. You say we have to cross the river. How is it possible?' I asked.

'I have arranged all sorts of equipments to cross it. You follow me a few more steps and just wait and watch,' Jang Po said throwing a broad smile at me.

Chhodan and Dolma joined Jang Po and soon their smile broke into laughter looking at my gloomy face. They said something in their dialect and laughed again and again. However, I felt no impurity and disregard in their laughter. I seemed to be the only member of caravan who was worried on account of the challenge flowing down in front of us, and this made others a laughing substance.

'Sir, don't worry. I shall take you to other flank of Parahio,' Chhodan came forward to rescue me. I grinned.

The caravan once stopped on the bank I dropped my rucksack. Chhodan started fumbling into her baggage and finally pulled out a rope. She climbed on a heap of stones. When she raised her hands with rope in the air I saw a wire stretched across the river. Chhodan tied the rope with the wire like a swing. She called Dolma and then tied her waist with the rope hanging from the wire.

Dolma started pushing her body forward by holding the wire one by one with her hands. The rope received most of her body weight. She caught the wire by her right hand and pushed her body forward. Then she caught the wire by her left hand and pushed again her body forward. She kept on pushing her body forward by holding the wire one by one hands. Once Dolma crossed the river the rope was pulled back on the wire.

The half of the caravan had crossed the river by the similar way as performed by Dolma. Now it was my turn and Chhodan called up me to follow the same technique of crossing Parahio. She advised me not to be frightened and disheartened.

'It is easy and simple. Look, Dolma has done it easily. Hold the wire. Don't look down on the river's flow while you are crossing. Keep on pushing your body forward by holding wire. Look up in the sky when you are moving forward. Put your weight on rope that supports your body to lift and move ahead,' Chhodan advised me before tying my waist with the wire and pushing me forward.

I remembered all my Gods, including the god of the gods, *Neelkanth*, and finally left my body to its destiny. While attempting to push my body forward, every member of the team kept on encouraging me. It was really a thrilling experience of crossing river with the help of a rope and wire.

'You people are really great. All you are full of courage and great like these mountains,' I admired the entire team once I had completed my turn of crossing Parahio.

We took our baggage and continued our journey to Gechang, which was not far from us.

Gechang, a summer settlement, was at a knoll with some flatland on the mountain slope. The team members, one by one, stepped into Jang Po's house, which was double storied like one at Sargam. The rooms were spacious. Apart from a bunker close to Jang Po's house, there was no second house. And the house was surrounded by agriculture fields.

After having a cup of tea I stepped on a narrow trail passing though the croplands. I felt the presence of some high scented plant species. I focused my attention on the plants growing on bunds, and plucked a plant leaf to smell. It had a strong aroma. I collected a couple of twigs and pressed them inside a magazine for making herbarium. I came across the fragrance of Hissopus and Artemisia quite often at the edges of crop fields. Luckily, I spotted couple of individuals of Eramurus – an endangered species of umbel family.

After dinner and lot of chatting I had a sound sleep in my sleeping bag stretched on the hard floor. Next day, before I set off my journey to the next base camp at Thango, the forest guard, who joined me one day before at Sargam, requested me to discontinue my further explorations.

'But I have just started my work. How can I discontinue without some information in my hand. It is just not possible. I came all the way from Dehradun to collect these valuable less known herbs,' I said.

'Sir, my wife is not well and I wish to be there with her,' he pleaded.

'Sir, I do have some important family commitment, and I have to go anyhow. I have not seen my family for past two weeks,' the second forest guard who accompanied me right from the Kaza intruded in the conversations.

I guessed that they wished to get rid of the explorations as they did not have any interest in trekking and the Pin Valley. If I continued trekking with them they would have spoiled our interest and explorations by creating trouble, time and again. Hence, I made up my mind to continue my explorative journey without their support.

Chhodan, Dorje and Dolma had to stay back at Gechang and I had to trek further in the lonely mountains with Jang Po. After enjoying a plate of Maggie I continued my journey to Thango with my lone assistant Jang Po.

Thango was located at the bank of upper reaches of Parahio in a broad valley. It was a village of thirty five households but the moment I reached here all houses appeared to be abandoned. I could not see a single person at Thango.

'What happened to this village? Did you see anyone?' I asked Jang Po.

'They all have shifted to their winter homes,' he said. 'Now only a few families practice transhumance. Living on move being a tough task people prefer to settle in a single village rather than moving seasonally from one village to other,' Jang Po disclosed the realities of tough life style and livings of mountain residents.

In the evening, I sat down on the bank of Parahio. Here in the rough and desolate world, the Parahio was flowing down gently, along the Thango valley. Just before sunset I spotted a group of Himalayan Ibex descending majestically on the steep and rugged mountains terrain.

I spent a week at Thango, straying around in search of medicinal herbs all the day. In the evening of every day, I enjoyed sitting at the bank of Parahio, watching birds and listening nature's music in the tune and resonance of rivers, rivulets, insects and birds.

The day I reached back at Sargam I saw both forest guards who left me at Gechang were waiting desperately for me. As soon as they saw me they appeared to be relaxed and glad. I thought probably my safe return had made them happy. By the time, it had been evening and they wanted me to travel to Kaza. Being tired I refused to travel further. I had also to survey southern valleys of the Pin Valley national park, and it was not a good idea to go back in the middle of my survey. When both the guards realized that I am no more interested to return Kaza, they disclosed the fact of their presence at Sargam.

'Sir, our chief conservator of forests wants to see you immediately. He came all the way from Shimla and, at present, he is at Kaza,' one of them said.

'Why does he want to see me?' I asked.

'He looks after research wing, and he has keen interest in medicinal herbs,' he explained. 'But there is no bus service at this time. It is not possible anyway to reach Kaza today,' I said.

'Sir we have arranged a taxi. Please sir. Anyhow we have to go otherwise we both will be dismissed from the service. We have families to feed. It is the question of our life,' a guard said on behalf of both.

I realized the reason of their happiness once they saw me trickling down at Sargam. They were asked to present me before their boss. They managed taking me to Kaza. On the way, they pleaded before me again and again not to disclose any such thing which went against to them.

I dropped my baggage at the Kaza's guest house. I walked to circuit house around eight o'clock in the evening to see Vinaya, the chief conservator of forests whom I had met earlier. Vinaya was a large hearted gentleman. He was a keen observer and had a faith in medicinal properties of herbs. He offered me to have dinner with him at the circuit house.

'Are you comfortable Chandra?' he asked.

'Yes, I am enjoying my stay and work,' I said.

'Do these forest guards stay with you during survey?' he asked. Probably he had smelt something wrong or perhaps someone had informed him or someone had complained about guards visit to their homes.

Now the ball was in my court. I did not want to harm the guards yet I was skeptical on the Vinaya's source of information. Looking my silent reaction to his question had made Vinaya to realize that his source of information was right. Before I say something he lost his temper and called up his staff, immediately.

'You people don't want to learn. I request people to upgrade your knowledge but you don't pay any heed. You don't deserve to retain your job,' before he finished I intervened. 'It is all right, they were with me initially but later on I allowed them to leave.'

This made him to calm down slowly but his concerns to make his staff knowledgeable remained, which reflected in his talk till we finished dinner late in the night.

Next day, I spent with Vinaya and his staff. We visited a nearby village where villagers were attempting to domesticate some medicinal herbs. I saw a nursery of medicinal herbs, which was raised by the forest department. Vinaya traveled back to Shimla and to continue my study I arrived again at Jang Po's residence at Sargam.

From Sargam I walked up in a valley which led me to a village called Mud. In the Mud valley the greenery was substantially higher than the Spiti and Pin valleys. Surprisingly, I encountered a dense population of Dactylorhiza hatagirea – a terrestrial medicinal orchid, locally called as Angbolakpa, at a place just before Mud village. In all my mountain wanderings I had not come across such a dense population of this endangered medicinal orchid.

Just before entering the village, on a relatively flatland, I was stopped by a group of teenage girls. They kept on repeating a term "Mehndok". I looked at Jang Po who was smiling.

'Sorry, I don't know your language. Please explain what does this mehndok stand for?' I asked.

'Mehndok, mehndok….,' girls continued.

I had become totally confused. I heard this term first time in Spiti. Jang Po was not disclosing me its meaning and he was still smiling gazing at me. After some time, Jang Po took out five rupees from his pocket and handed over the teenager's group. He said something in his local language and I felt that Jang Po was trying to settle down the matter. The girls were raising their eyebrows and fingers at me, frequently, while discussing with Jang Po. This made me to think that most likely I was the subject of dispute. I kept on standing at a corner trying my best to understand the situation. During the conversation with Jang Po the girls remained in the commendable position. At the last, the girls seemed to be agreed with Jang Po and they moved aside the trail.

'Let's go,' said Jang Po.

'What was this?' I asked while following Jang Po.

'Nothing special,' he said.

I presumed that Jang Po did not want to share and reveal the real cause of incident, at the moment, as all the girls started following us. I stared back where they all were chatting and laughing.

Mud was Dolma's village – the one who had trekked with us to Gechnag. Being Chhodan's friend Dolma happily arranged our stay in her own house, where she lived with her mother and a younger brother of twelve years old. I was unable to communicate directly with her mother as I did not know her language and she did not know my language. Dolma being bilingual helped us in passing our feelings to each other.

Like Jang Po, Dolma's house was double storied with several rooms. The room allotted to me was probably the best one. It was decorated with handmade carpets with some beautiful paintings on the wall. One of the paintings caught my sight in which His Holiness Dalai Lama was adorned with garlands. Ashes of agarbatti had formed a pile just below this painting.

'I think this paining is special in this room.' I asked Dolma indicating the painting of His holiness.

'We worship His Holiness Dalai Lama just like you worship '*Neelkanth*'. Worshipping His holiness wards off all evils,' Dolma said.

Dolma was a very caring girl. Despite cooking food, arranging warm water as and when required, looking after domestic animals, she also gave me company so that I did not feel lonely and boring for the period I stayed in her house.

I climbed up and down on the undulating land and mountain slopes around Mud in search of medicinal and aromatic herbs. A day I reached in an area, which was full of dense lush herbs. Though, here most of the area was under thick snow cover, I encountered the highest number of medicinal herbs in a small portion of land free of snow. Many medicinal herbs were quite similar to one which I had observed in the Valley of Flowers. I saw a group of shepherd grazing goats and sheep. They informed me the name of locality, which they called Tarbak. They camped here for two and half months during their movement in search of good pastures for their goats and sheep in the high alpine areas of the trans-Himalaya.

The entire day trek and excitements of spotting many medicinal herbs had exhausted my body. I could not sleep properly and fell sick. Being uncomfortable I called up Jang Po. Dolma and her mother too got up. On my enquiry about doctor, Dolma first time felt helplessness, as there was no doctor and no primary health care facility at her village.

'You must go back to Kaza,' Dolma suggested me.

'I think so,' I replied realizing the urgency of treatment.

'I shall drop you at Sargam. It is lonely mountain trail. Anything may happen on the way,' she said.

'I have Jang Po. We will manage.'

'I doubt as he is not much familiar with this area. I have to drop you,' she said firmly.

Next day, we set off our journey back to Kaza. Reaching at the spot where a group of teenage girls stopped us and Jang Po handed them five rupees, I asked Jang Po again about the incident.

'What was that secret, which you did not disclose yet? What is Mehndok?' I asked.

Hearing Mehndok Dolma laughed, all of a sudden.

'I think Dolma will explain you better than me,' Jang Po said.

I looked at Dolma she was still laughing.

'You were caught,' she said with a wide smile on her face.

'I was caught! Was I impertinent? Sorry, I did nothing,' I said in surprise.

'I know you did nothing. Actually, it is one of our customs. Whenever, two or more girls happen to be at a spot, and any man passes through that spot, the girls enjoy the right to demand for gifts from him. This custom is called Mehndok. It is upto the choice of girls to stake their claim or not. Generally, the Mehndok is applied on unknown people or the person from other villages,' she said with smile.

'Oh, my God! It was a custom. Very interesting!' I said.

Panting and prodding, I kept on pushing my body further up and downhill trails. My body had weakened, gradually, with every step, and I sat down on bare ground or boulders at every few steps. I constantly felt hard to push my body forward. I started losing control over my body. On many occasions, Dolma and Jang Po held my hands and supported me to stand. After throwing myself to a few steps I began to sprawl on the ground rather to sit down. Jang Po, finally, lifted me on his shoulder and strolled down to the Sargam.

I was admitted in the Kaza's hospital. The doctor, who hailed from Kerala, had diagnosed a severe deficiency of water in my body.

'It is a case of dehydration. You must drink adequate water. Also, mix some salt and sugar in the water. Drink water as much as you can,' he advised.

'Is there any serious problem?' I asked.

'No. Your all vital organs are functioning, perfectly. Drink water,' he repeated his advice.

'I am feeling too weak,' I said.

'It is only because of shortage of water in your body,' doctor replied.

The same day, I was discharged from the hospital. Jang Po suggested me to drink 'namkeen chai' – a local tea which contains some salt and butter, apart from the extract of some native herbs. Initially, I did not like its taste yet I kept on drinking it in anticipation of meeting water requirement of my body. Slowly, I had habituated to its taste.

Drinking namkeen chai several times in a day brought back my energy level and finally recovered my strength. I thanked Jang Po and Dolma from the core of my heart for taking care of my health. They had not only saved my life but also taught me a lesson that the secret of fighting with environmental vagaries might also hide in the local people's culture, customs and food habits.

Resting at Kaza's guest house for couple of days, I wished to survey the Kibber Wildlife Sanctuary. This sanctuary was named after a village in Spiti called as Kibber.

'It is difficult to catch bus to Kibber,' Jang Po said.

'Just like your village,' I grinned.

'It is not a joke. I mean it. Catching bus to Sargam is not a problem, generally. There are exceptions, always. But there is hardly any bus to Kibber. For many days there is no bus,' he said.

'Then, it is a real problem,' I said.

'Well, I go to market and explore if there is any mode of transport to Kibber, tomorrow,' having said this Jang Po left to Kaza's market. By the evening Jang Po returned with some news.

'I met a truck driver who may go to Kibber tomorrow for loading peas,' Jang Po said. 'I requested him to drop us.'

'That is fine.'

'He asked to be ready at five o'clock in the morning,' Jang Po said.

Next day morning, we stepped into the truck with our baggage without any hassles. The truck drove on the dusty mountain road. After over two hours of drive we were dropped at Kibber village. One of my colleagues from Mysore had hired a house here. He was working on the ecology of snow leopard. Since he was on tour, his assistant welcomed us and offered accommodation in the rented house, free of cost.

'I am Sushil,' my friend's assistant introduced himself.

'Glad to meet you,' I said, though, I was surprised to hear his name, which was not common in the land of Buddha I was travelling. Such a pure Hindu name seemed to be quite uncommon to me. For me his name was quite familiar and easy to remember.

I stayed couple of nights at the Kibber village while exploring medicinal herbs in the high reaches of this trans-Himalaya region. Sushil rendered all sort of facilities and support, apart from giving me company during the field visits, as and when required.

A day while surveying the high passes above Kibber at Minguit area Sushil asked me, 'We have amchis and shamans at Kibber, and they possess sound knowledge on medicinal herbs. Most of the elders in each family do have some knowledge of herbal medicine, and they use many herbs growing around as a home herbal remedy. But I don't understand what this aromatic herb's business is. Why are you at all after such herbs?'

'Aromatic herbs do also possess medicinal properties. Apart from their use for cosmetic purposes, they are also used in curing diseases. Aromatherapy is most sought treatment today. It heals mind, body and soul by using roots, leaves and blossoms of scented plants. Plants become aromatic as they contain some scented essential oils, which are quite powerful in their concentrated forms. Essential oils are also used for skin care, as they keep the skin moisturized and healthy. But they are not directly applied onto the skin in the concentrated forms rather they are diluted with carrier oils like apricot kernel oil and sweet almond oil before use. Such herbal-based skin-care products are very good for the people like me straying into your areas, which receive high solar radiation including ultra violet rays and hence burn the skin,' I explained.

'But I don't have any sign of sun burn,' Sushil suspected my explanation.

'Your body is acclimatized to this environment and solar radiations,' I said based on my own experiences. I had often noticed that whenever I went to the high altitude areas after a long gap, initially my skin showed sunburned signs for over a fortnight but thereafter I hardly noticed such changes in my skin.

While walking downhill slope at Minguit, I spotted a big herd of over hundred blue sheep to my right, grazing on the undulating pasture. I sat down on a knoll, full of grasses, for watching their movements through a pair of binocular.

'Does your livestock share the same pasture with these wild sheep?' I asked Sushil.

'Yes, they do,' he said.

'So both blue sheep and your domestic animals graze together. Don't they fight each other for food?' I asked.

'When our livestock are brought to these pastures, the blue sheep climb further up in the mountains into other high altitude pastures,' Sushil said.

'But obviously both are herbivores and eat same resource. Eating a similar resource by someone may create resource shortage to others. There may not be direct fighting yet indirect competition cannot be ruled out,' I thought and said. 'By the way, have you ever seen snow leopard?'

'I have seen twice. But it is very shy and elusive animal. We do have wolf here though people don't like and tolerate their presence, as they are very harmful for the domestic animals,' he said.

Sushil was a well-informed person. I enjoyed his company in the desolate sparsely human-habited mountains.

While trekking back to Kibber for night stay I asked him, 'Sushil, don't you feel that your name is slightly different from the commonly spoken names in Spiti. It is more similar to the one which we have in our villages around Dehradun.'

He smiled, and I waited for his comment. Since he had taken time to comment, I said again, 'please don't mind. I don't mean to hurt you. Am I impertinent?'

'No, no, not at all,' he said hastily.

'I felt so that's why I asked,' I explained.

'You are right. Actually, before joining school my name was Ghyaltse Tsering. When I joined school, then the class teacher was hailed from Shimla. Always, his accent of my name remained imperfect. This made him a laughing stock in the class. He became fed up with the pronunciation of my original name and hence within a week of my admission he changed my name into Sushil. Since then my official name has become Sushil. Though, my parents and relatives call me Ghyaltse Tsering, my class mates and people from outside Spiti call me Sushil,' he disclosed the secret of his name, which had been bubbling in my mind since I met him first time.

Other day I visited Chhichim – a nearest village of Kibber. A rivulet on the way had formed a microhabitat along the way it was flowing in this desert, which docked some good vegetation cover, including medicinal and aromatic herbs. Approaching close to the village I saw the villagers were busy in their farms. Both women and men folks were colleting sweet peas while singing Spitian songs. Without interrupting their rhythm I walked back to Kibber. My work had almost completed. I had collected over sixty medicinal and aromatic plants, of which twenty five were rare and endangered. I had to only arrange and label them systematically on the herbarium sheets before depositing at the forest department of Spiti.

In the afternoon, I was again in a truck, which dropped me at the Kye monastery. Since the herbal survey had almost come to an end, I had the opportunity to visit and see some more shades in the variety of well-known and wonderful monasteries constructed all across the land of Buddha. A year before my arrival at Kye monastery, his holiness the Dalai Lama was here for Kalchakra – a well known celebration of Buddhists.

At the dusk, I reached back to Kaza. Next day, I travelled in a bus to Tabo monastery. Tabo was one of the oldest monasteries I had ever seen in the Spiti. This monastery was constructed in 996 AD. Because of its breathtaking mural and stucco images Tabo was also called as 'the Ajanta of the Himalaya'.

In the first look, the Tabo monastery seemed to be an assortment of mud huts, connected with each other. The size of mud huts was unequal. Every room was full of wall paintings depicting various stories of earlier incarnations of the Lord Buddha. There were number of structure. Kalchakra was celebrated here a few years ago.

'Thousands of monks assembled here during Kalchakra. I have never seen before such a sea of people in saffron congregated in and around the monastery. His Highness Dalai Lama was also here. People from all walks of life and remotest villages also reached here to see and get blessings of His holiness,' Jang Po enlightened me about the Kalchakra and its importance to the region and society.

My stay in 'the land of many shades' had come to an end. I got into a bus with baggage in the early morning hours. The bus drove through the narrow and winding risky mountain roads. I passed through Kunzum la and Rohtang and finally dropped at Manali. The continuous restless bus journey further to Dehradun was quite tiring but overloaded with sweet memories of peace loving, honest and lovely people of this planet.

Living here in the land of Buddha, even only once in my life, it had become just like home for me. After the years of my visit, I still feel a bond and connect with Spiti, its colour, the culture and most of all, the Spitians. The hospitality and warmth I had received from Spitians remain memorable. They were generous enough to take me under their wings and looked after me like one of their beloved.

31.0

Om Mani Padme Hum

The city was reeling under extreme heat wave condition in a day of May, as mercury almost touched forty five degree Celsius at Bhopal. Hot winds swept the city in the afternoon had made the day quite uncomfortable.

'Why does summer so hot?' six years old Shaurya asked me. Before I began to response he answered himself. 'It becomes hot, so that children can enjoy summer vacation, especially in the hills.'

'It is time to brace for scorching days ahead,' I said while repairing cooler. Nevertheless, I too wished to get rid of the blistering heat. Shaurya's idea had finally clicked in my mind and I chalked out to visit a hill station. After a week, in an afternoon I was driving to airport with Shaurya and Richa. The city street wore a deserted look in the afternoon with most residents preferring to stay indoors. The airport road along the lake was sizzling, and after forty minutes of drive I got down from the vehicle to step into the airport.

'Intense hot wave conditions will prevail in whole of Madhya Pradesh till we come back from Sikkim,' I said while entering the Raja Bhoj Airport.

'Navtapa will come to an end in the first week of June,' Richa said.

'Delhi will be equally hot. Tonight we have to stay there. If there was any direct flight or even a connecting flight we would have flown straight to Bagdogra,' I pointed out.

At Delhi, we stayed at India International Centre and next day we flew to Bagdogra at eleven hours. Over one thousand and one hundred kilometers distance from Delhi to Bagdogra, we finished within one and half hours. Thanks to the technology and science and also to the Right brothers who made us to fly without wings. I hired a taxi to Gangtok at Bagdogra airport and within couple of minutes I was passing through the tea gardens on the undulating land. The scenic beauty of tea gardens remained visible for a very brief period, which was shortly replaced by the frequent human settlements.

Passing through the scattered forests encroached heavily by humans, I arrived on a bridge over the Teesta river. The landscape had worn a veil of clouds and rainfall was frequent all along the way. We had left behind the scorching days and the time to embrace the pleasant days had begun. I could see a hydroelectric dam on river Teesta. Both flanks of this river rose to hills predominated by thick broadleaf forests.

The vehicle began to gain heights on the winding mountain road. Still majority of countryside was shrouded in clouds. I could see through broken visibility the meandering road that brought and dropped tourists to various hill stations in Sikkim. Seeing a roadside vendor selling corns some km away from Teesta's bridge I asked the driver Sukraj to stop the vehicle.

'Do you want to click a photo here?' Sukraj asked.

'I wish to have some corns,' I replied.

'Don't buy here,' he said.

'Isn't it of good quality, here?' I asked.

He paused for a moment and said, 'here people roast them in dirty coal.'

'Dirty coal!' what does it mean?' I asked.

'Actually, they collect left out coal from the nearby crematoriums,' Sukraj whispered and drove ahead.

Passing through some dark forests, human habitations, frequent landslides, broken visibility, dense clouds, and intermittent rains, we reached close to the Tiger bridge over the Teesta river, which led tourists to Bhutan. Rambi – a place on the way to Gangtok was about twenty km from here.

The continuous driving on national highway Thirty One A had brought us at a place called as Thirty Two. Here Sukraj stopped the vehicle and asked me to enjoy corns. I looked through the window. It was rainy and again the land had worn a veil of thick clouds. In a row at the roadside several young women were selling corns while sitting under the roof of bamboo and cane made structure. The gentle hill slopes of both sides of road were under extensive farming of corns.

I stepped out from the vehicle, unfurled my umbrella and walked toward a young girl calling me to buy corns from her while roasting one on the fire. She appeared to be a humble but quite experienced businesswoman. She sold per piece of corn at the rate of twenty rupees. While eating the corns I realized that it was worth to pay twenty rupees for a corn, as it was really tasty. By the evening we reached at Dho-tapu – a guest house at Devrali - to stay for next couple of days.

Next day morning, I noticed a black and white photograph on the left wall of my room in Dho-tapu. As per inscriptions on the photograph, it was of a symposium held in New Delhi on 26 November 1956 on the occasion of 2500 birth day of the Lord Buddha. The title of symposium was Buddhism's contribution to art, letters and philosophy. The then H.R.H. Crown Prince Thondup Namgyal of Sikkim was sitting with the Jawaharlal Nehru, H.H. Dalai Lama, and H.H. Panchen Lama, and Rani Chumi Dorji of Bhutan. Realizing the influence of Buddhism in Sikkim, as depicted in the photograph, I wished to begin my sight seen at Gangtok from a monastery.

After breakfast at the guest house, we drove to Rumtek monastery about twenty four km from the Gangtok. At the gate of Rumtek monastery the solders only allowed us to walk further once I showed my identity proof. Rotating several prayer wheels to my left in the clockwise direction chanting "Om Mani Padme Hum", I stepped into the monastery. Though, I did not know the exact meanings of this mantra, I was sure it conveys my best feelings to the Lord Buddha. The strong spells of rain had drenched the miraculous monastery.

'We believe that when wind and rain bear down on prayer flags, the mantras and blessings inscribed on them are transmitted across the land,' a lama said at the Rumtek. It was really a beautiful monastery on the hill slope facing Gangtok city and guarded by the army personnel. I could see thousands of prayer flags on the sides of winding road from the Rumtek's courtyard. All these prayer flags were pitched with the hope of spreading peace and humanity.

'We perform here the sacred rituals in addition to the practices of Karma Kagyu lineage,' a lama informed me on my asking about his role in the monastery. 'It is a

Dharmachakra centre, which is a place of education and spiritual accomplishment and also the seat of glorious Karmapa.'

'Who is and where is Karmapa?' I asked him.

The lama paused. Looking at his face I presumed that my question had probably disturbed his thoughts. So I asked a different question, 'I heard something about a very popular Black Hat, which is kept in this monastery. May I know about it?'

'Yes, it is very much in the monastery,' he said.

'May I have a glimpse of it?' I asked.

'No. it is not for common visitors to see,' he replied.

'Well, can you tell me something about the history of this monastery?' I asked.

'It was built long back in sixteenth century by the ninth Karmapa. But the monastery was in ruins when the sixteenth Karmapa arrived here after fleeing Tibet in 1959. Since this locality possesses many auspicious and natural qualities, he rebuilt Rumtek, as his main seat of exile, with the help of the royal family of Sikkim and the Indian government. He inaugurated the new seat called Dharmachakra centre on losar, the Tibetan New Year's Day, in 1966,' he informed me the brief history of Rumtek.

'May I see the sitting Karmapa?' I came back to my earlier question, which was still unanswered.

'For the time being you cannot. This matter is in court. There are two groups, each supports a different candidate for the seventeenth Karmapa, and both candidates don't live here. The controversy remains between these two candidates for getting hold of the Black Hat and take over the Karmapa throne from the sixteenth Karmapa, who died in 1981. That's all I know,' he said.

Having seen and learnt a bit about Rumtek, we drove back to Gangtok and visited Do-duru chorten on the hill top surrounded by dense coniferous forests. Close to chorten was the 'Tibetology museum' depicting various stories of Buddhism and associated monasteries. It housed several Buddhist icons, paintings, statues, masks and religious objects of Tibetan art. The museum also owned a very good collection of rare manuscripts of Mahayana sect of Buddhism. Buddha was shown here in different postures, along with a story depicted through paintings of prince Gautam turning into the enlightened Lord Buddha. The story conveyed that by eradicating all defilements, ending the process of grasping and attaining realization of true nature of things, a prince became a Buddha - an enlightened or awakened one who fully comprehends the truth.

As indicated in the story, before being prince Gautam, the Lord Buddha had awaited for an appropriate time to appear in the human realm in order to attain Buddhahood and help to liberate mind. He then put the crown on Maitreya as his successor in the Tusita heaven and descended to the world. On the earth, queen Mayadevi dreamed that amidst the divine beings of spiritual world a Bodhisattva in the shape of a wandering white elephant approached her from the north and entered her womb from her right hand side. The Buddha was thus conceived on the full moon day of Vaisakha.

Besides the Lord Buddha, the museum demonstrated many other gurus who had proliferated Buddhism time and again. Here I learnt that Lhatsun Chanpo Namkhe Jigme was one of the principal Tibetan Lamas who came to Sikkim in the seventeenth century and became the patron saint of Sikkim. He was known for introduction of certain practices and revelation of certain hidden things which were later transmitted to the fifth Dalai Lama and the first Sikkimese king.

An attractive statue of a deity engrossed my attention as mostly I had come across the male gurus so far. It was a deity Tara or Dolma who was depicted as the most popular female deity in the Tibetan Buddhism. As per legends, the white Tara was known the giver of health and wealth, and the green Tara was the protector from all sorts of fears.

It was cloudy yet as per program we had to visit many other points. Most of these viewpoints were on Gangtok-Nathula highway. We drove to Tashi view point, which was constructed by one of the former kings of Sikkim, Tashi Namgyal. I was told that the Kanchendzonga could be seen from here apart from many other beautiful mountains and valleys. We waited for long to have a glance of Kanchendzonga but thick clouds all around us messed up our wish. A small cafeteria at Tashi viewpoint hence remained the centre of activities of all fellow tourists.

We drove further to visit Ganesh Tok, another vantage point. It was decorated with flags all around. At the top of the Ganesh Tok, there was a small temple of the Lord Ganesh. We entered the temple, which was small and could accommodate a limited number of visitors. The clouds had softened by then in some parts of the mountains and dales, and I could see, though in parts, the beauty of Gangtok. At a corner of the Ganesh tok, I saw some locals in makeshift shops renting out traditional attires for photography to the visitors. When asked a woman decorating a client for photograph in traditional attire revealed the rate of an instant photograph in the traditional dress was fifty rupees.

After enjoying a cup of coffee at Ganesh Tok, we drove to Hanuman Tok. I saw a part of Gangtok from this hillock due to patches of clouds hovering in the valleys and mountains. Here I bowed my head before the idols of Ram, Sita and Hanuman in the temple dedicated to the Lord Hanuman. The temple was neat and clean and seemed to be managed by the army.

The flower show at White House was the next point of our visit. Under a Japanese cedar, before entering the gate of flower show, I saw a young girl and a boy looking in one other's eyes and lost in chatting unnoticing visitors. Inside the gate I saw varieties of orchids and flowers, including Primula, Neorolgia, Lily, Hydenzea and Alstroemeria. One of the orchids, which attracted me most, was Paphiopedium hersutissimum. The hectic day visits and sight seen were ended at dinner table in a restaurant close to our guest house. Nathula was our next destination to visit, which formed the extreme north eastern part of Sikkim.

For visiting Nathula, the last border post of India in Sikkim, being a restricted and border line area inner line permits were required for Indian nationals. Foreign nationals were not allowed to visit this place without special permissions. I was told that any tour operator even drivers could manage to arrange permits on payment. I asked our tour operator who arranged a vehicle, including permits for a day visit to Nathula on eight thousand rupees. After picking up permits, next day morning we set off to visit Nathula at eight o'clock.

At the army's check post we were instructed to be back by half past three in the evening. While moving further to Nathula I was unable to see nature's beauty, which was hidden in the dense clouds. But this did not remain for long and at some point of time I could see nature's beauty in patches that had made free from clouds, sporadically. A few km away from army's check post, I saw pine and spruce in clusters at the lower elevation. Deodar began to replace such clusters while I was gaining heights.

I passed through some army camps on the way. The road on which we were moving was made on the steep mountain slopes devoid of human habitation. The road was risky and was under construction on many places due to recent landslides. Being a narrow mountain road in a very bad shape, it was a class act of the drivers to maneuver past each other while driving to opposite directions. The road condition had slowed down the pace of journey.

At a relatively gentle slope, I saw some shops in the row. This was the first human settlement with a market I came across on the way. Woolen garments and warm jackets along with coffee and tea were being sold here. Just below this settlement a river was flowing down. We had a cup of coffee and drove ahead. On way I saw a signboard of an alpine sanctuary and thought to visit it on our return trip.

After covering about forty km road distance we arrived at the Tsomgo lake. The lake seemed to be quite beautiful and eye-catching. Since Nathula was some eighteen km away from here and weather remained unpredictable in the high altitude areas, we continued our journey to Nathula. Fortunately, weather began to help us while gaining heights above thirteen thousand feet. I could now see the panoramic view of snowy mountain peaks, gorgeous valleys and stunted woody species bearing multicolored blooms. One of the most pristine and spectacular landscapes were lying before me.

Finally, we reached at Nathula. The army's check post was further hundred meters uphill from the road. I stepped out from the vehicle and began to climb the top. A bone-striking chilly breeze continued welcoming us. The fragments of snow accumulated on the mountain trail were creating hindrance to climb up. In addition, we continued fighting with low oxygen. The trail had become slippery due to continuous drizzling, and many tourists were unable to walk on the trail. I preferred to walk on the grassy slope parallel to the mountain trail, as the presence of tussock grasses made it less slippery.

Shaurya was very happy to see the snow far and wide. He wished to run and play in snowy landscape. Since it was biting cold and we did not have enough warm cloths, shortly Shaurya's rosy face began to turn murky. Just like me his hands and face had become numbed. I kept his hands in my trouser's pocket and wrapped a shawl around his face and head. This gave him some amount of relief but he remained upset.

Once I reached on the army's post I was thrilled being stepped on the borderline. Though, I had visited border areas before in Ladakh and Uttarakhand, I had never been so close to the Chinese soldiers and their check post. The borderline was marked with the barbed wire, and the Chinese army post was just at the hand's distance from the barbed wire. Generally, I had noticed no man's zone between the borders of India and China but here no man's zone was completely absent.

Walking over fourteen thousand five hundred feet above mean sea level at Nathula, my hands had become numbed and so that Shaurya's and Richa's. I saw four of our soldiers stood straight and alert. I felt deep appreciations to all of them who stayed in such inhospitable and insurmountable terrain to keep us safe from any untoward incident. I saluted to all such brave soldiers from the core of my heart.

I took few pictures of Shaurya and Richa at the top shrouded with clouds, intermittent rains and biting cold. I was without gloves and hence felt as someone had pierced thousands of needles in my hands and face. The piercing cold and instant drizzling forced us to walk back. Visibility of landscape remained unpredictable as within couple of minutes the dense clouds covered the entire landscape and in other few minutes they camouflaged in the mountains. As I walked down, I could see the winding road bringing lot of tourists in taxis to the Nathula.

Couple of minutes after stepping in the vehicle brought relief to my numbed hands and face. While coming back we visited Baba Harbajan's temple and thereafter a less-known but extremely beautiful lake - Kukup. The beauty of Kukup was further excelled by the blooming rhododendrons all around it. Yaks were grazing few meters away from the lake where ephemeral Primula had got hold of the ground.

At Shorathang, I saw a small hydropower plant which fulfilled the requirement of many battalions of army in this tough and inhospitable area. Within couple of minutes, once again we were driving back through dense clouds. Rough road and poor visibility had slowed down the vehicle's speed to about less than ten km per hour. Sooner or later we arrived at Tsomgo lake, which was about one km long and had oval shape. Like all other high altitude lakes of the Himalaya Tsomgo was considered sacred and remained frozen during winter. Enchanting flowers of Primulas and rhododendrons all around the lake were adding up in its pristine natural beauty.

As soon as we stopped close to the Tsomgo, several yak owners encircled and jammed exit of the vehicle. I asked Shaurya if he was interested in yak riding but his strong denial made me to understand his fears of riding an animal whom he had never seen before. A young lad who was nearest to my window I requested him to move a bit so that I could step out. He without uttering a single word moved away in search of other customers.

We walked around for some time while enjoying the beauty of Tsomgo. Its water was crystal clear. Many kids were taking pleasure in yak's riding. Watching their delight Shaurya's mood melted down and at last he agreed to ride the yak. I just looked around for a yak, and the lad whom I asked to move away from the vehicle was just behind me. He lifted Shaurya and placed him gently on his decorated yak's back. With some fear and joy Shaurya's yak riding was ended with a photograph in the background of Tsomgo.

While driving back we arrived at the entrance of the Kyongnosla Alpine Wildlife sanctuary. I got down to a glimpse of the sanctuary, which spanned over thirty one square km. A signboard at the sanctuary's entrance indicating the requirement of appropriate permits for carrying camera made me cautious. The gate was opened hence I entered the sanctuary's check post for permits. But it was locked and none of the employee was available. I read the last instruction, as written on the signboard in capital letters 'Defaulters are liable to be severely punished under the Indian Wildlife Act'.

I walked into the sanctuary. From ground flora to the top canopy, majority of the plants were quite familiar to me. Slowly the normal sound of forest resumed. The sanctuary endowed with varieties of rhododendrons. Many of them were blooming and others were preparing to bloom. The trailside was covered with wild strawberries and wild roses. At few places, the hood of snake lily was visible. Since there was shortage of time, I walked back within half an hour to get into the vehicle. We reached at Gangtok after six o'clock in the evening though we were instructed to reach before four o'clock.

Next day, I set off to explore Gangtok once again. Sikkim being famous for monasteries I began my exploration from the Enchey (Sang-nga-rab-ten-ling) – one of the historical monasteries founded in 1840 by Lama Drubthob Karpo. Karpo was known for his flying power. I drove through some of the fine coniferous forests of Gangtok before reaching this sixth oldest monastery of Sikkim.

On both sides of the path some huge conifer trees were planted in a row at a definite distance those appeared to be as old as the monastery. Thickets of bamboo had covered the hill slopes in front of the monastery's courtyard. Enchey had a unique architecture. Seven bowls filled with water were placed in row before and also both sides of the Buddha's statue in the monastery. Beautiful murals depicting various stories of Buddha's life had increased the Enchey's grandness and majesty.

The Himalayan Zoological Park at Bulbuli was my next destination. I saw many bamboo and cane species, including Perag and Rato nigalo just after entering the zoo's gate. The name plates hanging from these species described Perag as Arundinaria hookeriana and Rato nigalo as Thamnocalamus aristata. A few individuals of the well-known medicinal and edible timur shrubs (Zanthoxylum acanthopodium) were also planted on the roadside.

Passing through a spacious road surrounded by trees, I saw a signboard indicating an enclosure of clouded leopard. I had not seen clouded leopard before, even in the captivity. Imagining that I was going to see shortly such a fascinating leopard immediately brought a lot of happiness and enthusiasm in my mind. Walking a few steps further luckily I saw a big cat in the enclosure gazing at me. Reaching closure, I became skeptical on its identity, as it seemed to be a common rather than clouded leopard. Soon I realized the fact that the leopard I was watching was not the one that had depicted on the signboard.

I walked ahead where I saw another enclosure but there was no signboard and no animal. Walking further I passed a sharp band that led me to another enclosure with a signboard of Red Panda. I waited for a while and scrutinized the entire enclosure but could not locate a single Red Panda. Having lost my endurance I climbed up where I saw some civets and jungle cats in different enclosures. The intermittent rain had made the shortcut trail to further up quite slippery yet visitors were walking on the same trail. I walked first few steps quite cautiously as it was too slippery in the beginning.

At the end of the slippery trail the enclosure before me was of a great elusive cat, the snow leopard. I had seen once this fantastic cat a decade before in the Leh zoo. But I could not see this cat in wild even wandering in the Himalaya for decades. Snow leopard was sometime called as 'grey ghost' due to its ability to vanish into the surrounding rocks and mountains. But here in the enclosure he was lying ideally on the logs leaving past his shyness in the caves of snow clad mountains.

I walked up further into the forest on a trail made up of stones. Besides doves and babblers, I spotted a blood pheasant on one side of the trail. While coming back from the other route I reached at an enclosure of wolf but I did not see one. The moment I was passing through Red Panda's enclosure, once again, by chance I saw a Red Panda into an artificial den. After couple of minutes one more Red Panda came out from a bush, ran fast on the ground through bushes and slipped into the same den in which I had spotted one before.

Hundred meters down from the zoo's gate while eating chowmin at the lone shop, Richa noticed blood oozing out from her toe. Soon she spotted a leach sucking her blood.

This made us frightened and cautious, as well, as we had entered the world of blood suckers.

'Don't worry. These blood suckers are good for health,' looking us worried the shopkeeper said. 'You let them sucking your blood. You should not pull them out.'

'Why?' Richa asked shockingly.

'They unfasten themselves after sometime. Pulling them out creates itching on the spot,' he said.

'But how come they are good for health?' Richa asked.

'Because they suck impure blood and make you healthy. We use to place leaches on the boils, sores and infected organs. They suck all impure blood, which ultimately cures such ailments and also remove impure blood from the body,' shopkeeper enlightened us.

I had been unsuccessful for days for not being able to have a glimpse of Kanchendzonga. To retest our fortune we drove to Tashi Tok, once again. Reaching at Tashi Tok I waited for half an hour but it was of no use. Kanchendzonga remained hidden in thick clouds. We drove to Fambong Lho Wildlife Sanctuary after one more unsuccessful attempt to see Kanchendzonga.

On the way I noticed extensive farming of large cardamom on mountain slopes. There was a research institute also on the large cardamom. Driving further brought us at Pangthang where I saw the Sikkim Unit of G.B. Pant Institute of Himalayan Environment and Development. The sanctuary was quite close to this institute. I stepped out from the vehicle and walked further from this institute into the sanctuary.

The Fambong Lho had some dense forest cover. The ground flora was compact and often dominated by large and diverse fern species in patches. Polygonum polystachyum and Rumex nepalensis which I had seen in number of alpine meadows of Uttarakhand had got hold of the ground on many places. I walked deep into the sanctuary. Slowly the normal sound of forest resumed and I could hear the insects, frogs, birds and ripple of rivers and rivulets. But I could not see any big animal.

After spending some good moments in the sanctuary I walked back. Before getting into the vehicle at Pangthang, casually, I lifted up my eyes unto the Kanchendzonga and it was unbelievable. A patch of cloud had dissolved at the right side of Kanchendzonga, and a peak of this beautiful snowy mountain was peeping out from the thick clouds surrounded all around it. I had been chasing this moment for past couple of days and it became true unexpectedly when I had lost all hopes. I was mesmerized, captivated and thrilled. I was finally able to see the Kanchendzonga, which remained elusive to me for days just like snow leopard.

While descending to guest house at Devrali I could see the panoramic view of Gangtok as most of the clouds hovering here had dissolved in the atmosphere. The landscape was punctuated with waterfalls flowing down from the mountain forests. The city seemed to be congested in some pockets with high rising buildings whereas others still had some green cover. The construction of buildings was continued on the available spaces. I was afraid of the fact that if such rampant construction would continue, the charm of Gangtok, which attracted tourists from far and wide, would be lost.

I stepped out from the vehicle just three km before the guest house to visit MG Road. Being a commercial hub of Gangtok, both sides of the road were filled with consumer goods. A strip of garden in the mid of the road segregated it into double lane. The road's floor was made up of stones. Since the entry of vehicles was not permitted, I enjoyed walking here freely. Benches were placed on some regular intervals. I sat on one such bench to rest and also to watch market, tourists and their activities.

A brief rest made me stress-free and I started feeling hungry. A few steps away I saw a vegetarian hotel and within a minute I was before the hotel counter. It was too crowdy. Somehow I managed to order for a masala dosa. After finishing the early dinner I took one more round of MG Road before walking down to the guest house. All along the national highway there was a separate lane for pedestrian protected from iron pipes, which gave me a sense of security from the speeding vehicles.

Next day, I decided to go nowhere hence I just relaxed in the guest house. The room here was spacious and comfortable. A large colour TV with multichannel facility was enough to engage me throughout the day. After breakfast I sat on the balcony. I could see traffic remained disrupted frequently due to rainfall and last night's landslide on the serpent national highway. Jeevan, the guest house manager, saw me and came near for passing his time, as his all clients had gone for day excursion and he was free.

'You don't wish to go out, today,' Jeevan asked.

'I wish to relax,' I said. 'Your Sikkim is a nice place.'

'Yes, it is. But I am not Sikkimese. I am native of West Bengal,' he said.

'So what bring you here?'

'Employment, I have been working here for past nine years.'

'In the same guest house.'

'Yes, here in Dho-tapu only,' Jeevan said. 'We have tourists round the year. Being a favorite tourist destination, state government promotes nature tourism, water sports, paragliding, ice sports, adventure tourism...... You know we have casino too at Gangtok. This place was not like what it is today ten years back. But it remains a peaceful state of India.'

'It is naturally a beautiful state too,' I said.

'Have you visited Lachung?' Jeevan asked.

'Not Lachung, but I visited Nathula,' I said.

'Nathula is reopened on July 2006 only for promoting cross border trade. Being the shortest exit point to link Lhasa for Buddhist pilgrims and other visitors, the state government has proposed for regular cross border bus service through Nathula,' Jeevan said before leaving to attend a new client at the reception.

Having relaxed for over eight hours I walked in the irregular rains holding an umbrella along the highway and lanes to visit markets by the evening. I walked through Lal Bazaar where I saw a dried fish market apart from several other commercial goods. Lal Bazaar road connected MG Road and New Market to the national highway. Walking further up on the stairs of Lal Bazaar I arrived at the meeting place of New Market and MG Road. New Market was actually the further extension of the MG Road market. Being Saturday, the MG Road market was closed but New Market was opened. While coming back to guest house my interactions with shopkeepers at the Lal Bazaar made me to realize that it was cheaper than other two markets.

Next day morning, we checked out the Dho-tapu guest house and drove to Pelling via Nanchi in the south Sikkim. The driver seemed to be a teenager hence I asked the tour operator on phone about his age.

'He holds a valid driving license. Though, he seems to be teen, he is above eighteen. He has been driving for past three years,' the tour operator informed me.

On my asking the name, the driver showed me his fist. For a moment I could not understand his intension and rather looking at his fist I remained looking at his face, initially. Later, staring on his fist my sight was caught by a letter scribbled on the back of his finger and then I saw a letter on each of his left hand's finger. It began with C on back side of his thumb, which continued on rests of the fingers with H, O, N and G.

'This is my name,' he said finally.

'C H O N G, you mean Chong,' I exclaimed.

He seemed to be an interesting boy. His hairstyle was equally interesting, which was straight upright.

'How do you maintain this attractive hairstyle?' I asked Chong.

'I used jell to keep them straight upright,' he disclosed the secret with a broad smile.

On reaching at Thirty Two of national highway I got opportunity to buy some corns again from the women vendors. Leaving behind them with their job and beauties we passed by Sikkim Rehabilitation and Detoxification Centre and Ranipal bridge before reaching at Singtom - the confluence of Teesta and Ranipul. After crossing Teesta we drove on the uphill road that passed through the dense broadleaf forests with bamboo thickets. The continuity of these forests was broken by human settlements where plantation of guava and banana was common.

Chong hailed from a village of Namchi. There were two different roads to Namchi; one led through a famous tea garden and second passed through his village Turung. We selected the one that passed through the tea garden. While driving to tea garden, Chong made us cautious raising his finger to a vehicle coming from opposite direction. I saw a passenger of that vehicle peeping out through window with a hand raised in the air. Chong slowed down the speed and stopped before crossing that vehicle.

'There is a heavy landslide, which has blocked the road,' he shouted before crossing our vehicle.

'What to do now?' I asked.

'No option is left now. We have to follow other road. Sorry today you cannot see tea gardens,' having said this Chong turned the vehicle. He did not even wait for my reply.

We drove back on the same road for about fifteen km before to follow another road. The vehicle kept on gaining heights on the mountains covered with forests. From the heights I could see villages on the downhill slopes and dales. It was sometime hard to locate villages, as they were dispersed in the forests rather than congregated at some localities.

'This is my village,' Chong said.

'Well, I understand. Now you will be desperate to meet your parents,' I said.

He smiled but maintained his silence.

'I would like to see your home, too' I said.

He stopped the vehicle and soon I was in the courtyard of his house. Kids with curiosity were peeping out through a single window of a Primary School, which was just above Chong's house. His house was made up of wood. The kitchen, cowshed and chicken-shed were separated from the main house. Seasonal crops and fruit trees were growing on the land around the sheds. A lone litchi tree was overloaded with fruits. A large sheet of polythene was stretched over a pit of twenty by ten meters for harvesting rainwater to the right side of the house.

'How many households are there in Turung?' I asked Chong's grandma.

'Over two hundred,' she replied.

'But, I saw only yours and two more,' I said with surprise.

'They are in the forests on the uphill and downhill slopes, and not visible from here,' Chong's brother Surendra came forward to explain.

'What is your family size?' I asked Surendra.

'Twelve. All we live together,' he replied.

'What do you do?'

'I am in army. GR.'

'Gorkha Regiment or Garhwal Rifles.'

'Garhwal Rifle.'

'So you are on leave for two months,' I said that made him to smile.

'Over a week was spent in journey only from Ganganagar. Where are you from?' Surendra asked.

'Dehradun.'

'I have been in Shimla. Shortly my posting is due and I may be posted in Garhwal,' he said.

'Do you know some medicinal herbs?' I asked Surendra's father.

He paused for a while and said, 'neem.' Besides neem, he did not utter any other plant's name.

Having interacted briefly with Chong's family while sipping namkeen tea, we drove further to Namchi. The taste of namkeen tea had reminded me for a while the days I spent with the people of Ladakh. We drove through the Namthang forest range, which finally led us to Namchi via a small town of Namthang.

The Namchi town was a jungle of concrete in the mountains surrounded by natural forests. Many crowded multistoried buildings had sprung up here on the mountain slopes. To get rid of such a crammed place, I asked Chong to straight drive to the monastery Padmasambhav at Samdruptse. A huge idol of Buddha was placed here in open.

Being a new idol, a couple of well-trained painters were busy in drawing murals on the monastery's walls.

After watching the Padmasambhav, we drove to the site called as Chardham. Like monastery the Chardham was also a newly developed site for tourists. Most of the well-known religious shrines of Hindus were constructed here within a few hectares of land under the haven of the *Lord Neelkanth's* huge idol. I was fortunate enough to see within an hour the most venerated shrines of Badrinath, Kedarnath, Jagannath Puri, Rameshwaram and Somnath along with many revered jyotirlings of the *Lord Neelkanth*. In such a small state, it was quite astonishing how many choices were available here for tourists. After bowing head before these great shrines we drove ahead to the Buddha Park.

The Buddha Park seemed to be a picnic site. A huge idol of Buddha was placed here on a hillock surrounded by the beautiful gardens. The site was neat and clean. Though a picnic spot and quite attractive as well, I saw a limited number of tourists here. An old monastery was about half km away from the park's entrance. Six lamas of less than ten years old were playing cricket on the grassy lawns of the old monastery. Shaurya immediately joined them and played for couple of minutes before I called him to move ahead.

Pelling was our next destination where we had to stay for the next two days. The nature's beauty kept on unfolding, as we made our way across the unspoiled landscape to the hotel at Pelling. While passing through the dense forests, I saw a vendor selling vegetables in a roadside makeshift stall. Looking him alone in this dense lonely forest I surprised to think whom he sold his items. But soon I realized that people like me were his customers as I got down to buy some carrots. Having seen a bunch of different carrot colours, I asked the vendor, 'what is this?'

'Radish,' he said.

'But it is red, not white like radish,' I said.

He threw a broad smile and said nothing. Looking at some small green berries, I asked him again, 'what do you call it? Is it timur?'

'Yes,' he said. 'It is good for health and we use it as a spice in making of pickle.'

Apart from timur, red radish and carrot he was selling bamboo shoots, as vegetables. Leaving him with his drudgery in the drizzling forests, we continued our journey through dark woods and a few scattered human settlements. On the way I was unable to locate the bamboo made houses, even in the remotest villages. All along the road wherever I chanced upon a settlement or a lonely house I noticed that all were made up of concrete and cement.

Soft drinks, chips, kurkure, and all other junk food items that we had in Delhi, Dehradun and elsewhere were available in the roadside shops deep into the forest. I appreciated the marketing and advertising talents of their manufacturers who made it available at every corner of the Sikkim and elsewhere.

Having passed a large forest area and some small hamlets, I arrived at a small town of Rabong. Encountering some restaurants and hotels made me to feel hungry. To calm down my hunger without further delay I slipped into a roadside restaurant. A girl at reception welcomed me and assured to serve chowmin within twenty minutes. Soon after sitting around a table a woman at her thirties came forward to offer some water.

'Who owns this restaurant?' I asked her.

'All we four women,' she said.

'Well, this place is Rabongla,' I said looking at the signboard hanging from the roof of their hotel. 'The one we had just crossed was Rabong?'

'No, Rabong and Rabongla, both are same place,' she said. 'Rabongla is more accepted and respected. Rabong is the place and suffix la adds more respect in its name. We pay a great respect to this place, which gives us not only the shelter but also the livelihood and that's why we say it Rabongla.'

The chowmin they served us was quite tasty. Pelling was still away and dark had loomed large. We continued our journey in the dark and cloudy night. After driving into pitch dark night and heavy rainfall for two hours we arrived at the Pelling town. If Seen Villa, that was booked for our night halt was further three km away into the forest at Naku. For the next two days I had to stay at the If Seen Villa, which was a beautiful resort amid the dense forests.

Since I was informed at Gangtok that the Kanchendzonga was closure to Pelling, I asked the helper at If Seen Villa where I should go to see a clear view of it. He raised his finger to the window and said, 'peep out through this window in the morning. You will have a clear view of Kanchendzonga provided that it is not cloudy.'

I woke up early in the morning and ran to the window. But, alas! it was heavy rains outside and Kanchendzonga remained hidden in the clouds, as usual. I stepped back to my bed and slipped again inside the blanket.

Vivek - the resort manager – was a nice and helpful person. Next day, he spent most of the time with me. He walked with me into the nearby forest where I saw many birds including drango, woodpacker, dove, sparrow, finches, and many colourful sunbirds. Being the son of a herbal medicinal practitioner, he disclosed the indigenous uses of several plant species growing around his resort and in the surrounding forests. He had a fair amount of knowledge on the uses of plants as medicine.

'You know several medicinal plants,' I appreciated his knowledge.

'I know a bit but banjhakri knows better than anyone,' he said.

'Who is he?' I asked. 'Does he live close by? I wish to visit him.'

'Earlier, we had many but now it is a tedious task to find out one. One banjhakri still alive but he lives quite far away from here,' he said.

'You mean banjhakri is not a name of a person. Is it a profession?' I asked.

'Banjhakris are the practitioner of shamanism who diagnose and cure all sorts of ailments. They know innumerable medicinal plants. They also perform certain rituals during crop harvesting and also at wedding and funeral,' Vivek said.

'How do they possess such vital knowledge? Do they get this knowledge from their forefathers?' I asked.

'Banjhakri is a quite different person. He is not equated with an ordinary man. He lives in caves with his wife inside the dense forests. He seeks children who have potential to be a shaman. Whenever he finds the one he abducts him and takes him back to his cave. Though, he abducts child he does not do so out of malice. He takes care of the abducted child and teaches him all the knowledge he holds. But the child remains in danger of being eaten whole by banjhakrini, the wife of banjhakri. Banjhakrini is known as extremely brutal and blood-thirsty who carries a golden sickle in her hands. Banjhakri always protects the child from his wife. In case the child remained alive he returns home as a well trained shamanist. Such child becomes more powerful than the shamans trained by other people,' Vivek narrated in brief the whole story and history of banjhakri and banjhakrini.

'It is quite interesting and mystified, as well,' I said.

'Banjhakri is revered and celebrated as the god of forests,' Vivek said. 'He may be a spirit.'

I kept on noting down the names of medicinal plants and their indigenous uses as revealed by Vivek in the surrounding forests of the 'If Seen Villa'. By the evening I had a list of forty five such plant species, which included chestnut, pine, figs, large cardamom, wild cherry, wild daisy, young bamboo shoot, mint and morning glory.

'Have you seen flying foxes?' Vivek asked me.

'Yes, I saw couple of times,' I said.

'We have a nest of a flying fox,' Vivek said while serving evening tea in the courtyard. 'But it is very high up in the tree.'

'I can understand. Obviously, such thick forests are the ideal habitat of wildlife,' I said.

'We have Russell viper, as well,' Vivek said.

'Oh, so it is quite risky and dangerous to walk in these forests. Don't you afraid of such creatures?' I asked.

'They are nocturnal. But if seen in the day light kids use to enjoy playing with them,' he said.

'Kids play with Russell viper. I don't believe this,' I was shocked.

'Russell viper doesn't bite, generally. But once irritated it keeps on biting. We have varieties of snakes here, including the one who possesses gem, a precious stone,' Vivek said.

'Have you seen any such snake?' I asked as I was told many stories of such mythical snake in my childhood.

'Earlier, we had one such precious stone at home. It is believed that it makes someone prosperous and wealthy. My father was a very rich person. We kept it out from the home at the time of someone's delivery only. But one day because of our mistake the snake took back that precious stone. It requires to be placed on a pious site hence we place it under a banyan tree, which symbolizes the *Lord Neelkanth*. But once by mistake we forgot to put it under banyan tree during one of the delivery occasions,' Vivek said.

Having spent two days at the If Seen Villa and its nearby forests next day we loaded the luggage back into the Mahendra Xylo to set out for Darjeeling. We stepped out from the vehicle after ten km at the Padmasambhava monastery, one of the oldest monasteries of Sikkim. There was a museum in the monastery, which owns several ancient scriptures, masks, clothes, shoes of seventeenth century, utensils and weapons. Third floor of the monastery contained an old and colourful temple.

About three km away from the Padmasambhava monastery I saw the ruins of an old fort. On asking to a lama I was told that the fort was older than the monastery.

The monastery was on the hilltop and we had to drive on the downhill slopes. After about twenty km driving through a pine dominated forest I saw a group of students in school uniform planting trees on the mountain slopes. Soon I realized that it was the world environment day so I asked Chong to stop the vehicle. I walked on the slope and showed my interest to join them in planting a few saplings, which they accepted pleasingly. After planting a couple of saplings we drove further along the Rangit river, which brought us at Mailli – the confluence of Teesta and Rangit.

We left following Rangit at Mailli and drove along Teesta for sometime before gaining heights on the mountains. On the way to Darjeeling, we stopped at a vantage point where vendors were selling soft drinks, tea and some snacks. It was a beautiful area. The clouds had moved above the mountains which made us witnessing spectacular and fabulous views of mountains, forests and valleys. Deep into the valley I saw the confluence of Rangit and Teesta increasing the exquisiteness of already incredible landscapes.

The vantage point's name was the 'Lovers Point'. Such an interesting name made me to ask a vendor, 'Is there a story backing this name?'

'See down in the valley. The narrow river is Rangit and the broader one is Teesta. Rangit is a boy and Teesta is a girl. They are infatuated with each other. Both are lovers who meet down in the valley and one can see them from here. That's why it is called as the Lovers Point. The wishes of lovers are fulfilled at this point. Teesta and Rangit, the eternal lovers of each other, bless all the lovers who come here to see the confluence and wish to remain together,' he explained.

While the vendor was explaining the reason of being Lovers Point, Richa had arranged a couple of plates of Momos, Maggie and couple of soft drinks for lunch, which were ubiquitous in Sikkim. We enjoyed the lunch at the Lovers Point amidst the incredible natural beauty. Sikkim was blessed everywhere with the fantastic landscapes and amazing beauty.

On way to Darjeeling we passed through the extensive tea gardens. Women in colourful attires were busy in plucking mild twigs and leaves of tea bushes. While entering a dense pine forest I noticed clouds stretching across the landscape, and shortly the visibility had gone down to such an extent that it was difficult to see an object even at five meter distance. It was horrifying to drive in such a poorly visible mountain road having deep gorges and sharp bands, quite on and off.

It was merely four o'clock and sun had enough time to set. Chong, though, had switched on the headlight it was difficult to keep the speed. At a place I saw a narrow railway line leading along the road. The rail track crossed the road on many places. After an hour of driving with the speed of less than ten km per hour we arrived at a small railway station. Six not two train number having five small wagons stood at the station. The wagon size was so small that about sixteen persons could have been accommodated in one wagon. I had not seen before such a smallest train, except toy trains.

Finally, we arrived at the Rhododendron Resort for the night stay. By now we had been acclimatized to the rainfall, so we walked to the main city centre without caring of rains after dumping our luggage in the room. The city of Darjeeling and its main market centers were flooded with tourists. It was difficult even to walk freely. After a brief uncomfortable walk in the streets of Darjeeling we returned to the resort. I saw a few ladies like the one at Rabongla's restaurant looking after the resort. On request they served a simple, less spicy and home-made dinner.

'What brings you here?' one of the women seemed to be in her thirties asked me.

'We have to see the sunrise from the Tiger hill,' I said. 'I was told that one should be at Tiger hill before three o'clock in the morning.'

She looked at me and smiled. 'How long will you stay here?' she changed the topic.

'We have to go back tomorrow just after witnessing the beauty of sunrise,' I said.

'I am sorry to say but for past two months no one has seen the sunrise. It is too cloudy,' she informed.

'Well. Is it worth to wake up so early to see sunrise?' I asked.

'I cannot say. But the possibility of clear sky is quite dim,' she said.

I came back to my room. Since there was a least chance to see the sunrise, I made up my mind not to get up early. I slipped into the bed where I felt some bad smell. I inquired about the smell. One of the lady caretakers informed me that it was due to instant rains for past many weeks, and it was the smell of accumulated moistures in the air and beddings. Whatever was the reason I could not sleep comfortably over the night.

In the drizzling morning of next day, we set out to our return journey. We drove to Bagdogra via Khursiong, Matigara and Siliguri. The city of Bagdogra was quite crowded and chaotic, as well. Roads were in very bad state with innumerable pits and depths of despair. Quite often we stuck on streets for hours without any red light. Fortunately, we had started our journey early in the morning hours keeping high margin to catch our flight. Otherwise, in such a situation there was no chance for boarding the flight.

Ten days excursion in the peaceful land of Buddha had come to an end when I walked into the airport at Bagdogra for collecting the boarding passes at the Air India counter for flying back to hold my routine life at Bhopal via New Delhi. While fastening seat belt a sermon of the Lord Buddha echoed in my mind. 'Separation from what is pleasant is suffering. Involvement with what is unpleasant is suffering. Also, not getting what one wants and strives for is suffering. The origin of all these sufferings is bound up with desire, a thirst that makes us cling to possessions, to persons, to life itself. It is a thirst which can only be occasionally satisfied but not ultimately assuaged.'

Rumtek monastery in Sikkim

32.0

The Roof of the World

Kargil war had come to an end. I had got green signal in 1st week of September 1999 for my much awaited visit to survey herbs and herbal practitioners of Ladakh. I boarded in Air India at Delhi. After some struggle and ifs and buts in the air finally the pilot landed the aircraft at Leh. The city of Leh and its adjacent areas seemed to be altogether a different world for me. The mountains were beautiful but unlike the Garhwal Himalaya they were without green attires. The Leh valley had some green patches along the Indus. I had couple of months in hand for knowing this unique land on our planet.

Dorje – my assistant and guide, as well – had arranged logistics for my stay at Leh as a paying guest before my arrival. After few weeks of interactions with the local people of Leh, Rumbak, Choglamsar and Thikse I planned to visit the Karakoram Wildlife Sanctuary in Nubra valley, which was further north of Leh. Since it was a borderline area, the inner line permit was required from district commissioner's office to visit the Nubra valley. So I prepared the permit and also hired a taxi. Illiyas – the taxi driver - was a well built local young Ladakhi. To enter the Nubra valley one had to cross a pass – Khardung la. The term 'la' stands for pass in local dialect.

Next day on way to Nubra, I passed by army convoys, frequently. Human habitations were scanty all along the valleys and mountains. The serenity of these valleys and mountains were often broken by the sound and echo of army's convoys. The road was broken at many places due to heavy landslides hence was under repair. Even in the bone-striking cold, the labours were busy with their jobs. Local person was hardly seen in the labour's groups, as I could easily identify them from their distinct dialect and mongoloid features. While passing close to them I observed that they were mainly from Bihar. I contemplated and appreciated their hard work, determination, and struggle for existence, which had brought them here from the warm plains to such an extremely cold mountains in which temperature even went down to - 40 °C during winter.

When asked I submitted a copy of my permit at the South Pullu. The road beyond this point was in a very bad shape. I was about to reach at Khardung la, just 300 m away from the pass, suddenly I noticed that Illiyas was trying hard to drive ahead. The gypsy had almost refused to obey his orders and it was almost out of control. To keep in control, Illiyas slowed down the gypsy's speed to 1-2 km per hour. When it became extremely difficult to drive I got down and asked Illiyas not to take further risk. While I walked a few steps away from the gypsy I realized that the road had become extremely slippery. I felt as I was walking on a glassy wall or slope. The snowfall and its continuous deposition on ground had turned into a thick layer of hard ice. The army's convoys had pressed it further, which made it harder and slippery. Walking just a few minutes on this ice had numbed my hands and legs, and I was not able to move anymore.

Illiyas even being a skilled hill driver was also afraid of the sheer downhill slope. He got down and waited for couple of minutes to recoup his broken courage. We could see the remains of trucks met accidents in the dale and broken taxis hanging from the rock cliffs and boulders. We decided to push the gypsy further, as long as we could do so. Whenever Illiyas gathered some courage, now and then, he tried to drive the vehicle for few meters. Somehow with lot of struggles we arrived at Khardung la. It took us above 1½ hrs to cover just 300 m.

At Khardung la the roadside board reads 'the world highest motorable road; 5600 m above mean sea level'. It gave me a great pleasure and relief. I was made to understand that before meeting the goal one has to successfully qualify the hard work and patience is required.

I walked on the scattered fresh snow and took some snaps of Khardung la and the spectacular scenic beauty of hills lying in front of me. I had a cup of tea with some snacks in a café at the la. Close to the café a shopkeeper was selling memento of Khardung la. Some life forms could be seen surviving at this altitude of 5600 m. Leontopodium, Acantholimon and some aconites were visible amidst snow. The lines of colourful penchants unfurling at the summit had increased its beauty.

After this short break we drove to North Pullu and here I again submitted a copy of my permit at the army's camp. North Pullu onwards was continuous downhill drive for half an hour till we reached at a spot having 2-3 tea stalls. We crossed Khardung village, which was about 30 km away from Khardung la, and after about 28 km drive we arrived at Khalsar. Here we had our late lunch. The road bifurcated at the few km downhill from the Khalsar. We continued following the road leading to our left. The other road on the right was leading to Panamik – the base camp of the Siachen glacier.

Down in the Nubra valley along both the flanks of Shyok river some scattered bushes of seabuckthorn could be seen. A few individuals of Salix trees were also visible in the dale. Nubra valley was relatively flat, wide and crisscrossed by the winding channels of the Shyok and Nubra rivers. The landscape and greenery had changed with my progress to Diskit from arid cold desert to an oasis. Eight km before Diskit, I passed through a beautiful village named Hunder surrounded by agricultural fields, orchards and sand dunes. I could see a Gompa at Diskit on the top of a hill. At night, I stayed in a hotel of a small town of Diskit in the beautiful Nubra valley.

Since I had to stay long in the land of Ladakh, I had to be accustomed forcefully to eat Ladakhi foods, mostly chowmin and thuppa. Ladakhis used to prepare several varieties of chowmins, both vegetarian and non-veg. The delicacy of chowmin here was unmatchable with what I had earlier in Dehradun and other cities. Despite such delicacy I was always desperate to find out some hotel that could serve me rice and chapatti. After a long search in Leh, I found a shopkeeper who agreed to cook some rice and chapatti, especially for me. Though the way he cooked had made the food tasteless, I was satisfied at least having my routine meals. I asked hotel manager at Diskit if he could afford some chapattis but his answer in negative dissolved my hope and I was forced to compromise with chowmin again at the dinner.

The other day I walked in the narrow but clean and lonely road of Diskit. I saw men and women working hard together in their agriculture land while enjoying chorus equally. Some had ploughed their farms and others were still ploughing with the help of yaks. Yak seemed to be their major property, which they used not only in agriculture and transportation but also used as food.

Chatting with such happy farmers I got to know that they used to produce wheat, barley, peas, mustard, apple, walnut, apricot and even some almond. The orange berries of the *tsestalulu* (sea buckthorn bush) were also harvested seasonally by local people. In comparison to other parts of Ladakh Nubra valley was green and had good farming land. The original name of Nubra was Ldumra, which literary meaning was the 'valley of flowers'.

At the eastern corner of Diskit, there was a monastery surrounded by the grove of Salix. While walking on the edge of the farmland I saw a unique and healthy camel browsing spiny seabuckthron in the barren land. I walked further to look it from the close distance. There were four other camels, and all had double hump. These camels were uncommon and unique to me due to their double humps. They were also called as Bactrian camel or double humped camel.

At the lunch, I happened to meet a lama – a Tibetan monk, who was sharing the same table.

'Jhule,' I said with respect.

'Jhule,' he replied.

The term 'Jhule' was similar to Namastey for Buddhists in Ladakh.

'Nubra valley is beautiful. Where is the last boundary of our country's territory?' I asked.

'Turtuk is the last village of India in this valley. Beyond which is Pakistan. During last month's war Pakistan's army had supplied arms and ammunition to this village. Fortunately, our army had smelled the problem and raided the village overnight to seize such dangerous weapons,' he informed.

This fuelled my interest to visit Turtuk, and I informed the same to Illiyas.

'It needs special permit to go there', Illiyas informed.

'Why? I am not foreigner. I have submitted permits twice already. This is my country and I don't need permission again and again to walk in my own country. Anyway I am not going to cross the international border. Turtuk being in India can be visited by any Indian,' I said.

'Well! But this is the rule,' he said.

'Do villagers have such special permits to come down to Leh? How does army ensure their identity?' I asked.

'There is a limited bus service and securities deputed at check posts generally know all the villagers,' he replied.

'In case I am one of the villager's relative lives in Leh and out of Ladakh,' I quizzed.

There was a pause for some moment. 'Securities enquire if they find out any unknown person in the bus and make sure his/ her identity,' Illiyas replied.

The conversations had faded my hope. Looking at my face Illiyas said, 'don't worry sir. I am Ladakhi and they will not stop me. I shall take you there.'

Next day, we drove to Turtuk. Just after 3 km there was an army check post. We shut the window's glasses, which were coated with a light black sheet. No one from outside could see us now, and at check post no one had given any signal to stop us. We drove further and arrived at a broad open valley. Several army trucks, loaded and unloaded with soldiers and provisions, crossed us on the way. I was surprised to note that many soldiers had even saluted our gypsy, as we were not visible and they probably assumed that some army officer was patrolling in the gypsy.

There was no other vehicle on road except army's convoys. We passed through an army cantonment at Thoise. By now many questions had flooded in my mind. If I am caught without permit then god knows what will happen. This is not fair and reasonable. I should go back. I questioned myself. In contrast to me Illiyas was quite cheerful and laughed whenever any solder saluted the gypsy.

I asked Illiyas to return but he kept on speeding the vehicle. He tried to persuade and convince me. After some moments of dilemma I firmly asked him to turn back to Diskit. While coming back I was equally worried about our army. If some terrorist happened to be in my gypsy and if it was a terrorist's vehicle then .... If I was a terrorist ....

Having spent the night at Diskit, I backtracked to the bifurcation point from where I took the other road that led me to Sumur. Sumur being the village of one of my colleagues, Rinchen Wangchuk, who had shifted at Leh, I got down here to meet his family. His elder sister was at Sumur. She insisted me to stay at Sumur. I met couple of amchis of Sumur while staying at her house, and in the evening I visited the village famous monastery, Samstening Gompa. Sumur seemed to be an oasis itself in the middle of an extensive cold desert.

Next day, I drove to Panamik that was further twenty km away from Sumur. There was a hot water spring at the Panamik village. An old amchi at Panamik informed me the magical medicinal properties of the hot water spring. He used to advise his patients to take bath in the hot water spring, especially to the patients suffering from skin diseases. After chatting with villagers and amchis I visited an old monastery at Panamik that was known as Ensa Gompa.

The world highest battlefield, Siachen glacier, was located a few km away from Panamik. But I was not permitted to visit beyond Panamik. Kargil war had just come to an end but I did not come across any sign of conflicts wherever I passed through. I had to drive back through the peaceful area, full of flowers and friendly people.

Reaching back at Leh, I decided to visit the high reaches of Markha valley that was located in the south of Leh. Next day, I along with Dorje set off to see the best habitats of snow leopard in the wonderful high altitude areas of the Hemis National Park, which formed the upper part of the Markha valley.

There was motorable road upto Spituk from Leh, and after Spituk the road was under construction till Zincher. The bridge over Indus at Spituk had been dismantled due to flash flood just few days before our arrival in Leh; so we decided to follow the another way to Zincher via Kya. Though, there was no proper motorable road but somehow Illiyas managed to drop us three km before Zincher.

The Hemis National Park, from the place Illiyas dropped me, was approachable only by walking or riding on mules or horses. On my inquiry, a passerby disclosed the difficulty of getting horses and donkeys at the place we were dropped. I was told that at one km uphill a small mud house owner had a few donkeys. I requested Dorje to go there for hiring a couple of them.

After one and half-hour Dorje came back with donkeys along with their owner. I learnt then that Ladakhi used to say *Khote* to the donkey. Besides yaks, *khote* used for transporting goods in the mountains. *Khote*'s owner refused to go with us as he was preoccupied in seasonal harvesting of crops, mainly barley. He wanted us to drive his Khote but none of us was familiar with the way to Rumbak – our destination for the day; so we requested him again and again to accompany with us but he refused to do so.

At one moment he agreed to go with us on higher payment but in next moment he denied this deal too. I did my best to convince him but there was a lot of confusion, also due to poor communication, as he was not familiar with Hindi and speaking Ladakhi was milking a ram to me. Dorje, who was translating the Ladakhi into Hindi was also failed to convince him and finally the Khote's owner returned home with his *Khote*. Later, I came to know that he was the only person at that place with *Khote* and so that there was no possibility to get any mode of transport for further journey.

Sun had approached at the mid of the sky. Due to scorching heat, we took shelter under a small Salix shrub, as the place was devoid of trees. Many tourists' parties, mostly foreigners, were trekking up and down on the way to Rumbak. I asked almost every tourist guide to accommodate our luggage but my hope faded away with the time. I lost hope to reach Rumbak. I thought it would be better to camp at the very spot and hence I asked Dorje to gather and pile up the luggage on a relatively flat place.

Since morning I did not have meal except a cup of tea in the early morning, I was feeling hungry and had passed through couple of black outs. In such situation, it was difficult to climb further so we decided to pitch our tents for night halt in the hope of getting some mode of transport for further trek in the next day.

Dorje took out some rice and pulses and started cooking *Khichdi*. I stretched the tent and started pitching it. While doing so, I saw a tourist party of over two dozen of foreigners climbing to Rumbak, which again aroused my hope. I thought there is no harm to make one more attempt. I asked for help but the guide of that party showed his inability, as he had no free mule and space to upload our luggage.

During conversation I came across the fact that the guide was native of Rumbak. This tip led me to think that he might know one of my fellow researchers from Dehradun who had camped in Rumbak for over three years to study feeding ecology and home range of snow leopard.

I introduced myself as that researcher's colleague and tried to read his face. The guide thought for a moment and promised me to send few horses to carry my luggage as soon as he reached in Zincher. Needless to say, this really gave me a great relief. Later, I came to know that he was Namgiyal who happened to be one of the field assistants of that researcher during his study in the Hemis National Park.

Namgiyal extended his kind support to my visit in the Hemis. That evening he took me to Zincher and next day to Rumbak. While trekking to Rumbak, Namgiyal showed me a gorge where he had helped in radio collaring the first snow leopard. At Rumbak, I stayed in Namgiyal's house and enjoyed his unforgettable hospitality.

Rumbak was a nice high altitude village located above four thousand meter elevation. It was encircled by several mountain peaks, including Chhaslung, Lungtung, Choksti, Hushing-la and Sabgwat. On the very first evening at Rumbak, I spotted a large herd of blue sheep grazing on the slopes of Chhaslung. Being a small village Rumbak had eleven households and a primary school. Tourism and agriculture was the major occupation of the villagers.

The upper altitudinal limit of the human settlements in Ladakh was higher than the other parts of the Himalaya. The vegetation around Rumbak was mainly dominated by Artemisia, Nepeta, Causinia etc. In the river valleys presence of water gave way to the dominance of grasses and sedges with a few herbaceous species. The bushes of seabuckthorn were mostly seen in the lower river valleys.

I continued my trek from Rumbak to Shingo and Sku. Before reaching at Chillung I had encountered many marmots nibbling high altitude nutritious fodder. Chillung was located in the bank of river Zanskar. Here I had to cross the Zanskar by a trolley that was constructed by Leh Nutrition Department with the aid of UNICEF. The Youth Club of Chillung village took care of the trolley. They used to lock the trolley and only opened it whenever somebody went for crossing the river. As usual, the trolley was locked at the other side of river and the village was not visible from the point I was standing. I was quite tired but there was only one option to climb up on the mountain for calling up somebody to release the trolley.

Panting and prodding, somehow, I managed to climb up and after one and half hours of repeated callings a person heard me and came to release the trolley. Once I was pushed to the other side of the river, he asked me to pay four hundred rupees on account of using trolley to cross the river. I tried to negotiate but it did not work out and I finally paid the entire amount. At Leh, when I interacted with Rinchen Wangchuk, I was told that there was no such condition for crossing the river. He said that tourists might pay some donation for maintenance of the trolley but it was not mandatory. Anyway, this was one of the additions in my experiences of exploring the roof of the world.

It is relatively easy with pen or camera, to record the outward appearances of mountain, its scenic beauty, peculiar flora-fauna and its inhabitants. Many travelers do so but more is required to capture the essence of the land, the fragrance of the blooms, or to see into the heart of the local inhabitants. The land of mountains so hard and harsh, so empty and awesome, it troubles the mind and physical stamina.

The panoramic view of Leh

33.0

The Floating Heaven

On a pleasant morning I took off to Srinagar by Air India from Raja Bhoj Airport of Bhopal. There was no direct flight so I had to change the flight at Delhi. Kashmir being a first choice of tourists, there was a lot of rush and somehow I managed to book tickets a week before in SpiceJet from Delhi onwards. The flight from Bhopal got delayed by thirty minutes and I landed on Terminal III of the Indira Gandhi International Airport at 10.50 am.

The connecting flight to Srinagar was at 12.20 and I had one and half hrs in hand, which seemed sufficient to catch it. But when I came to know that SpiceJet was operated from Terminal one, which was quite away from Terminal III, I needed to get better speed. I had to collect my boarding pass forty five minutes before the schedule departure. Coming out from the aircraft and then from Terminal III had consumed twenty five minutes.

On the helpdesk I got to know that for transfer passengers there was shuttle bus service, which covered the distance between these two terminals in about fifteen to twenty minutes. As per this calculation every moment had become precious for me, and I was running short of time because I had to collect boarding pass forty five minute before the departure. Naturally, the panic loomed large.

I looked around for a shuttle bus, and ran to catch immediately as soon as I saw one at the stand. It was empty. Enquiring the driver I got to know that still there was ten minutes remained for the schedule departure of the bus. I was puzzled on account of this big obstacle in visiting my long cherished dream. I got into the bus with deep agony. I was not sure on my destiny whether to go back or stay in Delhi.

Three foreigners, by the time, had seated in the bus. The driver was laughing outside on some jokes with his fellow drivers. I was not in the position to share his happiness. Rather I got out from the bus and requested him to drop me as the time to depart was approaching fast. I was though skeptical on his reaction, but he realized my problem and hence consoled me. He assured to drop me at the stipulated time.

On reaching, frantically, at the Terminal One, I rushed to SpiceJet counter. There was a long line of passengers waiting for their turn to collect boarding passes. I stood for a minute in the queue but then thought to take a risk. I walked to a closed counter where a girl was talking over phone. I somehow managed to convince her to issue my boarding pass. The delight to visit Kashmir had returned in my heart and face while walking to security check holding the boarding pass.

I was quite happy to see the snow-laden mountains after long period. I remained in the air flying above and through the clouds for one hour and ten minutes before

I landed on the Srinagar's Airport. All fellow passengers, mostly from Bengal and Gujarat, became excited on hearing the announcement of crew captain that outside temperature was fourteen degree Celsius.

While collecting luggage from belt number two, I noticed that passengers had become busy in wearing warm cloths. I too wore my woolen sweater, cap and muffler. While dragging my luggage through the exit, a person asked, 'bus or taxi.'

'May I know the rates?' I asked.

'Five hundred rupees for taxi and fifty rupees per person for bus to drop at the Dal.'

I thought to travel by bus and bought three tickets; one for myself and one each for Shaurya and Richa who were traveling with me.

The bus dropped us at the TRC. While coming out from the bus soon I found myself surrounded by the men-folk. Soon I got to know that they were hotel boys, houseboat owners, rickshaw drivers, tourist guides, and their well wishers. After a lot of discussions, confusions, and negotiations, I decided to stay in the houseboat. I narrowed down my selection to a cheerful lad among the houseboat owners.

Driving to houseboat at the Dal, Zubic - the houseboat owner, showed me some houseboats down in the narrow gullies, which were cheaper. 'Sir, during season Amarnath pilgrims use to stay in these houseboats,' he said.

A boat, locally called as shikara, was waiting for us in the Dal. We got into shikara and within five minutes I was dropped into the houseboat. I gazed over the Dal, it was really beyond my imagination, and expectation. I had been in Nainital, Bheemtal, Hemkund, Kakbhusandi and was living in the city of lakes for past four years, but Dal was unique and larger than all I had visited earlier. Zubic served us a special Kashmir tea in 'the floating heaven'. The low temperature and extreme beauty of Dal had increased the taste of tea and pleasant atmosphere. There were four rooms in the houseboat and all were well decorated with carpets of maroons and red shades, mostly.

In the evening, I thought to have a round of the Dal. I rode into shikara with Shaurya and Richa at 5.00 pm, which carried us to a garden named after Pandit Nehru in the middle of the Dal. Besides colourful flowers, here I saw a couple of middle sized chinar trees and a few movable photographic shops. Tourists were busy in getting photographed, especially in Kashimiri attires.

We drove further in shikara to see 'the floating gardens' and 'floating markets' in the beautiful Dal. 'Here villagers grow vegetables during season,' raising finger towards the floating garden our shikara driver, Basir said. Many villagers were floating in their boats from one side of Dal to other. Dal was full of life floating on the serene and vibrant water. I purchased two grams of saffron by paying six hundred rupees from a floating shop close to a village. One of the shopkeepers was holding a 'kangdi', a small heating system. On my enquiry he informed me that it was a type of addiction in the winter and once someone started enjoying its warmth it was difficult to live without it.

The golden view of sunset resting on and in the Dal was mind-boggling and unmatchable. Gradually, the dark had started to fasten this tremendous beauty in its lap. Despite the brutal attempts of dark the Dal's beauty was not brought down, which remained attractive in one form to other. Dal's scenic beauty remained visible and had adorned by the lightings coming from the houseboats and impinging on its water. Many colours emerged and submerged in the lake, in the night.

At the dinner, I preferred to have some local Kashmiri dishes. Zubic helped me to select from the menu. I ordered for Kashmiri pulao, Alu Kofta and some chapatti with some mixed vegetables. The Kashmiri pulao was really tasty and had some unique flavor due to mixing of some local herbs. Though I was not tired, I went to bed early at 9.30 p.m. due to cold that made me to wrap myself in two warm blankets. Zubic had also given me a hot water rubber bottle to keep inside the bed. It remained warm till morning and I enjoyed its heat in the quite low temperature throughout the night.

Late in the night, my deep sleep was broken down due to sudden outburst of lot of noises just outside the houseboat. I removed blanket from my face and tried to listen and understand the situation. A day before of my arrival at Srinagar, there was a news in almost all the TV channels about a militant attack in a hotel Silver Star at Naugaun, just outskirt of Srinagar. I thought that militants had attacked again and that's why people were crying and shouting for help.

I got up and looked at my mobile for time. It was 5.30 am. I went to unbolt the door. Before I did so, I felt severe cold. I was not able to stand even for a minute without warm clothes. I got back into the bed but my mind was outside the room. After a long effort, finally I could make out a voice in the hullaballoo. 'Allah ho Akbar' that made me to calm down. It had become holier-than-thou time of 'namaaj'.

In the early morning hours, I came out to see the sunrise but the Dal was shrouded in the fog. It was severe cold and many water birds were bathing in Dal's freezing water. Watching them playing, swimming and bathing made me to feel more chilly.

While standing in the houseboat's balcony and watching the fabulous beauty of Dal, a shikara stopped just below me. A person riding in shikara greeted me and stepped up in the houseboat with a suitcase. He had opened and spread his shop before me, which was locked in the suitcase a minute before. He had shown me several colourful stones and jewelry wrapped in piece of papers. He wanted to convince me to buy at least something as a gift of Kashmir. But his smile kept on fading gradually with my constant unwillingness.

After having a warm cup of tea, I said goodbye to Zubic and left houseboat. For breakfast I looked around for a restaurant. In the busy road of Dal, there were many hotels but limited restaurants. I entered a busy restaurant in anticipation to get some fresh breakfast. I ordered mixed vegetable paranthas and by the time it was served to me I had time to browse the local newspaper lying on one side of the table. The headline in the Greater Kashmir read 'Silver Star shoot out, cops questions witnesses.'

The second major news was 'It is December in October.' To calm down my surprises on December in October I read further. 'Weather conditions worsened in Kashmir valley as temperature in summer capital fell by five degree Celsius to send people shivering much ahead of winter.'

I could see clouds hovering on the upper reaches of mountains, most of them had received fresh snowfall. The drizzle had forced people even at Srinagar town to take out warm cloths. Autumn generally remained a dry season in the valley, known for fading and falling leaves before the severe cold winter started in December. However, since the day I had entered the valley, weather was cold, particularly during morning and evening.

After finishing paranthas I stepped out from the restaurant and waived my hand for a vehicle. An auto-rickshaw responded quickly and stopped in front of me. I negotiated rates for hiring the rickshaw for full day and finally the rickshaw driver agreed on seven hundred rupees. I found Manjoor, the driver as well as the owner of rickshaw, a very cheerful and jovial fellow.

Manjoor first of all drove us to Sankaracharya temple, which was on the hilltop. The road was narrow and at the last stretch it was packed in the heavy traffic from all sides. 'Travelling in rickshaw is always better. It has advantage over taxi as it requires less space and one can drive and turn it even in crowdy places where taxi cannot move,' Manjoor said proudly while driving his rickshaw through the limited spaces among the stranded vehicles. 'Sir, you leave your camera and mobile in rickshaw.'

'Why,' I said. 'I have to take pictures.'

'Mobile, camera and electronic equipments are not allowed in the temple premises due to security reasons,' he said.

Once the rickshaw stopped I got down and started climbing the temple stairs, which was over two hundred fifty six in number. The view of the valley was quite broad and mesmerizing from the temple. I could see the wide range of Dal and other water bodies dotted with numerous houseboats on the fringes.

After Shankaracharya temple, Manjoor drove us to the Pari Mahal. On way I noticed army on duty at every hundred to two hundred meters interval. While driving rickshaw Manjoor Ahmad Malik seemed to be the happiest person of Srinagar. He kept on singing some local songs, at the same time he wanted to convey me all the information whatever he knew about the Kashmir, its historical monuments, gardens, lakes, peoples, politics and army. While talking politics, at a point of time, all of a sudden his smile faded down. He seemed to be highly unsatisfied with both state and centre government's functionary. He was worried on the depth of corruption in the country. And he was upset on the scams committed by politicians across the party lines.

Finally, he dropped us at the Pari Mahal. It was really the castle of fairies. Made on the mountain slopes it was one of the best vantage points adorned with colourful flowers. Besides thick forests and forests dotted with buildings, I could see the golf ground down in the valley. I wanted to spend some more moments in the fairies castle but we had to visit number of gardens and time did not permit to stay more at one place. We moved on to see Nishat Baag, the garden of gladness, made long back by mogul emperors. Nishat bag was adorned with myriad flowering blooms.

The Shalimar baag was the next garden we visited. It was beautiful as usual and was dominated with yellow, red, and orange hues. Many chinar trees planted four hundred years ago by moguls were visible here in couple of rows. All chinar trees had attained majestic heights and huge girths over the period of time symbolizing the grandness of mogul's kingdom. Standing beneath their huge crown cover had brought me in close proximity to feel those mogul emperors who had planted and enjoyed these royal trees.

I saw a lone chinar tree fallen on the ground. Tourists were playing and walking on its trunk and branches. They had probably met their unfulfilled desire of holding and climbing the standing chinar trees and its branches, which was otherwise not possible.

In every garden, the entry fee was same – ten rupees per adult and five rupees per kid below twelve. We had lunch in a dhaba just opposite to the Shalimar baag's gate. The dhaba was mainly crowed by Bengalis. Since evening had approached us and we had become tired, I asked Manjoor to stop the sight seen programme.

While coming back to Dal, Manjoor cautioned me about some undesirable things and incidences happened with tourists due to their ignorance. 'These shikara owners are very cleaver guys. They ferry tourists to the remote villager's shop where no one generally goes as they are almost disconnected from the main land. Shikara is the only way to reach upto them. Whatever tourists purchase there from the shopkeepers, twenty five percent goes to them. In Srinagar, everywhere, everyone's percentage is fixed. Ultimately, all such money goes from the tourist's pocket. In such situation, do you think they sell genuine items?' he informed me.

'It is surprising,' I said. 'Yesterday I purchased some saffron exactly in the situation you just have mentioned. The shikara owner did exactly whatever you speak.'

The accommodation for night halt was yet to be decided so I asked Manjoor if he could help me out. He informed me that he had already arranged one for our night stay. I was surprised as I had never asked him to arrange any accommodation for us. I was surprised on account that whoever I met in Srinagar he was a mobile shop of information and was able to arrange anyone's tour package and programme. Once I got into the bus at Airport, the bus driver was keen to book a room in hotel for us. When I got down from the bus at TRC, people started negotiating rates of hotels and vehicles. The houseboat owner was keen to arrange my rest of the tour programme. And once I left houseboat it was the turn of rickshaw driver.

Manjoor took us to Laxmi Guest House, which was cheaper and more spacious than the houseboat. The guest house owner was a Kashmiri Pandit, and Manjoor belonged to Muslim faith. I had heard and read about the riots and conflicts taken shape in the past between Kashmiri Pandits and Muslims in Srinagar but here the case was different. For past forty eight hours I had met Muslims only right from my stay at houseboat to shikara riding, hotels, dhabas, and auto rickshaw. Manjoor even being a Muslim arranged my stay in a Hindu's guest house. This not only touched me irrespective of the reason but also compelled me to contemplate what really was responsible for riots in the heaven.

I walked along the Dal, next day, and I was frequently asked by the boatmen and auto rickshaw to ride in their respective shops. I kept on denying and tried to make them understand that I had already enjoyed the same and I was willing to just walk. Without any negotiations they themselves started reducing the rates from three hundred rupees to two hundred and even one hundred fifty for one hour drive in shikara. In the beginning, I responded their queries but later on I just ignored extending my hands in the air. After half-an-hour of this exercise I began to feel uneasiness to respond them and so I decided to leave the Dal and hence turned to walk to the Badami Baag. Enjoying the sporadic sight and shadow of chinar, deodar and poplar I reached at the Badami Baag Cantonment area.

On my return from the Badami Baag, I saw ten to twelve goats surrounded by a group of people at the roadside. I stopped in the crowd and peeped in to understand the situation. When the crowd became relatively thin I inquired a person in beard holding the long hairs of a goat neck. I learnt from him that he came from Jammu to sell his goats here to the prospective buyers, as Id-ul-Juha or bakerid was scheduled just after five days on twenty seventh day of October. The cost of a goat ranged from eleven thousand to sixteen thousand rupees, obviously depending on the weight.

He used to point out goats as 'shawal' in his local Kashmiri language. His all 'shawals' had long hairs. One of the full grown adults 'shawal' weight was roughly around one quintal. The shepherds called as 'bakarwals' in Kashmiri language who lived on the move likewise other pastoral communities in the Himalaya. The bearded person, who was one of the goat's owners, informed me that he climbed to alpine meadows of Drass and Kargil with his flocks during the summer and descended to Shivalik hills near Jammu during the winters. The alpine meadows, locally called as 'Marg' in Kashmir, being rich with nutritious fodder maintained good health and growth of goats. All the 'margs', Sonmarg, Gulmarg and so on and so forth were also the beautiful scenic places in Kashmir and hence visited by a large number of tourists.

I left 'bakarwal' with his fate and moved further where I saw two girls of seven to eight years were saying ill to each other. Looking at me, they forgot to fight and jumped before me with folding hands. Before I could understand the situation they stretched their hands and started begging some rupees. In-spite of responding to their request, I imposed a question regarding the cause of fighting between them just before my arrival in the picture.

The girl who reached first in front of me for begging had explained that the other one had interrupted while she was begging from a customer. 'The customer took out ten rupees that he wished to hand over me but she grabbed the same before me. It is my money, which she did not want to return. She even did not want to share fifty percent of the money which is mine,' she explained. I advised them not to fight again like this and moved ahead.

In a narrow crowded market, I saw a few vendors selling lotus stalks on a roadside with other vegetables. At a small square, women were selling some local live fishes and on the right side of the road a person was selling apple at forty rupees per kg. Surprisingly, the cost of coconut, which brought here all the way from south, was cheaper than coastal areas like Goa.

I returned at Dal lake and was about to sit on the main roadside wall. A boatman, just beneath the road in the lake, came shouting toward me, 'photograph please. I am cheaper than any other in the Dal, and I make beautiful photographs.' He opened an album and tilted it to show me the photographs.

'What is your rate?' I asked.

'Per photo rupees hundred to hundred fifty only,' he replied. 'This rate is only for you otherwise I charge rupees two hundred minimum.'

'Thank you, I am not interested,' I said.

Along the Dal lake I could see different shades of houseboats in line however the grey shades had dominance over all others. Many shikara were floating before the houseboats in the Dal. My sight, all of a sudden, was caught by a signboard on a shikara 'Valley of Flowers'. This signboard reminded me the alpine meadows of the Garhwal Himalayas where I had stayed for several years to learn about flowers. I noticed that every shikara's name was quite catchy; Rosa, Mountain Beauty, Prince, Sapna, Moon Light, Golden Lily, Monalisa and Lotus were some of name attracted me.

Next day, after breakfast, I got into an auto rickshaw and purchased some more dry fruits at Lal square, before traveling to airport. The shopkeeper at Lal square, like any other shopkeeper, wanted to assure me that he had the best quality of dry fruits. He took a walnut and broke it into pieces by pressing between thumb and fingers without much effort. I had never been against of hard walnuts. Rather I always enjoyed breaking the hard walnuts, especially the way it engaged someone to take out its edible parts. I generally used needle to separate and drag out its tasty edible part.

The rickshaw driver dropped us just one km before the airport, and advised us to take taxi from there. Luckily, I saw a taxi on the roadside though there was no taxi stand. The taxi driver was kind enough to allow us to get into his taxi. I noticed that there was no passenger in the taxi having fourteen seats. Unexpectedly, without losing a second, the taxi driver drove us to the airport.

While driving, before I asked, he himself informed me that a party was waiting for him at the airport but he could not move in as no vehicle was allowed to enter without passenger in the airport's premises. He thanked me before I said something. There was strict security check in. We were checked at four consecutive entry points before reaching to the counter for getting boarding passes. I was advised at the counter not to take hand baggage as it could cause delay. The security might also not permit for the same.

Holding my boarding pass I again passed through three security check in before the final security pass. Since I had a small handbag containing my camera, binocular and couple of apples, the security asked me to open the bag and click the camera. I was instructed to finish the apples before final boarding and entering the aircraft.

At the airport, I found inadequate facilities for passengers. The signboards were not clear. Bathrooms were old fashioned, dirty and poorly maintained. The announcement was so bad and the sound system was so poor that I was unable to draw any meaning out of that voice. Overall, it was comparable with a railway station.

While I was thinking about the airport, all at once, I saw a fellow passenger in hurry dropped his luggage on the toe of a lady. She cried in pain like anything. Within seconds, her toe started bleeding but no one had time to pay any attention to her pain rather everyone was busy selfishly in getting their work to be done.

Prior to final boarding, I was called up again by security to identify my luggage before loading it into the flight no AI 822. I did so and came back into the waiting room. I had not gone through such a security system ever before flying anywhere, even to deliver a lecture at the Pennsylvania State University of the United States of America just before the nine / eleven terrorist attack on the World Trade Centre.

We had to fly via Jammu and just before take off a crew member announced, 'The distance to Jammu will be covered in thirty minutes. We shall stay at Jammu for another thirty minutes before our final departure to New Delhi.' The schedule arrival of flight at Delhi was 17.00 hrs but it had been delayed for thirty minutes.

My boarding time to connecting flight for Bhopal was 17.30 hrs and I had just landed at Delhi. I had to go through the security check again at Delhi airport. I rushed with Shaurya and Richa to the security, by the time I heard the announcement, 'This is the final call for boarding to Mr CP Kala travelling by Air India flight Number 836 to Bhopal.' I only heard my name and rest I had assumed.

Just after security check on transfer I ran hastily in the corridor, jumped into the elevator and arrived at a book stall. I ran through the bookstall and after passing through many shops finally I entered the air India boarding counter. The way I was breathing, the girl on duty with fine eyes did not take time to identify me. With a broad smile she welcomed and ushered us to the aircraft. I was the last passenger to take my seat.

After an hour, I landed at Raja Bhoj Airport of Bhopal. Here the temperature was twenty seven degree Celsius. With very relaxed mood I walked to the luggage belt. Different types and shades of bags and suitcases were moving on the belt. I could not see any sign of my bags even after twenty minutes of waiting. The belt had become empty, and my bags were still absent. My relaxed mood had gradually turned tense.

'What are you doing here? Please leave this place.' A person on duty ordered me.

'I have not yet got my luggage,' I said.

'Oh my God!' he said. 'Don't worry sir, it will be in hold. How many bags you have and what colour and size?'

'Two bags, one with grey and other one maroon.'

He ringed up to someone from his handset and asked me to wait. Within five minutes he got a message that no bag was remained in hold. He again consoled me and requested me to follow him to his chamber. He, without delay, sat before a computer and started making some entries in code words. Meantime, he tried to contact the Air India office at Delhi but did not get any immediate response.

'Sir, you sign here,' he said stretching a piece of paper to me. 'No problem sir, you will get your luggage by tomorrow morning'.

'How do you say this so confidently? You don't have any information about my bags. Even your own Air India people are not responding your calls. It is unfortunate.' I said nervously.

'Actually, sometime it happens. Since there was no time left in Delhi to unload and load your bags, it would be somewhere in Delhi. We will trace it,' he assured me.

I had become quite upset. The attraction of my entire tour had faded down. With heavy heart and without my beloved bags I came out from the airport to pick up a vehicle.

Three auto rickshaws were lined up on the roadside stand. A rickshaw driver came forward to inquire if I was in need of one. 'Can you drop me at Vanika, close to PNT square?' I asked. He thought for a moment and passed on his turn to his fellow rickshaw driver.

'How much will you charge to drop at Vanika?' I asked.

'Three hundred fifty only,' he said.

Without any negotiation I got into his rickshaw. He silently drove us to the residence. Sitting in rickshaw I was thinking about my bag, as I had deep doubts of getting it back. I was quite disappointed on the Air India and its functionary. I had almost lost my trust on Air India. I was so much lost in my thoughts that I did not even notice the moment of time I had passed through the beautiful Bada lake.

Reaching in front of my quarter at Vanika, I stepped out from the rickshaw and pushed my right hand into my jean's pocket to pick up the purse. I was about to drag my purse from the pocket, all of a sudden, I saw the driver bending down to his feet and shouting loudly. I could not see anything as rickshaw driver was just before me and there was no space to bow and gaze ahead of him since to my right was rickshaw and a wire wall was to the left side.

I was extremely confused. Pushing something away once he jumped a corner, I was shocked to see a black street dog growling in front of him. The dog jumped again before the driver to bite his legs. I started shouting instantly to chase the dog away from his legs, but the dog had become too rigid to leave the driver. I somehow opened the gate and pushed the driver in. Luckily, the dog did not turn to me and moved away slowly from the gate. The driver painfully lifted up his ragged trouser to knees. The flash of his legs was torn and his both legs were bleeding. Before I extended any help to him, the poor rickshaw driver had driven away and I entered my residence in double shock, although the dog menace had superseded the lost bag's episode.

The Air India person who assisted me at the airport had given me three telephone numbers to inquire the lost luggage. I made a call after an hour, as advised by him, but still there was no good news, as they had not yet located my baggage.

In the next day morning, I was surprised when I received a call on the 'lost and found'. The luggage was finally traced and dropped at the Air India office. The person at Air India office received me with great pleasure and satisfaction. And I had no other choice but to trust in their services for customers.

'What is your opinion on the Srinagar's tour?' I asked Shaurya when I entered home holding the bags. But He did not respond.

'Did you like Srinagar?' I rephrased my question.

'I liked nothing,' he said.

'Why?' I asked with deep surprise.

'I did not see snow. I had to play with snow, and I had to make snowman's statue. You are a liar. You had assured me to show snow but you did not keep your words,' he said with disappointment.

I had been in number of snowy mountainous areas but here Shaurya had missed his first chance to see snow. He made me to realize that the visit to Kashmir was incomplete without visiting snow-laden alpine meadows, including the Gulmarg and the Sonmarg. And above all, I realized that the visit of heaven can't be completed in a few days.

Author with Shaurya in the Dal lake of Kashmir

34.0

A Vagrant and the 'Queen of Mountains'

The political, administrative and landscape picture in and around Dehradun had changed a lot over the past decade from 2000 when I first left to Almora and subsequently to Delhi and Bhopal for making my living. Driving from Jollygrant Air Port to the Wildlife Institute at Chandrabani on 3rd week of May 2012, I noticed enormous changes in shops, markets, houses and even roadside sal forests. Thousands of sal trees had cut down from both sides of two lane road to make it four lanes between Dehradun to Rishikesh. Hither and thither, 3-4 labours in groups were struggling hard to uproot the remains of cut trees. In comparison to past, lesser number of monkeys were straying on the roadside, may be due to present disturbances of constructions.

Dehradun is a city of 'walas' as it comprises of many colonies whose name ends with 'walas' such as Jogiwala,

Lachchiwala, Bhaowala, Chukhuwala, Suddhouwala, etc. The fertile agricultural land had converted into concrete jungles in most parts of these 'walas'. The similar changes had crept in the areas leading to the Wildlife Institute from the T-Junction – a spot on the national highway to New Delhi. I thought the Wildlife Institute would not have changed, as they discourage changes and advocate generally for preservation of substance's originality. Alas, the Institute was not untouched with the changes crept in its surrounding areas. The earlier good-looking reddish roof tiles had been replaced.

Having spent two days in Dehradun, I set off to Mussoorie with my wife Richa and son Shaurya. I noticed similar changes on the way. The dense forests of sal and pine-mixed had reduced. I got down before Jhadipani – a small village - for some moment to drink some cold water of a natural spring.

On my arrival at Taxi stand in Mussoorie, a person, looking around desperately, stared at me perhaps with some hope and asked, 'Are you looking for accommodation?'

'Yes, what is the rent?' I said in Garhwali pulling my luggage from the taxi.

He gazed at me with surprise and leaned to pull my bag. I was thinking about my budget, which might and might not afford the cost of living in hill station, especially during summer vacation.

'You are a local person and we have very reasonable price to the locals. How much do you wish to pay?' he replied.

'Not more than 600 rupees per day,' I said.

'It is too low, at least 1200 rupees.'

'That's too much,' I complained. 'I am not in Mumbai.'

'Sir, the peak season is not yet started. In June, the same room is rented out on 2000 rupees. And the cost of each room sometime inflates upto double on Saturday and Sunday. What brings you hear?' he quizzed.

I ignored his question and moved ahead. He followed me a few steps and did his best to convince me. When he could not melt down my stand he called up other fellow hotel boy to take me further. After some negotiations with this new hotel boy, the deal ended up on rupees 800. Walking on the famous Mall road toward hotel premises I saw a vendor selling kafal fruits. Watching kafal after a long period of time, about 2 years, made me to smile. Its succulent red and blackish fruits watered my mouth. I bought 250 gm of kafal which costs 30 rupees. Five and half year old Shaurya had seen kafal first time in his life. His ever inquisitiveness had woken up, which contented only after having its delicious taste.

After necessary formalities at counter, I checked in the hotel room. I shut the door and went to wash in the bathroom. It was about 3 pm and the water was still cold. I switched on the geezer and waited for few minutes to warm up the water. I remembered my bathroom at Bhopal, where in summer the water running from the tape remained so warm that I had to fill up the bucket and then wait for another 20-30 minutes to cool it down before using to wash hands and face or to bathe. Once I had dried myself, I sat on a wooden chair, in front of the window to soak in the beauty of the 'queen of mountains'.

In the evening, I came out to walk on the Mall road which stretched from the Picture Palace to the Gandhi Chowk. Mall was full of colours. Tourists were shopping, negotiating with vendors, eating in the roadside shops, chatting with family members and a few were resting on the roadside benches. The diversity of languages at the Mall had revealed that the tourists had trickled down from different states and countries to feel the flavor of mountains of the Garhwal Himalaya.

Visiting mountains does not only bring peace and satisfaction in life but it also improves health and physical fitness. I remember the words of a person who once told me that climbing 500 m uphill improves appetite. Interestingly, despite eating frequently in the hotels and makeshift shops in the Mall, I felt hungry and returned to hotel. I ordered for dinner and finished it completely before going to bed.

Next day, my getting up late I credited to the cool nature of the 'queen of mountains'. After late breakfast, I opted to stroll on the Camel Back road via Kuldi, as the hotel I was staying in was close to Kuldi. A few scattered roadside horse chestnut trees were in full blooms. There were some houses, on both downhill and uphill slopes, mostly surrounded by the grove of deodar, oak and rhododendron. Indian barberry, Himalayan yellow raspberry, wild roses and Himalayan cherry principia were flourishing under the canopy of these trees. Stinging nettle and Nepal dock had encroached upon some roadside wasteland pockets. I could see some pine trees, with distinct brown colour, on deep downhill slopes and knolls.

Unlike the Mall, the Camel Back road was calm and secluded. During my 3 hours walk with intermittent rests on the roadside cemented benches I came across a newly married couple, two packed rickshaws, two families, and three boys in school dress who might had bunked the classes. I liked the tranquility spanned along the road, which had given me sufficient space to saunter and sufficient time to watch the scenic beauty while walking without fear of collision and subsequent conflicts with fellow travelers.

I had deep surprise why tourists walk on the Mall only and do not walk on the Camel Back. Do they remain attracted by shops, crowds, vehicles and other artificial objects even after coming here in the hills? What really compel them to climb mountains? I found only one shopkeeper, near a vantage point on the Camel Back, selling some cold drinks, tea, snacks and biscuits. Obviously because of lack of tourists there was even no street vendor.

I bought some snacks and cold drinks from the lonely shop and sat on the roadside bench once again at a vantage point. From here, while eating snacks, I could see the far and wide views of mountains. The hill slopes and valleys far away from me were almost devoid of forests. There were some terraced agriculture land yet most of the areas were barren. I felt the need of extensive afforestation in such barren valleys and slopes.

As soon as I got up to return, the shopkeeper asked 'Are you going back? The Mall is quite near from here. You have to walk just few steps further to reach at the Gandhi Chowk.' I did not find any reason not to believe his words and walked further. I reached at the Gandhi Chowk and took a kulhad of milk. I was extremely satisfied with a day walk on the peaceful Camel Back.

The Gandhi Chowk was a busy market square. Here under the statue of Mahatma Gandhi I saw some labours were resting on the floor despite a signboard instructing prohibited area to enter. On one side of the square there was an old library established in 1843 by the British Government.

Next day, while walking on the Mall I was interrupted by a rickshaw man. 'Kampty fall; Company baag,' he said.

'How far is company baag?' I asked.

'Only five km,' he explained. 'I charge you only two hundred rupees. The rate is fixed. Hundred rupees, to and fro, per couple and hundred rupees extra is for one hour waiting charge'.

I climbed into the rickshaw with Shaurya and Richa, and the driver had pushed its pedals hard to move ahead. The wheels squeaked due to lack of oil. Having known me a native of Garhwal from my language he said, 'Sir, my son has just completed M.Sc. How is his future?'

'In which subject,' I asked.

'Something called botanist,' he replied.

'Botany,' I flabbergasted, as the last word attracted my attention deeply. Being a person of same background, I was acquainted with the merits and demerits of Botany. The core science subjects had no more charm and had lost the glorified past, as they used to be considered in our student life in 1980s. The fascination to take up basic sciences for carrier advancement has lost somewhere in the race of commerce and business. I did not want to dishearten such a hard worker who drove and pulled rickshaw whole day so that his sons could get better education and employment.

'Does he plan to do B.Ed?' I asked rather than replying his query. Historically, there have been long traditions of employment scarcities in the hills of Uttarakhand. The youths migrate to plains in search of livings. And someone rightly pointed out that the water and youths of hills are not worth to hills itself, as both drift to plains. For past couple of decades, the youths have been getting some opportunities in education industry. This has brought some hope and has placed an advantage to the B.Ed. holders.

'He is doing B.P.Ed in the Garhwal University at Srinagar,' he said.

'That's good. He has bright future and will definitely get some good job. One day your and his hard work will certainly pay you both.' I admired his work and positive attitude.

He had driven us through some of the fine oak forests. Dropping us at the gate of company baag, he asked me to take the entry tickets. The Campany baag was a beautiful garden flushed with varieties of roses, pansies, and larkspurs. It was a good picnic place for children. I returned after an hour of site seen, as instructed by the rickshaw man.

I dismissed rickshaw at the Gandhi chowk and walked further to the hotel after having some snacks and soft drink. Mall's roadside was lined with deodar trees. I had to walk fast as the queen of mountains, generally, showered in the evening, almost every day.

I rushed to the hotel which was at Kuldi. Since the rains had stopped I cast my eyes round to see the Kuldi market. My sight was caught by an old church and I entered its premises to know more about it. This church was called as Central Methodist church, which was established on 28th May 1885 by Late Rev. Danis Osborne. Since its establishment 51 pastors had served here. I learned that there was a massive earthquake in 1905 that had destroyed many old buildings in Mussoorie. This church had also developed some cracks and its four clocks had to be removed as they had become wobbly. About 150 m down from the church there was a mosque, too. Close by the mosque was a school. Now the time was insisting us to take dinner and go to bed.

One more day light broke at the 'queen of the mountains' and I started preparing myself to climb the Landour ridge. If Mussoorie is a synonym of the 'queen of the hills' then the Landour ridge is the crown of this queen as it forms the highest point in Mussoorie. I set off with Shaurya and Richa to climb the ridge as much as we could. The road after Picture Palace was relatively steep on the hill slope. It was narrowed down further to the uphill. Panting and prodding, we arrived at the spot from where one road led to Dhanolti and other further uphill. At the place of bifurcation, there was a resting place for travelers. While sitting here on a cemented bench, I saw a monastery, in front of me. I got up and walked further to visit the monastery.

It was a small yet magnificent monastery, which reminded me my three years stay in Ladakh and the Lahual-Spiti – the lands of Buddhists and their monasteries. The monastery premises had embedded in the strings of colourful pennants unfurled all across. To one side of the monastery there was relatively a big ground encircled by houses from three sides. Some colourful flags unfurled before every house. Richa informed me here that the big flags are not unfurled in those houses which have females only.

The 'wheels of time' had sunken into all four outer walls of the monastery. While walking around the monastery and pushing every 'wheel of time' to revolve in its axis I chanted the sacred words, 'Om Mani Padmehom'. For Shaurya the entire exercise had become a nice game to play.

After walking further uphill to my right hand side I reached a vantage point. The scenic beauty lying before me had enthralled me, and I could realize why the Mussoorie was decked out with the name of the 'queen of the hills'. I could see an extensive view and myriad colours and hues of township and trees dotted along the hills. It was just fabulous and amazing.

Getting away from the Landour without remembering the great Ruskin Bond was not possible. While watching the enormous beauty all around I could imagine the fact that must have inspired this great writer. I made up my mind, at least, to see a glimpse of this great person. I stopped a boy running down swiftly to ask the Bond's address, and as mentioned by him I climbed some more steps to reach at the Doma Inn – a restaurant attached with the Bond's residence. The road bifurcated just below the restaurant, which brought some confusion in locating the Bond's bungalow. My imagination of his residence, as big as his name, had escalated my puzzles.

It was a bright sunny day. Mobile indicated half past two of afternoon. The road was deserted and there was no one whom I could get some clues. To confirm his residence from any passerby, who seemed to be local, I sat on a heap of pebbles beneath a deodar tree in front of the Doma Inn. Waiting for while, an old man appeared on the point of road's bifurcation.

With some hope I asked, 'Uncle, do you know Ruskin Bond's residence?'

'This is only in front of you,' he replied pointing his finger towards upstairs of the right side of the restaurant.

I looked up at the set of steps leading to the upper story. The stairway at a corner of the house was quite narrow. I followed a few steps and the doubts crawled again in. After crossing some 10-12 steps, I saw an entry to the house on my right but its door was closed. A nameplate confirmed that it was not Bond's residence but it was a room of some advocate. I shocked, and pulled my steps back. By the time, Shaurya's curiosity to see Ruskin Bond had climbed to such heights that it was difficult to bring him down without meeting the goal.

Shaurya kept on insisting which made me to climb some more steps further. At the end of the stairs I saw a swing in a closed small courtyard. The iron walls around courtyard were adorned with some good-looking creepers. I looked around for the call bell but I could not find one. Since it was about quarter past two I hesitated to knock the doors in anticipation of resting time, as generally people in hills go to bed after lunch, especially during summer. I persuaded

Shaurya somehow telling him that Bond was sleeping, as I thought so. I made up my mind to climb and explore further uphill, for the time being, and take a chance of meeting Bond while coming down.

The road to Landour ridge from Bond's residence was extremely steep. I was surprised to see the courage of drivers driving vehicles on such steep road. They were driving vehicles as usual speed despite the narrowness and steepness of the road. On roadside there were some beautiful old cottages with mammoth deodar trees. I saw a troop of langur close to the office gate of Landour Cant (Ministry of Defense) feeding leaves with their young ones. Within a short distance a group of monkeys were exploring foods and some of them had got some eatables in the dense deodar forests.

Being tired I sat on a roadside resting bench. Few visitors and residents were walking up and down. I could notice the sharp difference between the people climbing up and running down. Where one was highly exhausted due to nonstop steep climb and thus took rest at every few steps, it was difficult to stop the steps while running down. While thinking the uniqueness of hills, which had changed the patterns in human steps, I saw two women walking down with head load of fodder, firmly. Soon they left following the main road and stepped in a nearby old house.

Having climbed in a peak summer day, I had become thirsty and hence I was desperate for water. Since I did not find any water source on the way I asked Richa to follow them for getting some water. Richa and Shaurya entered their house and when did not turn up for long I walked to call them. They came out, followed by both the women with their kids. They not only gave water but repeatedly requested us very cordially to have lunch. The human values, affection to even an unknown person and high simplicity of hill people remain unmatchable, forever and a day. I was overwhelmed by their simplicity, generosity and hospitality. On the bade-adieu, they gifted us some kafal fruits. While climbing further their warmth welcome made me to recall, 'The Guest is the God'.

The steep climb was halted near the gate of the Sant Pauls church at Landour Cant. This church was constructed in 1840. The dense forests of deodar began from the church's were continued up to the mountain ridge. Situated at the altitude of 7,500 feet or 2,286 m the top of the Landour ridge was the highest point in the Mussoorie. This area remained the most secluded and beautiful area of this hill town, with spectacular views of the snow clad great Himalaya, dense deodar forests, and peaceful slopes.

Near the church there were five shops, including the Himgiri Restaurant where we had some snacks and cold drinks. Here I learnt that British forces occupied this region following the Gurkha wars in the second decade of the 19th century. Colonel Frederick Young, an army officer of the East India Company, had constructed the first permanent dwelling at Mullingar in 1825. The name Landour was taken from Llanddowror, a small town in Wales. Landour became a convalescent for British troops suffering from malaria and other tropical diseases in 1827. Those who did not survive had been buried in the cemetery on the north side of the hills at Lal tibba.

The road to Lal tibba was passing through some of the finest and dense deodar forests. I could see these forests were penetrated by some of the oldest settlements in Landour. In some places deodar had mixed with oak and rhododendron. The old trees of deodar had quite big trunk. Nonetheless, here I noticed that deodar trees of high girth class were low in number. It was quite possible that deodar had been exploited from these forests in the past as British Government had been quite fond of its timber.

Many familiar high altitude alpine flowering plants welcomed me on the slopes of Lal Tibba. The patches of Rumex nepalensis, of course, again reminded me its infestation and proliferation of land under intense anthropogenic disturbances. I walked around the Landour ridge and trickled down at Sant Pauls church. Walking downhill to Picture Palace was far easy than to climb Landour cant. I had seen some fantastic forests, landscape beauty and peaceful slopes and had met some nice hill people, yet I was feeling some imperfection in my daylong explorations. I thought there was no harm trying again to cherish the dream, which had been abandoned while climbing to Landour ridge.

An unknown energy had pushed me up step by step while reaching before Bond's residence. I reached at the door and without thinking for a moment I knocked it gently. There was no response. I knocked again and tried to perceive sound of any movement. Luckily, a boy unbolted the door and peeped out.

'I wish to meet Ruskin Bond Saheb,' I said.

He gazed at me and stopped for a while. I felt he wanted to say something but he went into the next room. 'Somebody wants to meet you,' I heard him saying.

'I am quite tired. Who is that?' I heard a slow but quite heavy sound coming closer to the door.

And suddenly I saw the great author. It was really a great moment to see such a great person so close to me that I could have touched him. It was not a dream but a reality in flesh and bones. I heard and knew he was tired. Fortunately, his one book – The Best of Ruskin Bond – was in my bag. I took the book out and requested for an autograph. The seventy eight years old eyes twinkled. 'Well, come in,' he said.

By the time I entered the room he had picked up a pen to scribble something on the book. 'What is your name,' Ruskin Bond asked.

'Sir, I am Chandra Prakash Kala,' I said.

He wrote my name. 'Is it ok?' he said showing the spelling of my name.

'Yes sir, it is ok,' I said looking at my name written by a great author.

After scribbling some words of blessings to my happy and peaceful life he gazed at me. I found time to introduce myself.

'Sir, I belong to a village of Pauri Garhwal. I spent years in Dehradun but could not make out to meet you, ...' I said.

Meantime, Shaurya and Richa had arrived at the door so I introduced both of them. Ruskin Bond kept on smiling most of the time. I took permission for his photograph, which he accepted without any hesitation. Having spent some time with him, we finally greeted him and walked down the stairs. I was extremely touched by the simplicity and greatness of Ruskin Bond. And I could understand why he loved hills and hills milieus.

Next day on 25th May, I packed up my goods and returned to Bhopal. Coming out from the Raja Bhoj Airport I had felt the intense heat wave conditions prevailed all along the road. The temperature was 43.9 degree Celsius and people were forced to stay indoors. The 'Navtapa' (the nine hottest days) had started, and the sun was beating down hard on the very first day of the nine days. While passing along the beautiful lake – the well known life line of Bhopal - I could feel some relief in the relatively moist and cool breeze.

The queen of mountains

35.0

Hidden Gem of Europe

Wondering in the mountains for decades exposed me to various colours and facets of mountain ecosystem and environment. These mountains harbored rich diversity of wonderful plants. The cultural milieu in these mountains was equally diverse and attractive across its length and breadth. While collecting literature on the Himalayan ecosystems and biodiversity, I most often stumbled upon the similar work on the Alps, which fuelled my interest on this beautiful mountain chain and its inhabitants.

An evening of January, I received an email from the University of Ljubljana through which I was invited to deliver a keynote speech on my experiences with the ecology and medicinal plants of the Himalaya. Being a keynote speaker, an excursion to the Triglav National Park of Slovenia was also sponsored by the organizers of the event.

I set off to Slovenia via Paris in the mid of June, and finally I landed at Ljubljana by the next day evening. Ljubljana was a beautiful city encircled with mountains and hillocks. The city's climate was cool and its extensive rangelands were dotted with forest patches. The traffic, even in the busiest roads, was quite low. I was surprised to know that despite being a capital of Slovenia, the city's population was only 276,000, of which one fifth were the University students.

Being a first keynote speaker, I delivered my lecture just after the inauguration of symposium by the Honorable Minister of Agriculture, Forestry & Food of the Republic of Slovenia. Number of delegates from different countries participated in the Symposium and discussed various issues related to conservation, cultivation and commercialization of medicinal and aromatic plants. Next day, all keynote speakers, including me and convener of symposium Dea Baricevic were taken to the city for its brief introduction and site scene.

The city's altitude was 298 m above mean sea level. River Ljubljanica, flowing in the middle of the city between a Castle and Roznik hills, was known to have a great influence on the city from past to present. Some well maintained footpaths led up the Castle Hill. To check the deluge in Ljubljanica, Grubner - a canal - was built. I was told that Joze Plecnik, a renowned architect of Slovenia, gave a new look to the riverbanks by designing walking paths with a promenade, and also renewing bridges – Triple, Cobbler and Trnovo. The city had number of grand buildings and churches that were the living examples of high quality skillful architect. Because of compact size, Ljubljana was a walking and environmentally friendly city, with a lot of green space.

'Slovenia has always been the most prosperous region of the former Yugoslavia,' informed the whitish lady guiding us. 'Though, it is a small country, it contains within its borders the best snowy mountains, thick forests, lush green meadows, and historic cities. The City Museum of Ljubljana has an extremely appealing oldest wheel.'

Being tired I wanted to take some break. Along the Ljubljanica, from Dragon Bridge to St. James Bridge, there were rows of cafeteria. I sat down in a café and began to enjoy coffee along with the panoramic view of the river and the sound of the city life. Young girls and boys were sitting on high stools by the river. While sitting and observing the water running past gradually I felt all my fatigue floating down the Ljubljanica.

Once I had finished coffee I got up and walked further in the old city. At the Preseren Square the whitish lady who was guiding us showed me a statue and said, 'it keeps alive an old romantic love story between the greatest Slovenian poet, France Prešeren, and his muse Julia. Prešeren met the burgeois beauty in the Trnovo Church. Though, she married another and never fulfilled his desire he dedicated to her his most beautiful sonnets. But at least Prešeren's statue and her bust on the house where she once lived are placed to look at each other till the end of time.'

The last day some selected participants were taken to the Triglav National Park - the only national park of Slovenia. Since we had about hundred national parks in India, I was bit surprised to know this fact. We drove to Triglav National Park by bus. On way I saw some small villages. The roof of houses was conical in the villages. I was told by a participant, Petra, that heavy snowfall in winter was the reason to make roof conical so that snow could not accumulate on the roof. In a village, I saw an old castle – the Bled Castle - constructed on a steep rocky hill top. The base of this hill was surrounded by a cluster of houses.

We crossed the wonderful Radovna river and entered the Radovna valley after about an hour drive from the hotel

Mons of Ljubljana. Radovna valley was within the border of Triglav National Park, cutting deep into the north eastern part of the limestone Julian Alps. In a narrow gorge of Radovna valley, we were shown the ruins of a bunker in which solders of Napoleon Bonaparte had fought with some intruders in the beginning of nineteenth century. There were some undulating grassland areas in the Radovna valley, which were leveled purposefully in past by its inhabitants for cultivation. Conifer forests dominated the gentle and steep slopes.

In Radovna valley, there was a small cluster of some old farmhouses, which was called as Pocar farmhouse. I was told by its caretaker that earlier this farmhouse was used as seasonal hamlet, just like high altitude summer settlements of the Himalayan people, but later on people permanently settled here. The Pocar farmhouse was converted into a museum, which contained traditional documents and equipments used for agriculture and routine household purposes. Some of the documents and instruments found inside the farmhouse were dates back to 1609 and 1672.

Cows were driven to the pastures, as it was summer season. I saw some of the best alpine meadows of the Alps spreading across the land full of flowers. Butterflies were flying from blossom to blossom. Petra Ratajc informed me that because of richness of wild flowers here the beekeepers were able to produce very tasty and high-quality honey. The locals also turned this honey into tasty and aromatic drinks.

'Almost every Slovenian will have some creative qualities. We have great painter, writer, dancer, musician, wine-maker or engraver,' said Petra.

'Yes, I heard a story of the greatest Slovenian poet, France Preseren and Julia, at the Preseren Square,' I said, showing off myself, as I was well versed with the history of Slovenia.

'Wonderful! Then, I am sure you know the Narcissus,' Petra asked.

'I beg your pardon. I have not heard it,' I whispered.

'Narcissus Fountain is in the mall near the square you visited in the heart of Ljubljana city. Narcissus was an extremely handsome and divinely beautiful boy. Numerous girls fell in love with him, but he didn't care about them. He kept on admiring whole day his stunning beauty in his reflection on the surface of a lake, until one day he became so entranced by his own image that he fell into the water and drowned. On the very same place he drowned, a flower grew that even today is called Narcissus,' Petra explained.

After an hour of rest with lunch, we moved to see the peat bogs at Pokjuca. The peat bogs were full of sedges and flowering plants. Now we had to climb a mountain peak - Galetovic. The elevation of Galetovic peak was, though, low compared to the Himalaya, but it was equally chill. On way we crossed some alpine meadows, and when I reached in the meadow, I was very glad to see the ground vegetation that was quite similar to the vegetation above the tree line zone of the Himalaya. Petra Ratajc having worked years in a Botanical Garden of Ljubljana had accumulated a fair knowledge of Alps plants that helped me to verify them and also set a brief comparison with the Himalayan plants.

The return journey was equally exciting and informative. A different route was followed to come back the hotel Mons at Ljubljana, and hence I got opportunity to see some more landscapes and hamlets on the way, besides a fabulous lake – Bohinj – with full of fishes. At the end of the day, I prepared a general list of approximately sixty plant species common in the Himalaya and the Alps areas of Slovenia I found within a day. Many of these plant species were medicinal as well as aromatic. The Slovenian Govt. had placed some important species, including *Taxus baccata* in the protected list in order to save these useful plant species. As a whole, the journey to this part of the Alps was quite useful and informative to me and almost a dream, which shaped reality.

I saw the diversity of landscape that changed in spectacular fashion. While coming in contact with the friendly people, fine cuisine, health resorts, thermal springs, tourist farms and sports, I noticed that Slovenia offered something for everyone.

While flying back over the snowy mountains I realized why the people call Slovenia as a 'hidden gem of Europe'.

Slovenia's landscape from Triglav

36.0

The Majesty of Mahasu

As soon as the train stopped at the Haridwar station I dragged my lone two wheeled bag and stepped out from the train. Being the month of May though the mercury had shot up, the outside weather was not unpleasant and I could walk comfortably. Before I leave station, a rickshaw driver came to me and asked to drop me at my desired destination. I looked at his face trying to read his sincerity. Since he appeared to be an honest and simple I asked him the rates for dropping at any hotel near Har-ki-Paidi.

'Twenty rupees,' he said.

'Per person,' I asked.

'No for you all,' he replied raising his hand toward Shaurya and Richa.

'Well, drop us at a cheap and clean hotel,' I asked.

'No problem, I shall drop you the hotel of your choice,' he said adjusting our baggage in the back of his rickshaw.

He began to pedal the rickshaw, which pulled us. Shortly he stopped before a hotel close to the railway station. 'This is a very nice hotel. Go in and see the rooms of your choice,' he said.

'Is it Har-ki-Paidi?' I asked.

'Har-ki-Paidi is close by, only at ten minute walking distance,' he said.

'But we wish to stay at Har-ki-Paidi,' I said.

'Sir, believe me, you go and see rooms. In case you do not like here I shall drop you at Har-ki-Paidi,' he said.

I got down and went into the hotel. The receptionist asked for my choices of rooms and in reply I asked for room rents.

'You please first see the rooms. We have both AC and non-AC rooms,' receptionist said and instructed an attendant to show me the best rooms.

I examined both type of rooms but I remained unconvinced. The room rent was also higher side for my pocket to afford. I walked out from the hotel and asked the rickshaw driver to drop us at Har-ki-Paidi. Despite obeying my instructions he persuaded me to see other hotels in the same locality. I thought there is no harm in checking some other hotels hence I walked with him and entered the next hotel.

I did not like couple of other hotels as shown by rickshaw driver and so that I asked him to drop me at Har-ki-Paidi but as usual he kept on insisting me to see and select the hotels in the very same locality. Finally, I became tired and hence I dropped my baggage in one of the hotels. Since the selection of hotel had consumed a lot of time I paid rickshaw driver fifty per cent more than the actual rate on my own.

Having relaxed for a while I came out from the hotel to visit the Har-ki-Paidi. I asked a fellow pedestrian about the way and direction to the Har-ki-Paidi who informed me that at least it took half an hour to reach there, as it was about three km away. I did not believe it as the rickshaw driver had spoken me that it was quite close and hardly took ten minutes. I walked to inquire a roadside shopkeeper who verified the distance which was three km only.

Though it was not quite far but having travelled for several hours I preferred to ask for a rickshaw to drop me at the Har-ki-Paidi. An old rickshaw driver with frail body came forward to drop us. He gathered all his energy while peddling rickshaw to drag us forward.

'What is your per day earning?' I asked.

'Three to four hundred rupees,' he replied. 'I work over thirteen hours from morning's seven o'clock to eight o'clock of the evening.'

Reaching at Har-ki-Paidi I took a holy dip in the most pious river of the world. I felt fresh and sat on the steps of the Ganga's bank. Hundreds of pilgrims were taking bath in the Ganga's water in anticipation of washing out all their sins. I saw a boy throwing a piece of iron tied with a long rope again and again in the river water. Initially, I thought he was fishing but when I saw him detaching coins from the hard iron piece it became clear to me that he was picking coins thrown in the river by the devotees.

'How many coins do you pick up a day?' I asked him.

'I gather coins equal to three hundred to four hundred rupees per day,' he said.

Since there was enough time for the Ganga's evening puja I began to stray in the Har-ki-Paidi. A person draped in blue emerged from the crowd. He unfurled a notepad and asked me, 'Tell me the amount you wish to pay for evening puja.'

'I shall offer after puja,' I said.

'You must pay, right now. So tell me how much rupees I should write on your name,' he ordered me quite rudely pretending to scribble in the notepad.

'You cannot compel me,' I said.

'Tell me the amount,' he repeated his words firmly.

'Get lost,' I shouted.

He murmured some words. Probably, he cursed me and immediately turned to catch another fellow pilgrim. I stepped up on the bridge over the Ganga to have a broader view of Har-ki-Paidi where I saw many beggars sitting in rows on the steps. A group of kids was gazing with all curiosity on the Ganges ever flowing water. A few women were selling flour pills at a corner. I bought a packet of flour pills and began to through them one by one in the water. I noticed some movement but I could not see fishes as the water was not clean. If the Ganga was not clean at the Har-ki-Paidi one could imagine the condition of the most sacred river after Haridwar to the Ganga Sagar where the filth and effluent of cities and industries are drained in its current.

With jingling bells and chanting mantras the Ganga's evening puja began at the Har-Ki-Paidi. I stood in the crowd and enjoyed the spectacular view of evening aarti. Bells ringed, lamps glowed and the mantras and bhajans rose at the Har-ki-Paidi. The event was a complete food for soul.

After offering puja's flowers to the Ganga I walked back to catch a rickshaw. The crowd had inflated several folds all along the roads. The rates of rickshaw had become just double and more than double because of oversupply of customers. I caught one and reached safely back at my hotel room.

Next day, I along with Shaurya and Richa set off to Dehradun. Within an hour and half we reached at Mussoorie bus stand of Dehradun. Since Dehradun was reeling under hot waves, we took a taxi to Mussoorie and within an hour we were at Mussoorie away from hot waves of plains. Cool breeze was blowing in the 'queen of hills'.

While getting down from the taxi, driver said, 'you will get good rooms at cheap rates even in best hotels.'

'Why?' I asked.

'Last year it was a terrific disaster all across the hills of Uttarakhand. Hundreds of people died and thousands became homeless. Now tourists scare to visit here. Hotels are deserted. People's livelihoods have shaken here. You know this is the peak season but the disaster has spoiled and collapsed everything,' explained the taxi driver.

We got a nice accommodation in relatively cheaper rate. In the evening, we set off on foot to visit Mall road. In comparison to my earlier visits Mall road had lesser number of tourists. Most of the shops in the market were deserted, which reflected the impacts of previous year disaster, as explained by driver.

Having spent a night in Mussoorie, we set off to Purola in a roadways bus. The bus was jam packed. Seats were full and some passengers were sitting on the bonnet and many others were standing in the narrow corridor between the rows of seats. Since there was no seat, I stood close to the bus gate holding iron rods above my head welded on the bus roof. Gradually, I became tired due to continuous jerks, as bus was moving on the uneven poorly maintained mountain roads. I felt to vomit but there was hardly any space to reach upto window. Shortly, I felt severe headache and I thought to get rid of the bus.

A fellow passenger wanted to talk with me but it was hard for me to talk due to nausea. He realized my painful condition and hence assured to arrange a seat for me at Nainbaag. He kept his promise and I got a seat at Nainbaag in the last row. After that, the journey became relatively bearable upto Naugaun. I peeped out through the window and watched neat and clean Yamuna flowing down in the valley. Bus had to drive further in different direction to Badkot hence we got down at Naugaun to catch some other vehicle to Purola.

We took rest for a while at Naugaun before stepping in a taxi. The taxi had hardly driven to a km all of a sudden it was stopped by a police van. Driver became nervous when he was asked by a young policeman to show taxi's documents. He showed some but did not produce all the necessary documents. On the spot policeman imposed fine and handed over five hundred rupees penalty slip to the driver, besides scolded him repeatedly. Driver had to pay the fine before driving to Purola.

Driver's extreme grief and anger out busted shortly that reflected in his actions of driving roughly in the hilly roads. Some passengers began to scream and others pleaded him to drive properly but he became deaf. Couple of passengers requested to drop them, as they did not want to meet an accident but he stopped listing and kept on pressing the accelerator. Despite to soak in the enchanting landscape and beautiful valleys, I got down at Purola bus station with all sorts of nightmare, finally.

It had become dark so my first priority was to find out a comfortable accommodation. I got one in a small market of Purola, which was relatively neat and clean. I preferred to stay in top floor of the Tilak hotel.

The hotel was attached with Kamal river flowing down in the middle of Purola market. Both sides of Kamal were encroached with high rising buildings. Its entire flood plain had been captured. It reminded me the last year's tragedy, especially at Kedarnath and all along the Mandakini,

Alaknanda and Bhagirathi that wrecked havoc and washed away many buildings constructed in the flood plains of these rivers.

I walked along the river bank, next day. People living in the houses along its course in Purola were throwing all sorts of garbage and filth in it. Kids were fishing in groups. At a place I saw some small fishes were flowing in its current. They appeared to be fainted or died. When I inquired from a young boy catching fishes I got to know that bleaching powder was dissolved by someone in the river, which was one of the several ways to catch fishes.

Kamal river seemed to be in unhealthy state at Purola itself. Shopkeepers, hotel owners, and all other residents used it as a dumping place. All along the market through which it ran down heaps of polythene, plastic bottles, and dirty cloths had not only distracted its natural flow but also had polluted its purity. Girls and women were spotted easily washing their clothes and boys remained busy in fishing. Some people defecated on its bank and pigs in groups roamed in and around its shallow water in search of food. Hotel sewage was set free through pipes into the river. Despite all this the same river water was taken through pipes back to the hotels without proper filtration. Removing of garbage and filth was not appeared to be the only solution for keeping the river clean. I thought that until unless the people were not educated enough about the consequences of water pollution, the situation would persist.

I left the river bank to climb up on the mountain slopes, expecting to have a broader view of the river valley. Scattered pine forest dominated all across the slopes wherever human habitations were either thin or absent. I encountered many medicinal and edible fruit plants beneath the pine forests, including delicious Himalayan yellow raspberry and Indian barberry.

The panoramic view all around me increased with gaining altitude. The valley, which was locally named as Rawain valley, was just fabulous. It was broad, spectacular and stunning. It was soaked in the green and brown shades of ripened and ripening crops. I had enough time to explore and enjoy the spectacular beauty of the Rawain valley. In and around Purola, I hardly encountered the old houses made up of wood and stones. Cement and concrete jungles had replaced all old environmentally and ecologically friendly houses.

While walking in the Rawain valley, a day I arrived in a village named Agoda. Likewise other villages in the valley all houses here were made up of cement. Old houses made up of woods and slates had become the part of history. Penchants unfurling from the houses intimated me the presence of Tibetan community. Pomegranate and apple were blooming in their kitchen gardens. On a grassy patch I saw about a three feet long snake crawling leisurely. A pedestrian joined me to have a glimpse of such a deadly creature.

'You seem to be an outsider,' he said.

'I am from Bhopal,' I said.

'But you don't look like from the plains,' he remarked.

'How do you say so?' I asked.

'Because of your look and language,' he said.

'Well, you are right, I belong to hills only,' I said.

'Which place?'

'Sumadi'.

'I see. I heard Sumadi has produced several well qualified officers. One of our District Magistrates was from Sumadi'.

Naturally, I liked his appreciations to my birth place.

'What do you do here?' he asked.

'I am on summer vacation,' I replied. 'Your area is simply fabulous'.

'The valley is more attractive and wide once you visit beyond Dunagiri,' he said raising his finger toward a hill in front of me.

'Is it Dunagiri?'

'It is believed that when Hanumanji was flying in the sky to Lanka holding Dunagiri mountain, a piece of mountain fell down here. This hillock is the same piece. Its soil properties are different from rests of the hills and valleys here. A Navodaya School has constructed on this hillock,' he informed.

I gazed at Dunagiri where I could see a huge tower and couple of buildings. Down in the valley the river flood plain was quite broad. I presumed that during rainy season lot of water would flow in the Kamal river. Both farm and grazing lands were being engulfed by the concrete houses all along the valley below Agoda village. I came across number of schools running in newly made buildings and roadside unoccupied shops.

Purola though a small town tucked away deep into hills seemed to be an education hub. People living in villages far and wide from the Purola somehow managed to accommodate their kids to study in schools here. Education was spreading like anything in the entire valley. While walking along the Kamal river I encountered some exotic tree species planted in the pine forests. The allergic bottle brush was flourishing along with some eucalyptus.

In afternoon, I saw groups of school girls and boys walking back home. I sat down in the shade of a pine grove gazing mountain slopes, valleys, and rivulets flowing down from the mountains. Some distance away from me a small girl draped in school dress with a bag hanging from her shoulder walking toward me. She was walking alone through the jungle but there was no sign of fear on her face.

'How far is your home now?' I asked when she reached close to me.

She looked at me and stopped but said nothing.

'Where do you live?' I asked again.

'Lok colony,' she replied this time.

'How far is your school? What is your school's name?' I quizzed.

'Bright Land School,' she said and walked on.

I followed her for a while in the desolate area before she left the main road and walked down in a narrow mountain trail. Shortly, she disappeared in a small colony. Realizing her safe return at home I sat down again under a pine tree. After sometime I heard some remote voices coming closure to me from the jungle. Soon I saw a group of young school girls walking on the mountain trail. They were chatting and laughing quite on and off.

'What is its name?' I asked raising my finger toward a village.

'Netri, Pujeli, Khaladi …..,' two of them replied one by one getting me introduced with the names of all villages visible from the spot.

'Which is the biggest one?' I asked.

'Netri,' a girl replied. 'I live there.'

'Your land is not only beautiful but seems to be quite fertile also. What are the crops you cultivate? ' I asked.

'Paddy, wheat, sweet pea, millets, pulses, seasonal vegetables …..' they informed.

They answered all my questions and enjoyed chatting with me just as I enjoyed their company. They appeared fearless and unhesitant. Interestingly, they chatted with me for more than an hour.

'I am sorry I have taken your lot of time. Had I not interrupted, you would have reached at home,' I said in view of closing the talks.

'It is all right,' they said. They appeared as they wanted to continue chatting. Realizing that their parents would have been worried I got up and said goodbye to them all, though my desire was to continue chatting with them.

Next day was the international biological diversity day. I thought to celebrate the day with students. So I walked to the Govt. Inter College and requested its Principal to allow me to interact with the students. He accepted my request and I was taken to the senior most class. After brief introduction I talked about biodiversity and its importance. Thirty five minutes of interaction was a small period for me in comparison to sixty and ninety minutes lecture at my parent institute.

Since my lecture had become over before the interval, I decided to interact with the students of other schools at Purola. I walked down to the Govt. Girls Inter College and requested its principal also to give me some time for interaction with the students.

'Today, actually health check up is going on in the classes,' principal said.

'Well, so may I interact with those students whose check up is either over or is scheduled after an hour?' I requested.

Meantime, two staff members of the health check up entered the principal's room. While talking with them for a while I came to know that most of the girls were anemic in the school.

'Quite often some students become faint and fall down during morning prayers. Hemoglobin level is quite low in most of our girls. Unfortunately, parents remain careless. When their wards faint at school they believe that it is either due to ghost's attack or tantra-mantras of their relatives or neighbors. They are highly superstitious, and rather doing proper treatments at hospital they prefer to consult some tantric,' principal expressed her feelings.

I got two classes together for interaction. Just after interval I began to deliver my lecture under a huge tree in the open ground, as there was insufficient space for over hundred students to accommodate in a single class. I was happy interacting with students having both beauty and brain together. The interaction lasted for two hours under the shade of a huge tree surrounded by splendor eye-catching landscape. I saw a girl in one of the rows whom I had met a day before while walking in the Purola's outskirts. She was seemed surprised to see me again. I got to know during interaction that over seven thousand students were getting education in various schools at Purola. I bade adieu to the students and walked back to the hotel.

I sat in the balcony looking at various shades in the horizon. A hotel caretaker came out from a room and threw a polythene bag full of garbage in the Kamal river. When I tried to interrupt he simply refused to hear me and said, 'nothing will happen. Water is made to clean all. No one can clean water'. Once he went off a young girl came to balcony and flung rappers in the air toward river. When I looked at her she smiled shyly.

'Do you work here?' I asked.

'Actually, my mother works here. Today, she is not well. I am on summer vacation so I came on her behalf,' she said.

'In which class do you study?' I asked.

'I have given tenth exam. I am waiting for my results,' she said.

'Good, I am sure you will be passed,' I appreciated her hard work and positive attitude. In mountains people are taught to work hard from the childhood and she was one of the several examples.

'Do you have any subject on environment?' I asked.

'Not now, but we had when I was in eighth standard,' she replied.

'Did your teacher then say anything about cleaning river?' I asked.

She shied again and dropped her eyelids yet smile rapped on her face. 'We have picked up garbage from this river on many occasions,' she said.

'Do you think selective removal of garbage clean up the river?' I asked. She looked at me and the river but said nothing. She appeared to be surprised on my silly question. 'I think if we stop throwing garbage in river it will remain clean,' I continued.

She nodded her head probably in concurrence and went off to continue her task of cleaning rooms. In Purola, except education industry and a few hotels no other industry was set up however the river had become polluted and its water was not proper for drinking. One could imagine the situation in the cities where the population was quite high and industries were discharging enough pollutants in the river. I thought for a moment.

Next day, I walked to a village named Khaladi. I saw here many vegetable farms, apart from standing wheat crops. I saw a young lad in his farms weeding out carefully.

'Earlier, I use to grow a few plants of tomato in my kitchen garden. Now, I grow pea and tomato in my limited agricultural land', said the young lad named Vinod Kumar on my inquiry. 'Those who have adequate land here in the village earn good money by producing and selling vegetables'.

I walked into the village where I met number of farmers. I came to know that the landholding of farmers like any other hill areas of Uttarakhand was small and scattered. The majority of farming was operated in the rainfed land. In order to reduce the degree of risk and vagaries of climate and weather, traditionally they grew many crop species together. This practice was called as 'Baranaja' cropping system (growing over twelve varieties of crops), which led to a symbiosis relationship between different plants and hence contributed to increase the productivity of crops. In past, all crops were grown for own consumption and not for sale. Many constraints in marketing farm produce, including poor accessibility of market, discouraged hill farmers for growing cash crops.

'In the beginning, switching over to vegetables from traditional crops brought up several doubts in our mind, especially about its taker. Therefore, we formed a farmer association to tackle the all possible hurdles,' said Brijmohan who was a member of the Fruits and Vegetables Growers Association. 'We then approached to Mother Dairy to buy our produce, especially pea and tomato, through an agreement with growers and association. Since then farmers bring vegetables at the local collection centre from where it is transported to New Delhi office of Mother Dairy'.

I was told that since plenty of water was required for cultivation of vegetables, especially tomato, the villagers began to concentrate more on their irrigated land in the river valley. 'We have migrated from uphill village to river valley as there was scarcity of water for irrigation. Can you imagine that there is negligible migration from our village to the cities, as we have productive farming system,' stated Dharamveer Singh.

'Being old and broken at number of places, immediately what we require is to renovate the network of canals in our irrigated agricultural land. I have tabled a plan of thirty five lakhs before the members of gram sabha for repairing all canals of our village under the scheme of MANREGA but it was differed," expressed Brijmohan.

Despite good economic returns, there was dark side of vegetable farming. Synthetic chemicals, as fertilizers and pesticides, were used heavily for high yield. In comparison to tomato less quantity of pesticides were used in pea farming, as it was grown in the winter when the pests remained low in number. In early stages of growth, less quantity of pesticides was sprayed in tomato crops but once flowering stage began frequent sprays of pesticides was done at regular interval of ten to twelve days.

The leaf litter from adjacent forests was collected for making manure by spreading it as an overnight bed for cattle, which was mixed with cow urine and dung. It was swept in the morning and was piled up at a distance from the cowshed to let it decay for couple of months before to use for raising crops productivity. 'Our village is surrounded by pine forests and pine needles litter is less fertile than oak leaf litter. Therefore, our dependency on chemical fertilizers is more,' stated Ravindra Singh.

Use of high yielding varieties, which relied mostly on use of fertilizers, was another cause of concern. It had changed the indigenous cropping system and had also reduced crops diversity, as well. However, cultivation of vegetables was a profitable business in the Rawain valley. Having enlightened with the traditional farming system and subsequent changes, as made by the people of Khaladi village, I returned to my hotel at Purola.

A day I wished to see beyond the Rawain valley. In the next morning, I caught a bus to Mori, which was located beyond Rawain in the Tons valley. The bus first climbed up on the mountain top at Jarmola. Oak and rhododendron were intermingling with pine in some places at Jarmola whereas on others oak and rhododendron had got hold of the ground. The forest was dense and dark yet the apple orchards had interrupted in their monarchy. After Jarmola the road led to the downhill slope, which brought me in the Tons valley. Soon I could hear the roar of river and waterfalls.

The scenic beauty of the Tons valley had increased several folds by the river Tons flowing in the middle of the valley. Tons river water was bluish and awesome. I got down at Mori, which was in the valley on the bank of river Tons surrounded by high rising mountains. Both sides of a lone road were packed with shops at Mori, which was a very small market. I hired a taxi service from Mori to visit the Mahasu temple at Hanol, as public transport was hard to obtain.

The road led along the Tons river to the Mahasu temple. Dense forest of chir pine dominated both sides of the river. Many villages were hidden in these forests. I saw places where river rafting was going on in the Tons. Camping and picnic sites had mushroomed in the riverbeds. And the narrow road continued to meander through the pine clad mountain slopes and valleys.

After about seven km drive from Mori I was dropped at Hanol. The Mahasu temple was located just below the road. Like old houses of Uttarkashi, the base of the temple was made up of stones and the roof, tomb and upper half were made up of wood. Its architect was unmatchable. Several high intensity earthquakes and disasters in this fragile ecosystem had not harmed a bit to this temple. The temple was made in the perfect harmony of the nature.

'I think Mahasu is a synonym of the Maha Shiv. The Mahadev! The *Lord Neelkanth*! So we are in the land of *Neelkanth*,' expressed Asharam who accompanied me in the bus and then in hired taxi to visit Mahasu temple.

'Well said, I did not know it,' I agreed.

'This temple was built in ninth century. It is believed that Pandavas escaped from the Lakhmandal or the Laksha Graha via Hanol to Himachal Pradesh,' Asharam informed me.

I entered the temple to offer my prayers to the Lord Mahasu. The frame of entry door was covered with coins nailed over one another. A large room was before the sanctum which had sacramental objects. The temple had four rooms in row and each was roofed separately. I noticed goats straying in the temple premises. Most of them were extremely frail. When I asked the priest I came to know that earlier goats were sacrificed here. 'Local people have extreme faith in the Mahasu and as per traditions they still offer goats to their deity. But now they don't kill these goats in the temple premises and let them loose here after puja,' informed the priest.

'May I know some more about the Mahasu?' I requested the priest.

'This village Hanol is named after a Brahmin, Huna Bhatt,' he said.

'Panditji, I was talking about Mahasu,' I said presuming that he did not hear me properly.

'I know. The story of this temple and the deity resides in begins with Huna Bhatt. With the beginning of Kaliyuga after Dwapar, a demon stayed here in Hanol who used to eat humans. He ate whosoever came in contact to him. On request of villagers he agreed to eat one person a day. Accordingly, he devoured seven sons of that pious-hearted Brahmin, Huna Bhatt. He did not stop here rather he wished to have Huna's wife Kirtaka. Huna and Kirtaka then prayed to the Hatkeshwari Devi of Hatkoti who suggested the couple to offer prayers to the Lord Shiva in the high hills of Kashmir. They followed the deity's advice, and then at last

Lord Shiva granted them their wish to make them free from the demon,' narrated priest.

'I see, and then Lord Shiva killed that demon,' I interrupted.

'I am not finished. Have patience. The story is not ended here. On his return from the Kashmir, while worshipping a day the goddess emerged from the earth and told Huna Bhatt to plough a part of his field every Sunday with a plough made up of silver having gold blade. While doing so, four Mahasus sprang on the sixth Sunday from four furrows in the ground he made by the plough. The first one was Botha, second Pavasi, third Vasik and the forth one was Chalda. All four are called by a common affix of Mahasu, Char Mahasu. From the fifth furrow their heavenly mother Devladli Devi appeared. The demon was then killed by Mahasu brothers. Thereafter, the land was divided among the Mahasu brothers so that they could take care of the people, land, forest, water and above all the nature in their respective territory,' he paused for a while and then continued.

'The day on which the Mahasu appeared first time on the earth is considered very pious. Being extremely pious, the birthday of Mahasu is celebrated by local people with great pleasure. On this occasion, the Mahasu is ritually bathed and then placed in the sanctum sanctorum. No one other than priest is allowed to enter the sanctum sanctorum. After sunset, a tall blue pine pole with a flag of deity hoisted on its top is planted on the ground. The whole night, men and women dance and sing in the ground with the burning torches of resinous woods in their hands,' he said.

'Mahasu is the supreme deity among all other deities in this region. On his name disputes are settled among the local people. In the name of Mahasu, water is poured in a metallic goblet by a neutral person and the disputants are asked to drink that water in the name of Mahasu. The party who gives the false statement is believed to suffer on drinking the water,' a person sitting close to the priest said this time.

I saw a couple of astrologers encircled by groups of people were sitting in the temple premises. In the compound, groups of tourists were playing with two rounded stones. I asked Asharam, 'do you know the speciality of these rounded stones?'

'You go and try to lift one of them,' Asharam replied.

'It is quite small. A kid will lift it up,' I said.

He smiled and said, 'let's try'.

When I began to do so it became too heavy to lift. I was surprised. It was quite small but extremely heavy. I felt that someone was pulling it against me. Finally, I bowed my head once again before the Mahasu and travelled back to Mori along the glittering Tons river.

'People here generally don't drink the water of Tons,' informed driver while driving to Mori.

'Why?'

'It contains lot of sand particles. Also its water is less tasty than the spring's water. We have plenty of natural springs so there is no need to drink its water. Its water is not even used for irrigation, as it is hard to draw water from this river because of its precipitous banks and deep gorges. As per a local belief the water in this river is the tears of Bhabruvanan. Two other major tributaries of Tons are Rupin and Supin. And one of them even is not used for washing hands and body,' he stated further.

On my query he informed, 'it is believed that it causes skin diseases, especially white spots on the body (leucoderma)'.

To my surprise, in all my mountain wonderings I heard just opposite of this about the rivers originating from the Himalaya. After coming out from the glaciers all these rivers pass through naturally-growing meadows and woods having innumerable medicinal plants that are believed to pour curative properties in the river water. And by and large people climb here take medicinal bath in these rivers.

During my three weeks excursion in the valleys and mountains I soaked in countless hues of nature's beauty, its cascading waterfalls, magnificent rivers, enchanting valleys, lush green pastures, thick forests, superbly carved terraced fields, antique temples, and also the simple, sincere and hardworking mountain peoples. Above all, I had been blessed to know about one more incarnation of the *Lord Neelkanth*, as the Mahasu. All in one go.

Mahasu temple deep in the hills of Uttarkashi

About the Author

Chandra Prakash Kala was born and brought up in Sumadi – one of the popular villages of Garhwal in Uttarakhand state of India. He studied Life Sciences at the HNB Garhwal University, Srinagar before doing his PhD on the 'Ecology and conservation of the Valley of Flowers National Park' at the Forest Research Institute (Deemed University), Dehradun. He has published over one hundred seventy five articles and half a dozen of books, which include "The Valley of Flowers: Myth and Reality" and "Medicinal Plants of Indian Trans-Himalaya". His decade long strenuous study of the 'Valley of Flowers' laid the foundation stone for tagging it in the list of World Heritage Sites. He served many institutions, including the Wildlife Institute of India, the G.B. Pant Institute of Himalayan Environment and Development, the National Medicinal Plants Board, and the Indian Institute of Forest Management with various capacities. In two decades of wandering, he visited widely across innumerable valleys and mountains of the Himalaya and the Alps.